AF593273

ROYAL PROGRESS

BRITAIN'S CHANGING MONARCHY

DANIEL COUNIHAN

CASSELL
LONDON

CASSELL & COMPANY LIMITED
35 Red Lion Square, London WC1R 4SG
and at Sydney, Auckland, Toronto, Johannesburg,
an affiliate of
Macmillan Publishing Co, Inc.
New York

First published 1977

ISBN 0 304 29793 3

Printed in Great Britain by
Butler & Tanner Ltd, Frome and London

TO
MY LONG-SUFFERING
FAMILY

In England, our traditions and our liberties are closely connected, and so it should be possible to treat the two at once.

E. M. FORSTER: *Abinger Harvest*

Contents

Acknowledgements

For permission to quote from copyright material the author is grateful to the following:

A. D. Peters & Co. Ltd for 'Elegy on His Majesty King George V' by Edmund Blunden from *Poems of Many Years* (Wm Collins Sons & Co. Ltd). Reprinted by permission of A. D. Peters & Co. Ltd.

Mrs Reichmann for extracts from a poem by Sir Max Beerbohm.

Illustrations

Illustrations

Author's Note

I am grateful to H.R.H. The Duke of Edinburgh for making room in his busy schedule for me to have a conversation with him while I was preparing this book. He provided me with much valuable information and many insights that I could not otherwise have acquired; he also nearly made himself late for Royal Ascot, and for that I beg his pardon.

I have also to thank many members of the Royal Households for their ready help and courtesy during my years as Court Correspondent, and especially, at Buckingham Palace, the Queen's Press Secretary, Mr Ronald Allison; the Assistant Press Secretaries, Mrs Michael Wall and Mr Rodney Moore, and their charming and efficient staff; and at Clarence House, the hospitable Major John Griffin, Press Secretary and Extra Equerry to Queen Elizabeth the Queen Mother.

The B.B.C. must be thanked for giving me the assignment which brought me in contact with the Monarchy at work closely and frequently enough to justify my attempting to write a book about it.

My friend, Mr Douglas Dumbrell, Court Correspondent of the Press Association, will already know how grateful I am to him for letting me pick his brains, as well as for his kindness to me, especially when I was new to the job.

Not least to be thanked is my former assistant at the B.B.C., Miss Pamela Griffin, now of the Department of the Environment, who gave much time and thought to helping with research.

It hardly needs to be said that I alone am responsible for any errors of fact or judgement that the book may contain.

1. Twenty-Five Years a Queen

'We do now hereby with one voice and Consent of Tongue and Heart publish and proclaim that the High and Mighty Princess Elizabeth Alexandra Mary is now, by the death of our late Sovereign of Happy Memory, become Queen Elizabeth the Second, by the Grace of God Queen of this Realm and of all Her other Realms and Territories, Head of the Commonwealth, Defender of the Faith, to whom her lieges do acknowledge all Faith and constant Obedience, with hearty and humble Affection . . .'

The words of the Queen's Proclamation, read on 8th February 1952, announced with all the solemn ceremony of ancient custom a new reign which had begun at an uncertain hour about three days before with no ceremony at all, unknown to the Queen, and for her, in a setting wild, strange and incongruous for the greatest and gravest event of her life.

On 5th February, King George VI was at Sandringham with his wife, Queen Elizabeth, his younger daughter, Princess Margaret, and a small party of friends. He believed himself almost recovered from recent severe illness and, carefree and happy, he had been out in the fields on a dry, cold and sunny day, shooting hares. He went to bed peacefully at about midnight after planning his programme for the next day. At some time very early in the morning of 6th February he died in his sleep. At that moment, his elder daughter and Heir Presumptive, Princess Elizabeth, was with her husband, the Duke of Edinburgh, in Kenya, at the start of a tour which had been intended to take them on to Australia and New Zealand. After official functions at Nairobi, they were now in bush country, and were spending the night which began on 5th February at the observation resthouse, Treetops, near Nyeri, built in the branches of a huge fig-tree which overlooked a waterhole in a forest clearing. Dressed in russet slacks and a shirt, with a cardigan over her shoulders, the Princess spent much of the night filming the great variety of game gathered at the waterhole, which was lit by artificial moonlight. Earlier, as she had walked along the rough track to Treetops, a large elephant emerged from the shadows and stood in her path. She did not hesitate, but walked quietly past it and climbed the ladder to the platform in the tree. Mr Sherborne Walker, owner of Treetops, said, 'Ma'am, if you have the same courage in facing whatever the future sends you, as you have in facing an elephant at ten yards, we are going to be very fortunate.' All her courage was called upon during the afternoon of the next day when news of the King's death was confirmed in a telephone call from London. It was her husband who broke it to her with great gentleness and, alone with him, she became aware that she was now the Queen.

The Britain over which the Queen reigns today is a country in some ways startlingly different from that to which she hurried home from Kenya a quarter of a century ago. It is a United Kingdom manifestly less united than it was then; it has willingly, though with some travail, shed its empire; it is less of a power in the world; it has chosen to seek its future partnership with its neighbours on the Continent of Europe; and its chief and vital preoccupation is its struggle to rescue its economy and its trade from the most perilous decline they have suffered in modern history.

Of course, with hindsight, the signs of what Britain was to become are apparent in much of what happened in the first year of the Queen's reign; indeed, although World War II, a fundamental cause of Britain's present troubles, had been over for seven years, some wartime conditions still prevailed in 1952. For example, it was only in the first month of the reign that identity cards, a very un-British wartime institution, were abolished; tea remained rationed and controlled until October; and only in that month were restrictions on the lighting of shops removed. Also in October, there was a portentous acknowledgement of a new and perilous era when Britain exploded her first atomic weapon on the Monte Bello Islands off Western Australia. In November, a guarded statement by the United States Atomic Energy Commission about a series of tests at Eniwetok Atoll was taken by press and public as meaning that the tests had included the first explosion of a hydrogen bomb.

In the summer, President Truman had laid the keel of the first atomic-powered submarine, the U.S.S. *Nautilus*. There had been warning signals in a new balance of payments crisis in 1951, but a drop in world prices of raw materials had enabled the Government to keep the economy on a fairly even keel. An almost holiday mood of hope had been created by the Festival of Britain in that year; but as 1952 opened, there was again need for something to rekindle patriotism and a spirit of endeavour in the people, who were at heart still depressed by the recurrent crises, domestic and external, that had continued to plague them since the war, and which had their sources deep in the inescapable facts of international economic and political life.

There was deep and general sorrow at the death of King George VI; but the accession to the throne of his daughter, a pretty, vulnerable-looking girl, who was a wife and the mother of two small children, had a high romantic appeal to most of the nation, not simply at the time but for long afterwards. She evoked protective feelings in most men, particularly those old enough to be her father, and affectionate solicitude in all. I remember being amused to observe strong reactions of these kinds among some of the more grizzled and ostentatiously hard-boiled of the then senior men in the B.B.C. news-room when the Queen visited Broadcasting House early in her reign. She stood, a smiling but rather shy Sovereign, on the stage of the large concert-hall, looking very tiny indeed among the generally rather tall men who made up the top brass of the B.B.C. in those days, and who buzzed about her combining a wonderful mixture of the respectful and the avuncular with the desire to be noticed.

Among the Queen's most ardent elderly admirers in those days was that incurable romantic, her first Prime Minister, Winston Churchill, back in power, after six years in Opposition, at the head of a Conservative Government pledged, as it claimed, to 'set the people free' from the results of the Socialist measures that Labour had industriously pushed through since the end of the war. In his broadcast commemorating the late King, his salute to the young Queen was laden with his imaginative feeling for history. He said: 'I, whose youth was passed in the august, unchallenged and tranquil glories of the Victorian era, may well feel a thrill in invoking, once more, the prayer and the anthem "God Save the Queen".' It is unlikely that he did not also take pleasure in the fact that as an old, worldly-wise and fatherly Prime Minister to a very young Queen he was repeating history, acting out again the charming relationship that had been established 115 years earlier between the youthful Queen Victoria and the ageing Lord Melbourne, who had been not only her first Prime Minister but also her confidential friend, teacher and adviser.

The attitude of protective affection towards Queen Elizabeth II was widespread throughout her realm. The glories of her Coronation, an event which was seen by many millions on television and charmed and impressed the world, added another dimension to the public enthusiasm for the new reign. Everything that surrounded the occasion—including the splendidly-coincidental announcement to the Coronation crowds that a British team had at last conquered Mount Everest—contributed to a growing mood of euphoria which some of the newspapers took up as a stunt. We were all to be 'New Elizabethans'. With a young Queen on the throne, we were entering a new age of British glory which would rival that of Elizabeth I, Shakespeare's Sovereign and Spenser's 'Faerie Queen', England's ruler when Drake singed the King of Spain's beard and sent his Armada packing, the Queen who was 'only a weak woman' but had the 'heart of a king, and a king of England, too'. It was heady stuff, but it grew out of the hope that wishing would make it so rather than from any roots in sober fact. It was a good story, and the papers plugged away at it. In March 1953, the *Daily Mail* had M Christian Dior exclaiming: 'The Coronation of the young Elizabeth II has filled not only the British but, rather strangely, the French, too, and much of Europe, with renewed optimism and faith in the future . . . ' The *Daily Express* published a picture of modern Elizabethans, including Sir Frank Whittle, Mr T. S. Eliot and Miss Margot Fonteyn, all in Elizabethan dress, as well as five other figures with blank faces to represent other moderns whom readers were invited to choose for themselves.

That reduced the whole thing to what was, alas, its proper level, that of a game. Real life was a much more serious affair, but as Elizabeth Longford recalls, it took the country some years to realise that there were no short cuts to Utopia. As she says, 'The impresarios could bill a star cast for "The New Elizabethans", but the stage would remain empty.'

The Queen herself was not playing games, but from the start of her reign fulfilled her constitutional role as befitted the daughter of George VI and the granddaughter of George V. Her approach was deeply serious, conscientious, dutiful, dedicated. So it has remained, as over the years her ministers have grappled with essentially the same recurring difficulties—inflation or the fear of inflation, the depreciation of sterling, rising prices, the demand for higher wages to meet them and more than meet them, growing unemployment, almost seasonal strikes, struggles to achieve a more equitable balance of payments. Abroad they contemplated the growing power and military strength of the Soviet Union as overwhelmingly the central development in foreign affairs, which it remains to this day. Other international problems preoccupying them at the start of the reign are still with us, in spite of years of diplomatic exchanges, international conferences, United Nations debates, summit meetings. Such subjects as Berlin, Cyprus, friction between Greece and Turkey, the Middle East, Rhodesia, South Africa, Korea, could all become at any time as much matters of urgent international and British concern as they were very often in the Fifties. New problems have been added to them, such as the strain on the economy brought about by the ability of the oil-producing nations to dictate terms, the long-enduring troubles in Northern Ireland which keep British troops constantly engaged to the detriment of wider defence commitments and the ordinary people of the realm subjected to terrorism. Regional and racial tensions have started to show, reflecting in varying degrees resentment at the political records of successive central governments.

During the first twenty-five years of the Queen's reign, as Britain has completed her withdrawal from empire, independence has come to almost all those vast pink areas on the world map over which the sun never set. To most it came bloodlessly. It is sadly ironic that one territory to which the movement towards independence was heralded by a wave of murders and other violence was Kenya, where the Queen succeeded to the throne, where during her last days as Princess Elizabeth she had been enthusiastically welcomed by the Africans as well as the white settlers, and where on the February day on which she left to attend her father's funeral and take over his task, the Africans lined the roads with bowed heads as she passed. The Mau Mau terrorist campaign began that very year and was not quelled until 1957. Kenya became independent in 1963, and the Duke of Edinburgh represented the Queen at the celebrations.

The first of the African territories administered by Britain to become independent was the Gold Coast, which became the sovereign state of Ghana in 1957. The new state had been launched with high hopes under the leadership of Kwame Nkrumah, and with a well-trained judiciary, an army that showed no disposition to interfere in politics, and a fair amount of money in the kitty. It was thought that it could become a model democracy for Africa. In 1960 it declared itself a republic within the Commonwealth, with Nkrumah as President. Thenceforth his rule became increasingly authoritarian, and his country almost a police state, and it was evident that Moscow was showing a great interest in it. A visit to Ghana by the Queen was planned for November 1961, but such was the country's condition, with the President arresting both opponents and erstwhile friends, and threats of reprisals against him, that many influential people in Britain, including some members of the Cabinet, feared for the Queen's safety if she went there. It was suggested that she could well be hit by a bullet intended for her host. The Queen was maintaining firmly that, in spite of all this, the visit should not be cancelled; and then, only five days before the date fixed for it, there came news that a big explosion had rocked the Ghanaian capital, Accra. The Queen insisted on remaining calm. She reportedly said, 'How silly I should look if I was scared to visit Ghana, and then Kruschev went a few weeks later and had a good reception.' It was decided that the Commonwealth Secretary, Mr Duncan Sandys, should go out to Ghana and, so to speak, test the water. He did so, rather gallantly, driving beside President Nkrumah along the projected royal route, and suffered no mishap. I well remember the news conference he gave to diplomatic correspondents on his return, and that there was great scepticism still among those who heard him about the probability of the Queen's being as safe in Ghana as he had been. This feeling was shared in the House of Commons where there was much alarmed speculation. It was suggested, for example, that the House might vote against the visit; the Prime Minister, Mr Macmillan, might then resign; the Queen might refuse to accept the resignation; and so on into realms of considerable fantasy.

In his memoirs Mr Macmillan recalls that such matters, including the possibility of his own impeachment, if the Queen left after a hostile vote in the House, were discussed at considerable length and 'with a sort of mock seriousness'. He says, 'It all seemed too absurd to be true.' In the event, there was no division in the House and Mr Macmillan advised the Queen to adhere to her programme. Her visit to Ghana was an outstanding success, and the Prime Minister recorded in his diary, 'The Queen has been absolutely determined all through. She is grateful for M.P.s and Press concern about her safety, but she is impatient of the attitude towards her to treat her as a *woman*, and a film star or mascot. She has indeed "the heart and stomach of a man". She has great faith in the work she can do in the Commonwealth especially. If she were pressed too hard, and if Government and people here are determined to restrict her activities (including taking acceptable risks) I think she might be tempted to throw in her hand. She does *not* enjoy "society". She likes her horses. But she loves her duty and means to be a Queen and not a puppet.'

It is entirely probable that the Queen's determination to be a queen within the limits that the Constitution requires has often been made evident in her relations with the seven Prime Ministers who have held office during the first twenty-five years of her reign; but it will probably be many years before anything is made public about that. Although she is quite certainly entirely conscious of her constitutional duty and right to be consulted, to encourage and to warn, the aspect of her arduous tasks that is most obvious is that concerned with her public appearances—on State occasions, such as the opening of a Parliament; when she appears before her people in person or on television, both as their Sovereign and as the mother of the most exalted family in the land; and when she represents them, either as Head of State and hostess on their behalf to foreign rulers and other dignitaries paying State visits, or herself carrying out tours overseas both within and outside the Commonwealth. In all these matters she is indefatigable, and she has certainly travelled, at home and abroad, enormously more than any other British monarch. Successive Prime Ministers have borne witness to the political and, frequently, economic value of the Queen's foreign tours. That they are tiring and exacting, often to the point of exhaustion, I can testify myself, having followed a number of them, even though everything possible is done to lessen the burden on the Queen. Often they impose real sacrifice, which was particularly severe in the early days of the reign when the Queen had to accept separation for long periods from her young children.

Immediately after the Coronation, for example, on top of visits to Scotland, Northern Ireland and Wales, and an exceptionally heavy programme of other royal activity throughout the summer and autumn of that year, the Queen and the Duke of Edinburgh set off on a Commonwealth tour in which they would circle the world and be six long months away from their children, Charles, then aged five, and Anne, then aged three. They left London by air in November, and in the still prevailing enthusiasm produced by the Coronation thousands of people lined the road out to London Airport, waving and cheering and at times almost blocking the way. The royal party put down first at Gander, in Newfoundland, for refuelling, at 3.25 a.m., local time. But even at that hour, and in that fairly remote place, crowds had assembled to see them; so, sacrificing planned sleep, they made an appearance and were ardently welcomed. From there they went on to Bermuda, where the Queen, among other things, opened Parliament, and attended a Government dinner at what, in London, was two o'clock in the morning. Next they flew to Jamaica, where the refitted liner *Gothic* awaited them; for the new royal yacht *Britannia* was not yet in commission. Then followed three weeks of comparative rest as the liner cruised the Pacific on its way to Auckland, New Zealand, where the main tour was due to begin.

The Queen broke new ground by broadcasting from New Zealand her Christmas message to her people all over the world. But before that there had been an adventure in Panama. When the *Gothic* was making its way through the Canal, the Queen and the Duke decided to cross the isthmus by car. On their way, travelling in separate cars, they were completely surrounded and lost sight of each other when scores of thousands of people, in a frenzy to see for the first time a reigning queen, flooded into the streets of the town of Colon. The police totally lost control and the Queen and the Duke could have been in great danger. It was midnight before they were able to rejoin the *Gothic*.

On the *Gothic*, the Queen and the Duke were able in theory to maintain some contact with their children; but the powerful broadcasting transmitter over which they could have spoken to them from anywhere in the world was found to electrify the whole of the ship's after end, and it was dangerous to touch anything linked to the electrified mainmast. It was therefore decided to wait until a less exciting radio-telephone call could be made from Auckland. This was done on Christmas Eve when the Queen and the Duke spoke to their children, who were staying at Sandringham.

I remember that at this time the B.B.C. was broadcasting a special bulletin of world and domestic news especially beamed for the royal travellers and, for a time, I was responsible for its preparation. Naturally enough, it was given the working title 'the *Gothic* bulletin'. One evening, near the desk where I worked in the Broadcasting House news-room, a cartoon drawn by some artist among the sub-editors appeared on the wall. It depicted a dank, stone dungeon in which a living skeleton, chained to a bench, pecked with bony fingers at a strange typewriter which soared grotesquely, festooned in spires, pinnacles, gables, crockets and gargoyles, and which might have been designed by Pugin and would certainly have delighted John Betjeman. Leaning out from beneath a cobweb, a rat gnawed at the parchment which protruded from the typewriter's carriage. In the half-open doorway, a bearded gaoler was saying to a royal couple: 'And this is where we prepare our Gothic bulletins.' I think that drawing ought to have been sent to the Palace; but it was filched by someone on the staff, and I last saw it framed behind the bar of a pub in Essex.

The royal Commonwealth tour also visited Tonga, where the Queen and the Duke were anxious to meet again the smiling Queen Salote who had won the hearts of the London crowds on the rain-soaked Coronation route by waving all the way from Westminster Abbey to Buckingham Palace, completely ignoring the downpour. The tour continued into the New Year, and included nearly two months in Australia; a visit to the Cocos Islands, on the way to a stay of eleven days in Ceylon; three days in Uganda; and stops in Libya, Malta and Gibraltar, before the arrival home in the second week of May. The Queen and the Duke had travelled on this tour 43,618 miles.

The Queen, usually accompanied by her husband, has carried out foreign and Commonwealth visits in every year of her reign so far, and by now she has been to almost every part of the world. Her visits, except for a few undertaken privately for family reasons or for a holiday, are made on the advice of the Government; more often than not their political purpose and political success are apparent, sometimes they represent some very new departure. One in this last category was in 1961, when in the course of a State Visit to Italy the Queen and the Duke called on Pope John XXIII. This was ranked as a State Visit to the temporal ruler of the tiny Vatican City State, as well as a visit of courtesy to the spiritual leader of many millions, among them large numbers of the Queen's subjects.

When the Queen and the Duke went to Yugoslavia in October 1972 it was the first State Visit to a Communist country. Almost inevitably there was speculation that, in the then popular climate of *détente*, it might be the forerunner of a series of visits to Communist countries behind the Iron Curtain. This has not so far been justified, although the Duke of Edinburgh and Princess Anne have been to the Soviet Union in connection with international equestrian events, and not in their capacity as members of the royal family, and Princess Alexandra, daughter of the late Duke of Kent and cousin of the Queen, made a largely cultural visit to Poland in October 1975, which was seen as marking a thaw in Anglo-Polish relations.

President Tito of Yugoslavia had made a visit to Britain in 1953 about three months before the Coronation and had lunch with the Queen, and it was then that he invited her to visit his most westernised of Communist countries; he was in London again in 1971, once more lunching at the Palace. When it was decided at last to take up his invitation this was seen, at least by the Yugoslavs, as an endorsement of their independent attitude towards the Soviet Union and a reaffirmation of Britain's wish to see them remain outside the main Eastern European Communist bloc. The tour was a great success, thousands turning out to welcome the Queen, and the only disappointment was when bad weather prevented the Duke of Edinburgh from flying by helicopter up into the mountains to meet some of the former Partisans who had fought the Germans and

Italians in World War II. The Queen and the Duke were given an enthusiastic reception in Belgrade, Dubrovnik, Titograd and Zagreb, and the Queen's personal interests were catered for by a visit to the world-famous stables at Djacovo where the Lipizzaner horses are bred.

The Queen has relatively often made private visits to France, but a State Visit there in 1972 was regarded as setting the seal on the newly-improved Anglo-French relations and the success of the British Government's bid to join Europe. President Pompidou was host to the Queen and the Duke on that occasion, which both Governments regarded as an outstanding success. Perhaps even more of a success in the strengthening of good relations between France and Britain, which have certainly had their ups and downs in the years since the war, was the visit to Britain in July 1976 of President Pompidou's successor, President Giscard d'Estaing. On this occasion, of course, the Queen was so to speak playing her reverse diplomatic role, that of Britain's most exalted hostess. The atmosphere that prevailed during this visit could hardly have been more favourable to the cementing of existing friendship and, in practical terms, the political talks that took place produced an agreement to hold discussions once a year, alternately in France and Britain, particularly about matters arising from membership of the European Community. These would be between Foreign Ministers, and there would also be periodic talks between other Ministers. But probably the main achievement was a new warmth in the way in which the two Governments now dealt with each other, and in securing this there is no doubt that the Queen played an important part.

The highly-experienced and well-informed Paris Correspondent of the London *Evening Standard*, the Australian journalist Sam White, had written before the visit that probably the best, and possibly the only card that Britain had to play in negotiations with Giscard was the Queen. Later he wrote, 'I never realised then the full truth of what I was saying half ironically: the fact is that Giscard and his wife and the entire French party have returned to Paris in a positively lyrical state about the British Royals. So much so that if the visit can be pronounced an outstanding success which, for the time being at any rate, has transformed Anglo-French relations, then the credit must go almost entirely to the Queen, with side credits to the Duke of

Edinburgh and notably enough to Princess Margaret.' Sam White said the Queen succeeded not only in charming Giscard but in impressing him with her air of relaxed position and authority. 'There was always,' he said, 'a subtle interplay between the formal and the informal which greatly fascinated the French.' Another columnist, the former Labour M.P. Woodrow Wyatt, concluded, in reviewing this French visit, that a Monarchy has to be conducted in some style or it is pointless, and that the way in which the Queen brilliantly combined pomp and splendour with informality had captivated the French President, who, he claimed, had come to Britain cautiously neutral, almost hostile, and had left with a glow of goodwill. Wyatt said, 'It would not have been quite the same if the President and the Queen had ridden on bicycles down the Mall instead of in a gorgeous carriage. At a time when so much in Britain has declined the value of the Monarchy to us has actually increased.'

I cannot remember a foreign State Visit to Britain which could have been considered a real failure, and during the Queen's reign there must have been getting on for forty of them. Invitations to make such visits emerge as the result of deliberations by a committee of members of the Queen's Household, the Cabinet Office and the Foreign Office; and they are never issued unless it is certain that they will not be declined and that the Foreign Office favours them. After that, long and well-tried machinery slides into motion, but preparations can take as much as three months. The British have acquired an international reputation for managing such things supremely well because their experience has accumulated literally over centuries and produced such a body of specialised knowledge that few difficulties are likely to arise in a State Visit which have not been encountered and overcome in the past. Vera Watson, in her fascinating book, *A Queen at Home*, based on months of research into the records of the Lord Chamberlain's Department of Queen Victoria's days, described some of the more outlandish problems encountered then in connection with State Visits. For instance, some splendid correspondence was occasioned by the great social event of the season of 1873, the visit to Britain of the Shah of Persia as a guest of Queen Victoria. Clearly, though his impending arrival caused the wildest excitement in London, the Shah was very much an unknown quantity there. Letters from the Foreign Office to the British Legation in Persia wanted to know if it was true that the Shah would bring three wives with him, and if he did, what was to be done with them? Would he expect them to be lodged at Buckingham Palace? Would they have to be shut up, invisible to all but female eyes? Was the Shah an early riser, because he would have to leave Brussels, *en route*, by six in the morning in order to catch the tide at Ostend? Would he eat anything set before him, or did he have special food? Did he like wine, or must he always be given something stronger, spirits of wine, for example? Did he sleep on the floor or in a bed, a 'regular 4-poster'? Did he sit on chairs or sofas, or on the floor? It was all sorted out satisfactorily in the end, and no doubt the Shah had a good time. It seems unlikely that the Palace would have comparable problems today in a much more boringly uniform world, but if they did, I have no doubt they would find a helpful precedent somewhere.

If the State Visits by foreigners to Britain are almost always successful, the same is not entirely true of the Queen's visits abroad, where the local political situation can sometimes be more influential on crowd behaviour than the chivalry due to a woman and the honour due to a Queen. Agitation for separatism in Canada worked to some extent in this way, in spite of great efforts by the Queen to demonstrate her deep regard for her Canadian subjects, and this was already apparent during her second visit there in October 1957, just before a State Visit to the United States, the first of her reign. Young men of Quebec demonstrated round the royal car, and threw at the Queen's feet something that might have been a bomb but was, in fact, a petition that a new hotel in Montreal should be named not for the Queen but after its French founder. Accusations were made in Canada that during her visits the Queen saw too many officials and dignitaries and too few ordinary Canadians.

In 1959, undaunted, the Queen went to see her Canadian peoples again; and she saw to it that her programme was designed to bring her in touch with all manner of citizens. A main official purpose of the trip was that the Queen would open the St Lawrence Seaway; she also made it the occasion for her first-ever television broadcast. This broadcast is famous not simply because it was the first, but because of a mysterious private joke that is still a mystery but which had a remarkable and salutary effect upon the Queen. The producer found that she was intensely nervous before the cameras, so much so that he feared for the success of the broadcast. The Duke of Edinburgh told him, 'Remind her of the weeping and the gnashing of teeth.' This cryptic message was passed to the Queen in a desperate, try-anything spirit, but it worked. The Queen smiled and relaxed and all went well. This cannot be said of this Canadian visit as a whole. The Queen began to seem below her best in health and more easily fatigued than was normal. She was, in fact, expecting her third child. The Canadian Prime Minister, Mr John Diefenbaker, was privately told of this, and he suggested that the rest of the tour, which the papers were describing as 'a punishing programme', should be cancelled. The Queen would not allow this, but the tour was shortened slightly, and the royal party flew home instead of sailing as planned in *Britannia*, because the Queen wanted to consult her doctors.

In nine of the seventeen years since then the Queen has visited Canada, in some years going more than once. The year 1964 was her most trying year there; for the separatist movement became very violent in expressing its opinions and focused some of this verbal attack on the Queen. There were rumours in some of the British papers about Cuba-trained terrorists with plans to kill a Canadian member of the royal party. One of the French separatist leaders said some people were resolved to let the Queen know brutally that she was not welcome in French-Canada, which he told a questioner could be 'another Dallas' [the city where President Kennedy was assassinated]. The Queen was no more to be moved than she was over the reported dangers to her in Ghana, and the visit went ahead. There was little trouble close to the routes along which the Queen travelled, but intense Canadian security measures away from them led to the manhandling by police not only of demonstrators but of innocent onlookers, so that in press controversy later the day became known as 'the Saturday of the truncheon'.

It was on a Canadian visit that the Duke of Edinburgh made a statement about the Monarchy which has been much quoted. He said, 'I think it is a complete misconception to imagine that the Monarchy exists in the interests of the Monarch. It doesn't. It exists in the interests of the people. I think the important thing about it is that if at any stage people feel it has no further part to play, then for goodness' sake let's end the thing on amicable terms without having a row about it.'

The Queen was again in Canada in 1976 to open the Olympic Games in Montreal as the country's Head of State. This time there was little if any open hostility from the French-Canadians, and crowds along her route were friendly, though not large. The French-language papers adopted a nice usage to avoid referring to her as Head of State. A shade ponderously, they called her 'the Head of the Commonwealth, which includes Canada', but some of them found polite things to say about her under this title. English-speaking Canadians regarded the visit as an opportunity to demonstrate to the Prime Minister, Mr Trudeau, that they were enthusiastically determined to retain the Monarchy. It is clear that many of them suspected him of wishing to court the French separatists by seeking to end it; and it has to be said that this is a suspicion shared, rightly or wrongly, by a number of highly-placed people in Britain who believe that while he is ready to make use of the Queen for his own political purposes, he would like to sever the link if he could.

I have never myself gone to Canada with a royal tour, but I have twice been with the Queen and the Duke to Australia, which the Queen likes to visit whenever she can in spite of its great distance from Britain. She has been there five times since the beginning of the reign, mostly for tours of several weeks. When the Queen goes to Australia, she does so, of course, as Queen of Australia, and Australian officials take over all the organisation of her visit as soon as she arrives. I have found them enormously efficient, with a scrupulous eye for detail and timing, and imaginative knowledge of the needs and difficulties of pressmen.

The first of the visits that I reported was that in October 1973, in which the central event was the official opening by the Queen of the controversial Sydney Opera House. At this time, I gained the impression that Australians, in the early stages of the Government of Mr Whitlam, who was removed from office in dramatic circumstances by the Governor-General just over two years later, were in a somewhat divided frame of mind about their links with Britain, and consequently a trifle uncertain about the precise attitude they wished to adopt towards the

Queen. I doubt if this was very apparent to the royal party, because the Queen and the Duke were cheered wherever they went, and official speeches, including those made by Mr Whitlam, were fervently loyal. The central fact was that Australia was in a period when it was exceedingly anxious to assert its own identity, its individuality, the totality of the independence that it had, in fact, possessed for many decades; and no one could quarrel with that. At the same time, it was evident that there was at least a considerable minority, presumably Australians of British stock, who while they were as keen to assert their independence as anyone else, felt strong emotional ties with Britain, and so were concerned about a number of developments, such as the plans to change the National Anthem and to have a new flag from which the Union Jack had been removed, and to put an end to Australia's connection with the Privy Council. It was at this time that a decision had been made to change the style and titles of the Queen in Australia, so that there she would be first and foremost 'Queen of Australia', and I was a guest at a parliamentary luncheon in Canberra at which both the Queen and Mr Whitlam spoke of the desirability of this. The Loyal Toast was uttered not just as 'The Queen' but as 'The Queen of Australia'. At that moment, I was astonished to hear the angry and incontestably Australian voice of a woman at the next table exclaiming loudly, 'The Queen of England!' I don't think she was seeking to demonstrate a conviction that the Queen ought to have nothing to do with Australia, because if she felt like that, she would presumably not have accepted an invitation to the luncheon; so I supposed that she was deploring one more nail knocked in the coffin of the British connection.

All this may give the impression that Australians are rather pompous and stuffy in their reaction to visits from their Sovereign. Nothing could be further from the truth. They manage things smoothly and efficiently, but they can introduce an easy informality that seems impossible for many British people, who become insanely-officious stuffed shirts when they get within a stone's throw of royalty, as I have discovered in many a British town visited by the Queen. I treasure particularly an incident that occurred at a small party the Queen and the Duke gave in Sydney mainly for press people who had been reporting their visit. After the formal presentations, the Queen moved round from group to group, chatting and smiling with a vivacity and friendliness that gives great pleasure on such occasions to everyone, and not least to Australians. When she was a couple of yards from my group an Australian near me was being handed a glass of whisky, and I heard him say loudly, 'Easy on the water, sport. Fish fornicate in that stuff.'

I would love to hear somebody say something like that on a British royal occasion. In fact, somebody did once, but that was also an Australian, one of a number of visiting sportsmen who had been invited to Buckingham Palace at short notice straight from training. The lady from whom this story comes was not a member of the royal family, but one of the visitors, collapsed wearily on a sofa, evidently thought she was. When she said to him sympathetically, 'You must be terribly tired', he replied, 'Tired, Princess? Tired? I'm buggered!'

It was a largely Australian occasion when I followed the Queen and the Duke, Princess Anne and Captain Mark Phillips and Lord Mountbatten on a tour of Pacific islands and Papua–New Guinea in the spring of 1974. It was as gruelling a programme for most of the press party as it was for the royal party, with a very strict time-table and innumerable short flights on aircraft that left at unearthly hours. I and a New Zealand correspondent were luckier than most, because we travelled most of the time on the Australian destroyer *Torrens*, which escorted the royal yacht *Britannia*, and I am unlikely to meet better hosts anywhere than the officers and ratings of that ship. They earned our admiration as well as our gratitude, because they had adopted a self-denying ordinance not to drink alcohol while on this escort duty, but they insisted that I and my colleague must not imitate them.

That South Seas voyage was full of excitements and incident from the moment of arrival at remote Norfolk Island, where leaders among the two thousand or so islanders were descendants of Fletcher Christian, the *Bounty* mutineer. Somewhere in the vicinity a cyclone named 'Pam' was blowing itself out, and the island, called, because of its steep cliffs, 'a place fit only for eagles and angels', had been cut off by heavy seas for five days. It looked as if the islanders might be disappointed of their first-ever personal visit by a British monarch. The waters were still rough when *Britannia* arrived off the landing point, Niggerhead Reef, but the royal party decided to risk going ashore in one of the island launches specially designed for the treacherous local seas. They did so safely, but between ship and shore the launch sometimes seemed to disappear completely in the troughs of the waves.

At sea, afterwards, on their way to the New Hebrides, the Queen and her family had some relatively calm days, but I was told that she herself was kept very busy dealing with telegrams from Britain, which was in the full tide of election frenzy. Unbeknown to the Queen at the time, there was tragedy during a performance put on for the royal party at Pentacost Island in the New Hebrides. Islanders were demonstrating earth-diving, a spectacular sport peculiar to them, in which men with their ankles tied to jungle vines dive head first from a tree platform towards heaped mud below, the springy vines checking their fall just before they reach the ground. It was alleged that no one had ever been killed or injured taking part in this perilous-looking sport; but as the Queen watched, the vines holding one diver broke, and he plunged into the mud. The Queen, looking clearly shocked, was told that he was not seriously hurt, but that he was being evacuated by air for further medical examination. Thereafter, as the tour continued, the Queen asked daily for news of him; but she was several stages further on her journey before confirmation was received that he had in fact died.

The next ports of call were in the British Solomon Islands, scene of fierce and prolonged fighting in World War II, where the party adhered strictly to their open-air programme in spite of a drenching tropical storm. The Queen and Princess Anne kept fairly dry under umbrellas, but the men of the party—the Duke, Lord Mountbatten and Captain Phillips—striding ahead in tropical uniforms, were soaked to the skin, as were the majority of performers and spectators in the various displays organised to welcome the Queen. The joyous blowing of conch shells and the beating of island drums drowned the sound of the heavy downpour which continued for most of the day.

During the rest of the tour, the Queen had to do a good deal of island-hopping by air in weather that was less than ideal, and there was at least one uncomfortable-looking landing. I never saw her look even slightly alarmed, and she was rewarded with some rapturous and exotic welcomes by peoples for whom her coming was the event of a lifetime. But I have seldom seen her greeted anywhere as enthusiastically as she was in Papua–New Guinea, then an Australian trusteeship rapidly approaching full independence. The territory had a big mass of political preoccupations, including a powerful movement for the secession of Bougainville Island, which is rich in copper, from the rest of the country, and there were rival groups making all manner of demands. But whatever else they wanted, everyone seemed to want the Queen and, dancing and singing, the people thronged roads and arrival points wherever she went.

For me at least, the high point of the whole programme was the visit to the rugged but potentially-prosperous eastern highlands of Papua–New Guinea, which had scarcely been explored in the late Thirties and contain some of the territory's most primitive tribes. In the township of Goroka, the royal party saw, almost as soon as they arrived, and in a manner that had nothing to do with contrived entertainment, some of the startling contrasts of this developing area. Outside the small, but sleek and modern airport lounged large groups of almost naked warriors, wearing towering head-dresses of bird-of-paradise plumes, their bodies painted in bright patterns, bows and bundles of arrows in their hands. They were not ceremonial dancers brought there for the occasion, of whom the Queen must have encountered hundreds during the Pacific tour, but tribesmen who had walked into the township from many miles away in the surrounding hills to see her. Many of them, with their wives and children, were among the crowds in the streets which watched the royal party drive from the airport. Some stood, gazing absorbed, in the entrance to the township's supermarket, with large advertisements for 'today's special' pasted up behind them. I was told that as many as eighty thousand tribal people had entered the township for the great occasion. For a large part of the visit, once again, a tropical storm discharged rain in drenching torrents, but nobody seemed to mind.

At a reception, Lord Mountbatten, who is always considerate of correspondents' needs, took me aside and said, 'There's someone over here that you simply have to meet,' and he introduced me to a small, quiet and respectable-looking middle-aged man, who wore the O.B.E. on his dark-blue lounge-suit. This was Councillor Wamp Wan, a respected 64-year-old member of the local government; and that was also what he appeared to be. What did not show in his appearance was that in his youth, as 'Fight Leader' of the Mogi tribe, which he still was, he had been a famous killer of men, probably of at least forty. He couldn't remember the exact number. 'Plenty,' he told me, when I asked. He had accompanied and helped the earliest European explorer of the area in the early Thirties. He said he had had six wives, of whom three were still alive, and twenty-four children. He told me that he intended to be baptised a Christian soon. He had once gone to London to visit the Queen, but on that occasion he had failed to see her.

The next day produced the most compelling spectacle of the tour, when several thousand people from many tribes massed to receive the Queen on a showground about the size of two football pitches. I was told that it was doubtful if they had ever been seen in such numbers before, ranked according to their tribes. Each group was decorated in a highly-imaginative and often beautiful fashion to make itself entirely distinctive. Coloured plumes, shells, grasses, leaves, bones, carved wood and tinted clays were intricately used to produce an astounding variety of appearance. From one district came so-called mud-men, carrying spears, wooden tridents or bows and arrows. Their bodies were coloured an eerie greenish-grey with dried mud, and their heads were completely hidden in disproportionately-huge masks of the same mud, with gaping gashes for mouths and eyes. They capered and gestured in a weird, slow mime, suggesting the spectres they were meant to be, or monsters from science fiction. There were moss-men, swaying figures entirely shrouded in moss. Another group looked like walking haystacks. Yet another had narrow, pointed, two-foot-high head-dresses, painted, as were their faces, in horizontal stripes of pink and grey.

As the tribes waited for the Queen, they danced and pranced, and kept up a sing-song chanting against a continuous throbbing of drums, working up an intense excitement that reached a climax when the Queen, the Duke of Edinburgh and Princess Anne and her husband arrived, and standing in an open parade vehicle were driven slowly round the astonishing assembly. Asking questions around the town later, I was given to understand that the whole affair had given great satisfaction to all concerned as a great and historic occasion. I heard only one adverse comment: 'Everybody else was dressed up; so why

Queen Victoria receives the Shah of Persia. His visit was the social event of 1873, but a headache for the Foreign Office

The young, radiant Queen Elizabeth goes to open Parliament in the second year of her reign. We were all to be 'New Elizabethans'

The Queen meets a world champion in Washington. 'How are you?' asked Muhammad Ali. 'How's your leg?' said the Queen

A competition for a monument to the Queen's Silver Jubilee produced some fanciful suggestions—for instance, that a giant corgi should be carved on the South Downs

didn't the Queen wear her lovely crown?' A very fair observation, I thought; and I passed it on to the Queen's entourage.

I suppose the most complete contrast to the primitive wonders that made up much of the Pacific tour would be the Queen's visits to the world's most technically-advanced nation, the United States, where she is held in very high affection and respect and has beyond doubt made an incalculable contribution to the continued friendship between Britain and that country on which, for the British certainly, so much of importance depends. Her first visit there as Queen was in 1957, when President Eisenhower, an old war-time friend of the British royal family, was in office. It was also a time when Anglo-American relations were impaired by the Suez crisis of the previous October. The Queen probably did more than anyone else on the international scene to restore them. Once again, she undertook an extremely heavy schedule, stressing in the sites she chose to visit and in her speeches the past that Britain and the United States shared. She was obviously enjoying herself. 'My, you look pretty!' was Mamie Eisenhower's greeting to her. The Queen in New York had the rather remarkable experience of receiving on the same day a ticker-tape welcome from Broadway and a standing ovation from the United Nations, where so many wanted to hear her speak that every seat in the General Assembly was filled and people were standing nine deep. At a press reception she was asked, 'How do you survive your terrific schedule of appearances?' She answered, 'I survive by enjoying myself every minute of the day.' Almost all the Americans who saw the young Queen either in person or on television were charmed by her. Those who may not have been charmed were at least impressed by her energy and her tireless devotion to her job, a quality that most Americans are traditionally expected to admire. A well-known, and exhausted news commentator said after she had flown away at two o'clock in the morning, 'Strong men have broken covering this royal runaway race. There isn't a clear eye left except Elizabeth's.'

It was an older, more experienced, but still immensely-dedicated Queen who visited the United States again in its bi-centennial year, 1976. There had been considerable clamour for her to provide a boost for the British aircraft industry by flying there in the Concorde aircraft. But once again, she saw the wisdom of underlining, especially in that historic year, matters that belonged to the history of both countries; and she chose to step ashore in Philadelphia from the royal yacht on the quay where William Penn, founder of Pennsylvania, landed in 1682. There was another ticker-tape welcome in New York, and Mayor Beame made her an honorary citizen. He told her in his speech that America and New York owed more to Britain than to any other country whose peoples had made their way to the United States. At a dinner given in President Ford's honour at the British Embassy in Washington there was an apparently unscheduled meeting between the Queen and the world champion heavyweight boxer, Muhammad Ali. Wearing a coloured, frill-fronted shirt, he approached her through the crowd, his hand outstretched. 'How are you?' he said. 'I'm all right,' said the Queen, perhaps a trifle startled. Then warming to him rapidly, she said, 'I'm glad to see you. How's your leg?' Delighted by this evident knowledge of the injury he had sustained in a recent contest with a Japanese wrestler, Ali said, 'Fine, fine. I'm glad to meet you, too. I love your country and I have many friends there.' At a White House banquet for the Queen and the Duke of Edinburgh, Bob Hope sang:

> Thanks for the memory
> This dazzling affair,
> This gracious royal pair;
> Their presence on our birthday
> Brought joy beyond compare...

And he went on to some felicitous rhyming about Great Britain, the greatest literature ever written, the Beatles and Benjamin Britten, the B.B.C. and four o'clock tea. There seem to have been only two American groups unwilling to make the Queen welcome. These were some Boston Irish, who demonstrated against the continued presence of British troops in Northern Ireland, and some fundamentalists who objected to the fact that a bell cast in London and presented to Philadelphia, whose famous Liberty Bell is cracked, did not carry a biblical text. Overwhelmingly, the Queen seemed to have scored a personal diplomatic success. A correspondent of a British paper, who evidently believed patriotism to be either outmoded, immoral or sissy, complained that the Queen had caused him 'a sharp twinge' of this affliction. 'That lady is great,' an American colonel told a B.B.C. colleague of mine in a Boston bar. 'I'm really British,' he went on, 'we all are here; we came from there.' The colonel's name was Murphy.

It is easy to criticise the Queen, especially if you are one of the many people whose understanding of what she really does is far from complete. But if you watch her carrying out her duties from day to day, working her way methodically but gaily through one exhausting programme after another, as one can see her on a royal tour, it is impossible not to admire her. When one observes the expertise she has for so long displayed in what must be one of the world's most difficult jobs, a job in which there are really no complete holidays and which has no retirement age, it is hard to credit that she had almost no special education or training for it. It was not originally envisaged that she would ever be a reigning Queen.

The Queen had a tranquil and sheltered childhood; and although she and her sister Margaret were darlings of the nation in the late Twenties and early Thirties, they would not have been overwhelmingly aware of this. They did not go to school; for in those days that would have been unthinkable for princesses of the British Royal House. They were taught by governesses. They had a happy family life. They adored, and were adored by, their mother and father. Only their grandmother, Queen Mary, ever sensitive in the service of the House of Windsor, saw to it that the small Princess Elizabeth was given some special instruction in history against the seemingly-remote possibility that she could succeed to the throne. They played some part in grand occasions; for instance, they were small bridesmaids at the wedding in 1935 of the Duke and Duchess of Gloucester. That was really the last year in which the future looked calm and unweighted by the prospect of great responsibility for Princess Elizabeth. Her grandfather, George V, died in the first month of the New Year. The Prince of Wales, the beloved Uncle David of the two princesses, succeeded him, but abdicated, and their father was King after the signing of the necessary documents on Thursday, 10th December, 1936. For ten-year-old Elizabeth, now Heir Presumptive, a new life began; but she was not made deeply aware of it yet. The children's governess coached them to make a proper curtsey to their father as he returned from the Accession Council to their home at 145 Piccadilly. That was possibly the first really appreciable sign for them of the momentous change. But by the time she was eleven, Princess Elizabeth was being introduced to the future when she was taken to watch a State Opening of Parliament, and not very long afterwards, she took the salute at a rehearsal of the Aldershot Tattoo. But it was still a tremendous treat for the two small girls to be taken on the London Underground, as they were in 1939, the year which was to bring war in the autumn.

Clearly, royalty in those days were really very remote indeed from the people they served. Princess Elizabeth developed closer and more frequent contacts with ordinary citizens when, at her own request, she became a junior officer in the Auxiliary Territorial Service, the women's branch of the Army, in 1945, when she was nineteen. She became a driver of lorries and staff cars, and learned how to service them. Increased contact between the Sovereign and a wider spectrum of the people has quite obviously been something that the Queen has sought increasingly ever since she came to the throne.

In this she has been encouraged by her husband, who had his own strong ideas about what has been called 'bringing the Monarchy to a crash-landing in the new age'. Princess Elizabeth and young Prince Philip of Greece and Denmark met for the first time when he was a Royal Navy cadet of eighteen, and she was only thirteen, paying a visit with her parents, the King and Queen, and her sister, to the Naval College at Dartmouth. Philip amused the two girls by joining them to play with a model railway. By 1941, the Prince and the Princess were writing to each other regularly, and Prince Philip called at Buckingham Palace whenever he was on leave from the Navy. Gradually they met more frequently. When they wanted to marry in 1946, the King urged patience, and the following spring he took his daughters away on a tour of South Africa. Princess Elizabeth was separated from Prince Philip from the beginning of February until the middle of May and, by all accounts, was privately rather miserable. Matters moved quickly when she returned to London. The couple became officially engaged, and the wedding was announced for 20th November 1947.

The nation was still deeply gripped by post-war austerity. The economy was in a bad way. The Labour Prime Minister,

Mr Attlee, felt the country could not afford to give people time off from work to make the wedding day a public holiday. The Princess had to surrender her whole allowance of clothing coupons to obtain her wedding dress, which was, nevertheless, designed by Norman Hartnell and made from silk produced by loyal British silkworms. On the day, thousands of people forgot all about its not being a public holiday, and lined the streets of London cheering and waving, revelling in the first bit of real British pageantry that they had been able to see since before the war. Somehow the War Office discovered enough breast-plates and other martial finery to deck out the Horse Guards in their old splendour, though at first it was feared they would have to appear in khaki. The wedding was a tonic for all. The royal couple departed with fifteen pieces of luggage, two hot-water bottles and a corgi for an austerity honeymoon in Hampshire and Scotland.

The marriage has without doubt been a very happy one. Beady-eyed pressmen, seeking for a rift or a flaw, were compelled to invent. This is precisely what some of them did. They took advantage of some of the Duke's absences from his family as he sought to develop useful work of his own that his position, influence and considerable talents could foster, beyond that support of the Queen which he has always put first in his life. He was away on a Commonwealth tour from the autumn of 1956 until the following spring, mainly engaged in studies in Antarctica, in the Galápagos Islands, and on conservation problems; so rumours were put about that this long time away from home was indicative of trouble between husband and wife, or the cause of trouble, or anything else of a similar unpleasant sort that might be suggested by a hint or a leer. It was all lies; but they were circulated so assiduously and with such unwholesome glee that the Queen's secretary felt compelled to issue a denial. It is not astonishing that for a long time the Duke regarded journalists with a jaundiced eye, and that he complained to one of them about 'those bloody lies that you people print to make money, these lies about how I'm never with my wife'.

The Duke, born in Corfu in 1921, five years before the Queen, is the son of Prince Andrew of Greece. He had rights of succession to both the Greek and Danish thrones, but he renounced these in the year of his marriage, when he also adopted the name of Mountbatten. He had been educated at Gordonstoun, in Scotland, as well as at Dartmouth, and he was commissioned in the Royal Navy when he was eighteen. He served throughout World War II in the Mediterranean and the Far East, and he continued with his naval career for some time after his marriage. But as the health of King George VI gradually worsened, the Duke undertook with his wife more and more public duties. Essentially he appears to have seen it as his task to be her supporter in her royal office, taking the weight from her shoulders where this has been constitutionally possible; but he has fulfilled over the years a large number of independent public engagements, and he has shown a special interest in young people and in scientific matters. In his private life he has demonstrated that he is very much the head of his family.

No one likely to know is in any doubt that the Duke's influence has been enormous in shaping the Monarchy to become what it is today in the life of the nation. It went beyond the purely practical matters that he took in hand soon after his wife's accession to the throne, such as various modernisations and labour-saving improvements in the Royal Household. It is probable, to give a small instance, that he has had much to do with gradual but definite changes in the manner of royal speeches, which are much less stilted than they were at the start of the reign and far removed from the conviction of George V that they should never contain jokes. The Duke was influential in the abolition of some of the more outmoded and class-ridden functions of the court, such as the presentations of *débutantes*, and with the institution of some new ones which keep it more in touch with the nation at large, such as the luncheons at which the Queen meets all manner of interesting people from many spheres of life.

Contrary to report, the Duke is an approachable and amiable man. The reputation he acquired for naval bluntness at one period no doubt arose from the fairly numerous occasions when he felt he had been goaded, as he was over the rumours of a marital rift in the Fifties. It has often been said that to take his place as the husband of the Queen he studied assiduously the record and methods of Prince Albert. I once asked him if this was so, and he firmly denied it. He said that he had not thought about doing so, because he and the Queen had not expected that her father, George VI, would die so young as he did, and the time of her accession had seemed remote when they were first married. He said recently in an interview, 'I doubt whether I've achieved anything likely to be remembered.' I think future historians may prove this estimate to have been over-modest; for he has probably been instrumental in giving the ancient British Monarchy a new lease of life.

That it has a new lease of life was seen to be a matter of public fact when the Queen and the Duke celebrated their Silver Wedding in 1972 and again on the Queen's fiftieth birthday in 1976. It was notable that in the newspapers and magazines, which almost without exception had praise for the Monarchy, and especially for the Queen herself, some of the nicest things about both were said by young people or those regarded as spokesmen for the young. For instance, the modish Miss Janet Street-Porter wrote in an *Observer* Supplement article on the birthday that while the mystery of the Queen continued the people were happy to pay for and to prolong the role she has to act out. She noted shrewdly that in these times of economic crisis 'complaints about royal pay come not from the mass of the country's wage-earners stuck on a £6-a-week rise limit, but the same old M.P.s who drearily trot out the same old arguments'. It has become clear that the Queen in middle age is seen by the people over whom she reigns and by those with whom she works as not only a good woman but also a wise and dedicated Sovereign. There is an instinctive national awareness that the majesty she embodies is that of her people, their history and traditions, their laws and their democracy.

Plans were maturing in 1976 for the celebration of the Silver Jubilee of the Queen's reign in the following year. It was announced that the Queen would attend thanksgiving services in St Paul's in London and in Glasgow Cathedral; and that there would be Addresses to her by both Houses of Parliament, a Naval Review at Spithead, a Review of the British Army in Germany, and visits by her and the Duke to places all over the kingdom, including Northern Ireland, during the summer. These and other events were to be supplemented by festivities organised by local authorities and groups all over the country.

Some of the more curious ideas for the occasion emerged in a competition for a Silver Jubilee monument. They included proposals for carving a giant corgi on the South Downs in the manner of the White Horse in Berkshire and the Long Man of Wilmington, for planting a forest at Balmoral in the shape of the Queen's head, and for re-digging and flooding gravel pits near Heathrow to make a water portrait of the Queen which would be seen by travellers from abroad arriving in London by air. Some of these won prizes, but press opinion about them was more amused than enthusiastic. It was decided to run silver-painted buses on sixteen London routes during the Jubilee year, and there were plans to make Leicester Square look more attractive for visitors by introducing a bandstand, closing approaches to traffic, putting down coloured paving and providing floodlighting and more seats. The Prince of Wales was to be Chairman of a panel to select well-designed souvenirs, but the Design Council said nothing could be done to prevent the sale of bad designs, and a fair amount of rubbish was on offer by the autumn of 1976. London's thirty-three Mayors promised 'a great spontaneous festival of the people'; and there were plans for jazz, pop music and opera, street parties, regattas and fireworks. Four special postage stamps were designed to be issued when the Queen made her Jubilee tour. The Prince's most important duty was to lead a national appeal to commemorate the Jubilee. The Queen wanted this to be focused on young people and, particularly, to give them opportunity and encouragement for service to the community. Clearly, too, there was a general hope that the celebrations would foster and concentrate the spirit of patriotism in the British people at a time when their economic difficulties and their reduced world status made great demands for sacrifice to restore the country's prosperity and its reputation as a modern, enlightened and viable democracy.

2. Royal Jubilees

The idea of the Jubilee comes from biblical times, from the Hebrew custom by which every fiftieth year all debts were remitted, all who had lost land within the period had it restored to them, and those who from poverty had hired themselves into bondage were released from it. The first Jubilee in the Christian Church was inaugurated by Pope Boniface VIII in 1300, and he offered plenary indulgences to pilgrims to Rome who fulfilled certain conditions.

Only three English monarchs before Queen Victoria could have celebrated publicly the Golden Jubilee of their reigns—Henry III, Edward III and George III—but they did not.

Queen Victoria's Silver Jubilee year followed close on the death of her husband, Prince Albert, and there could have been no question of any celebrations; but her Golden Jubilee, in 1887, came at a time when the Queen had started to emerge from the shadows of the long retirement from public duty that accompanied her mourning and made her for a time unpopular. She had during the Eighties been seen regularly enough in public to have become a well-loved part of the London scene, and she had also made official visits outside the capital, notably to Birmingham and Liverpool, where she was received with enthusiasm.

Quite apart from the Jubilee celebrations, 1887 was an interesting and exciting year. Politically, Ireland and the campaign for Home Rule was the issue that caused the most general excitement, with the Irish Nationalist members keeping Parliament on its toes in scenes that the Queen's diary recorded as 'shameful'. What unquestionably was shameful in that context was the publication by *The Times* newspaper in 1887 of the forged letter which sought to link the Irish leader, Parnell, with a double assassination in Dublin.

The country was at the height of its industrial power, ahead of all other nations. Compared with the beginning of the reign and the still-remembered 'hungry' Forties, there was for a great part of the nation real prosperity. G. M. Trevelyan says, 'Manners were gentler, streets were safer, life was more humane, sanitation was improving fast, working-class housing, though still bad, was less bad than ever before.' Income tax varied from twopence in the pound to sixpence halfpenny at the highest.

There was enough money about for life to seem good to many, and plenty to buy with it, including quite a lot of fun. Seaside holidays, for instance, were available to the many rather than the few. The painter of 'Derby Day', W. P. Frith, brought out his reminiscences in 1887, in which he tells how Victoria more than thirty years before had bought his crowded holiday beach scene, 'Ramsgate Sands'—which is, incidentally, still at Buckingham Palace, hanging at present in a little waiting room used by many who call there. Had Frith painted this in the year he published his book, he would have found an even more crowded Ramsgate, and a crowd not exclusively middle-class. It was rather a good year for books; for in it, Sherlock Holmes's name was heard for the first time with the publication of young Dr Conan Doyle's *A Study in Scarlet*. Hardy's *The Woodlanders* emerged in that year; so did Rider Haggard's *Allan Quatermain*. Two books published in 1887 were from novelists aware that beneath the sunny surface there were social stirrings, George Gissing's *Thyrza* and *The Revolution in Tanner's Lane* by William Hale White ('Mark Rutherford').

These stirrings did, indeed, exist. The year before, the Trade Union Congress had decided that it lay within its province to set up some machinery for labour representation in Parliament; and now, in the Jubilee Year, most people knew who Keir Hardie was, though it was to be another five years before he entered Parliament as the first Labour member, a one-man party. However, the ordinary working man might not have known it quite as well as he knew the names of the Aston Villa football team, the winners of the F.A. Cup that year; for the age of mass spectator sport had begun. The music halls were packing people in every night. Also there was a new, very English style of opera through the collaboration of Gilbert and Sullivan, who had a different offering almost every year through the Eighties; for the Jubilee Year it was *Ruddigore*. It was a year when the young could look hopefully at the future; and schoolboys all over the country were reading Jules Verne's *The Clipper of the Clouds*, which was being serialised in *The Boy's Own Paper*. It seemed Jubilee Year indeed.

As the day for the official celebrations grew closer, Queen Victoria herself was feeling less jubilant than most. She had been receiving treatment for very painful rheumatism. One spring day she recorded in her Journal that she had fallen asleep in her chair after tea—'a very rare thing for me'. She modified for the Jubilee the very strict regulations as to who might be admitted to Court, so as not to exclude ladies who were innocent parties in divorce cases; but when she wanted to extend this concession to foreign visitors, her Prime Minister, Lord Salisbury, advised her not to do so, because of 'the risk of admitting American women of light character'. She signed remissions of sentences in honour of the Jubilee, but withheld her clemency from one suppliant convicted of cruelty to animals. There was a great deal to do. She was glad to let the Prince of Wales help her, as she would not do over any question of politics or policy.

In the House of Commons, someone was indignant about a decision that London pubs could stay open until 2 a.m. on Jubilee night. An Irish member, Arthur O'Connor, urged on the other hand that the practice of some historic royal occasions be resumed, and that the fountains should run with wine. There was an exchange of great charm during a fuss over the sending to Rome of a present from the Queen to Pope Leo XIII and the reception at Windsor of Papal envoys bearing the Pope's Jubilee congratulations. The Member for Kirkcaldy asked if any other great Ecclesiastics, Christian, Mahommedan, Hindu, or Buddhist, the Moderator of the Free Church of Scotland, or the Grand Imaum of Mecca were permitted to follow this example. The official answer was, 'Whether his Imperial Majesty, the Sultan of Turkey, can properly be called a Great Mahommedan Ecclesiastic I am unable to say. The Moderator of the Free Church of Scotland does not come under the category of a Foreign Potentate.'

The day before the great day, 21st June, on which an old lady was to be the centre of the events, *The Times* newspaper carried an interesting and portentous item about a young lady.

It said, 'The Great Classical Tripos which was published at Cambridge on Saturday was remarkable for the success obtained by a Girton student. The lady, Miss Ramsay, beat all the male students, she being the only one of either sex to pass in the first division.'

In the meantime, the old Queen continued to feel some trepidation about her Jubilee. The essential Jubilee ceremony would be a service in Westminster Abbey, which she had not entered since her Coronation there forty-nine years before, when she was a girl of nineteen. She hoped it would not be too hot a day. She told the Archbishop that the service must not be too long; for 'the Queen feels faint if it is hot'. She went to the Abbey to discuss the arrangements and see how it had been made ready; and now she began to enter into the spirit of the thing and, perhaps remembering that last visit so long ago, felt positively youthful; at all events, on her way back to Windsor, she drove to Earl's Court to see Buffalo Bill's American Wild West Show. The *Observer* had described this early in May: '. . . the Indian village hard by is the acme of order and primness . . . The "Wild West", which is characterised on the programme as "America's National Entertainment", begins with a "Grand processional review", in which all the members of the company take part. The *mise-en-scène* presented by this march past is exceedingly striking . . . Mexicans in velvet, cotton, and silk; and Indians in paint, clothes, and every colour of the rainbow . . . Shooting has its exponents in Miss Annie Oakley, who uses a shot gun, and Miss Lilian Smith, who exhibits a most unerring aim with a pea rifle, and Buffalo Bill himself, who performs some remarkable feats with a rifle on horseback.' The Queen found the show 'very extraordinary and interesting'.

There were still problems to be settled, and about one of them Victoria was being very firm indeed. Nothing would induce her to wear robes of State, as the Prince of Wales, for one, wanted her to do. She would not wear the Crown. She would not carry a sceptre. She would not drive in the ceremonial glass coach, because its movement made her feel sick.

So what the people saw, when the Queen with her cavalcade left Buckingham Palace for the Abbey in golden weather for a golden anniversary, was a tiny figure in black in an open landau which, by contrast with the dazzling display that surrounded it, took on the paramount dignity and importance that was appropriate. There was a trifle of glitter when the sun caught the diamonds in her bonnet of white Spanish lace, a touch of colour from the Orders she was wearing, the Garter and the Star of India. She sat with no one beside her in the landau, but she was faced by her daughter, the Crown Princess of Germany, and her daughter-in-law, the Princess of Wales. Indian cavalry formed the immediate escort; but there were also in the procession Life Guards and Hussars. There was a separate procession of sovereigns. On horseback, ahead of the Queen, rode male members of her family—three sons, five sons-in-law, nine grandsons and grandsons-in-law. In carriages behind came princesses. Also in carriages were Indian princes in cloth of gold, their turbans blazing with jewels. It was all so immensely gorgeous that the old lady at the heart of it was proved right in her instinct to appear less so—in spite of the grumbles of Lord Rosebery, who thought the Empire should be ruled by a sceptre, and not a bonnet; of Lord Halifax, who said people wanted gilding for their money; and Mr Chamberlain from Birmingham, who said a Sovereign should be grand.

At the Abbey the tiny, plump old lady, leaning on a stick, walked up the nave slowly to give public thanks to God for the fifty years of her reign and for all His mercies to her and to her people. She thought much of her dead husband, for whom, she said, this would have been such a proud day. She was glad that the choir sang the *Te Deum* he had composed, and that the anthem incorporated his chorale, *Gotha*, which he had once played to Mendelssohn. The service lasted about an hour.

Later in the day, there was a luncheon; a naval march past, which the Queen watched from a balcony; a dinner at which Scottish pipers played; a reception for the Diplomatic Corps. The sky all over London was popping and blossoming with fireworks. The Queen watched them for a little while, and then asked to be pushed to bed in what she called her 'rolling chair'. She said, 'I was half dead with fatigue.'

London continued with its celebrations. Enormous crowds had packed the streets all day, cheering loud enough to drown the brazen voices of the military bands, the blare of the trumpets. For days an army of carpenters, upholsterers, gasmen and floral decorators had been transforming the town. Now there were illuminations everywhere in the principal streets and squares. A lot of money had been made by those with space to let overlooking the processional route. A first floor in Piccadilly cost £700 of what was then a currency all the world wanted. Single seats went at from five to fifteen guineas. It cost a golden sovereign to risk breaking your neck on an overlooking rooftop. Clubs along Pall Mall made a killing from members and guests. All night, beacons and bonfires blazed from end to end of the country.

The newspapers were almost uniformly ecstatic about the success of the Jubilee. It is true that *Vanity Fair* struck the hint of a sour note at the start of its report, 'The procession to the Abbey was too disjointed to be really impressive, and the Queen looked scared and ill-tempered.' But it concluded that the return journey was 'one of the finest sights that have ever taken place. . . . As to the Queen, she was crying and laughing by turns at the wonderful reception accorded her along the whole route. Never was there such a success.'

It had been a tremendous ordeal as well as a triumph for an old lady. But from Windsor, four days later, she issued a message of thanks to her people for the enthusiastic reception they had given her, and praised 'the wonderful order preserved on this occasion, and the good behaviour of the enormous multitudes assembled'.

In the ten years between Queen Victoria's Golden Jubilee and her Diamond Jubilee in 1897, a great deal that was significant happened in the Queen's family affairs—which were also European affairs, because of the complex ties of so many royal families with the British Royal House—as well as in British domestic matters, political and social, and in Britain's relations with other powers. Although she was lamed and often in considerable pain from her rheumatism, the old Queen during these years seemed to grow in vigour and enterprise, in spite of having reached her seventieth birthday in 1889.

The Queen made several foreign visits, notably one to Berlin on family business of wider import. This included a meeting with Bismarck in which the Iron Chancellor clearly came off second best. Her son-in-law, Crown Prince Frederick, succeeded to the German Imperial throne, but died from cancer within three months. Victoria's grandson, who was to become the 'Kaiser Bill' of World War I, succeeded his father, and immediately began flexing his political muscles. He took objection to the avuncular fashion in which the Prince of Wales still treated him, and was generally such an embarrassing nuisance to everyone that it required all the efforts of the Queen and Lord Salisbury, a Prime Minister with immense Foreign Office experience, to prevent real international trouble. In all this there loomed a menacing portent of horrors which the Queen would not live to see and which her imagination could probably not have encompassed.

In those years, Gladstone's second Irish Home Rule Bill had been rejected by the House of Lords, and was 'out of the way', as some of the unforeseeing said with relief—but a chain of events had been started which stretched into the future to Sinn Fein, the partition of Ireland, the birth of the Irish Republic, and onwards to the exploited hatreds which kill Irish people and British troops in Ulster and by-standers in London streets more than seventy years later. Industrially, the late Eighties and Nineties were a period of great strikes, of which the most important was the London dock strike of 1889 and the engineers' strike of the Diamond Jubilee year. Keir Hardie had founded the Independent Labour Party in 1893, and with this, and other developments, the political power of Labour was forming itself, though not yet fully poised to launch itself effectively on the parliamentary scene.

There were glimpses of the future, some ominous, some inspiring, to be detected in much that happened in the Nineties; with hindsight, one can even see the first strains that are at the heart of the economic difficulties that Britain struggles against today; but the surface mood of the country was even more self-confident in the year of Victoria's second jubilee than it had been in that of her first. Prices were down; wages and living standards were up; there was a high level of employment. Britain, though it had for so long been the centre of an empire, was for the first time self-consciously imperialist not only in the policies of its Government but also in national sentiment at all levels of the population. There was a lively interest in the white man's burden, in distant places, in travel and adventure, and in the sea; and there was also an inward conviction, strengthened by writers of quality as well as by popular magazine literature, that in a decent, honest and manly way, the British were uniquely qualified by nature, or God, or both, to lead the world in such matters. At that time, of course, and for many years previously, a good deal of factual evidence did seem to make some such belief at least understandable; and schoolboys of the bulldog breed, thumbing through the latest G. A. Henty, must in the Diamond Jubilee Year have been at their wit's end to think of new places where the planting of the Union Jack against fearful odds would be a tonic for the natives. A thoughtful few, no doubt, did wonder if all this *hubris* was really a good idea, and peered into the shadows to see where Fate might be waiting with a loaded sandbag; indeed, interestingly, one such was Rudyard Kipling. His fictional offering for 1897 was *Captains Courageous*, in the general spirit of the times, but the Diamond Jubilee itself occasioned him to write his well-known verses entitled 'Recessional', which included the lines 'For frantic boast and foolish word,/Thy mercy on Thy People, Lord!'

The possibility of having a great national celebration in 1897, when Victoria would have been sixty years a Queen, was first discussed after the Jubilee of 1887, but it was not until 1896 that public interest was fully aroused. It was agreed that the central event should be the Queen's going in procession to St Paul's Cathedral to thank God for the blessings of this longest reign in British history, and this was announced in March of the Jubilee Year. There then came from the Colonial Secretary, Joseph Chamberlain, the idea that the celebrations should be given a specifically imperial character. It was decided that not crowned heads, but the Colonial Premiers should be invited, and that representative detachments should be present from various Colonial forces and from other troops serving in the Empire. The Queen approved of this; apart from anything else, she dreaded the prospect of yet again being faced with the problems of precedence involved in accommodating a whole collection of monarchs; it would be bad enough sorting out the princes. Above all, she would on no account have her unpopular grandson, the Kaiser—'so fearfully and senselessly violent', as she confided to her Journal. He had already started angling for an invitation. Noting in her Journal his fortieth birthday, the Queen wrote: 'I wish he were more prudent and less impulsive at such an age.'

Work started on decorating London for the occasion, and there seems to have been no grumbling about the large sums voted for this by the civic authorities and other organisations concerned. To the great benefit of posterity, Fleet Street and the publishing houses also planned their arrangements imaginatively; and one consequence is that the Jubilee is remarkably well-documented. At the time, it must surely have been the most thoroughly-photographed event in history. One can see what the street decorations looked like along the processional route as Jubilee Day approached and, of course, the streets themselves. It is a pleasant surprise for the modern Londoner to discover that, in spite of two world wars, including the heavy bombing in World War II, the London of today is still quite recognisably what might be thought of as Sherlock Holmes's London. At all events this is true of, for instance, the clubs area, along Pall Mall and St James's Street, which seem hardly changed at all; St Paul's and the Bank of England; and by the Law Courts in Fleet Street, which were only fifteen years old in the Diamond Jubilee year, but already had a settled look of long exposure to the London fog and smoke of those days. Messrs. Cassell and Company published for the Jubilee a book of photographs called *The Queen's London* with more than 400 full-page scenes of the capital which are even more fascinating to examine now than when they were taken. They make it evident that in many parts of London a television or film company that could afford to stage the crowd scenes would be able to reproduce the Diamond Jubilee with almost perfect verisimilitude on the real and hardly-changed sites. London is still very much Queen Victoria's London.

The official decorations comprised garlands and swags of evergreen slung between Venetian masts surmounted with Imperial crowns; flags and banners; bouquets of flowers and pots with palms; and electric lamps to make the display show up even more brilliantly at night, a refinement noted with evident pride in contemporary descriptions. Some streets added their own touches of grandeur. St James's Street had massive twin Corinthian pillars at either end of it, with globes on top of them and massed floral arrangements at the base; and along the street itself were festoons of evergreen, baskets of rare flowers, birds in flight, and globes of red, white and blue glass. The south side of the Thames had flowers interspersed with golden eagles with outstretched wings. Larger buildings all the way from Buckingham Palace to St Paul's were outlined by tiny gas and electric lamps, as were others in the City area. Private houses along the processional route provided their own decorations, mostly of coloured draperies, mainly red. Days before the event, people were wearing red-white-and-blue Jubilee favours, the drivers' whips of horse-drawn London carried pennants, bicycle handlebars sported coloured streamers.

All hotels and boarding houses were crammed by the swarm of visitors who came not only from all over Britain but from every country in the Empire and from others all over the world. The principal Empire Premiers stayed at the Hotel Cecil. The foreign royalty went to the royal palaces or to private mansions which had been rented or lent. There were imperial troops at Chelsea Hospital, Hounslow, and Woolwich, and Imperial officers at the Star and Garter Hotel at Richmond.

The increased press of traffic in the streets made them almost impassable and it became hourly more difficult to get from one part of town to another. Vast, good-humoured crowds surged, wide-eyed, along the most important routes. Movement was further hampered by the colossal stands built for spectators along the processional way at almost every possible vantage point. The photographs show a huge one in the forecourt of Charing Cross Station and another nearby in the churchyard of St Martin-in-the-Fields. There were very elegant covered stands outside the Travellers', the Athenaeum, the United Services and other clubs in Pall Mall. A fine stand in Whitehall opposite the Horse Guards cost £7,000 for rental of the site and £5,000 for construction. It had solid concrete foundations from 3 to 6 feet thick, and incorporated 150 tons of timber and 15 tons of 45-foot steel girders. It contained, in addition to 5,000 seats, promenades, reception rooms, a luncheon room to hold 400, ladies' rooms, telephones and a smoking gallery. This amazing edifice took six weeks to build. For a tall stand in St Paul's Churchyard, focal point of the celebrations, a warehouse on one of the most valuable sites in the City was bought—by J. N. Maskelyne, the famous conjurer from the Egyptian Hall—and pulled down. As had happened at the previous Jubilee, very high prices were demanded for positions along the route; but most of the big speculators in seats lost money, some heavily.

The Queen had been much worried by the possibility of accidents to spectators—perhaps thinking of the 3,000 Russians who had been trampled to death at the Tsar's Coronation a few years earlier. She sent numerous messages about this to the Home Office, and local authority officials examined all temporary structures very carefully, condemning some. Crowd control was so well planned that no life was lost.

As happened at the Coronation of Victoria's great-great-granddaughter, Queen Elizabeth II, more than half a century later, crowds began forming for the Jubilee procession at dawn and some had been in their places at the roadside all night. Photographs taken just after first light show groups on the steps of the Duke of York's column in Waterloo Place and near St Mary-le-Strand Church. In fact, they could have found a viewing point somewhere had they arrived considerably later; for the route was six miles long, and except in the heart of the West End and at some famous points in the city, where the photographs show the people packed as for a Cup Final, the onlookers were fairly evenly spread all the way.

The royal train, which brought the Queen from Windsor to London the day before Jubilee Day, had been refurbished for the occasion: it was polished chocolate-and-white on the outside; satinwood, cream silk, white cord, green cord and lace on the inside; on the front of the engine was the Royal Arms; and the Royal Standard flew when the Queen was on board. 'Our Hearts Thy Throne'—an inscription that seems to have taken the fancy of most writers about the Jubilee—was written above a triumphal arch at Paddington beneath which the Queen passed on her way from the station to Buckingham Palace. In the photographs, one can just make out that another, in the Edgware Road, says more simply, 'God Bless Our Queen'; but one has no difficulty in reading the four tiers of, one suspects, fresh advertising on the Floral Stores beside it, which in huge letters announces, among other things, 'All Funeral Designs'. Mr Goodman, a St Paul's Churchyard dentist ('Single Tooth, 2s. 6d.—5 Years Warranty') may also have had an eye to the main chance, and certainly has come down to posterity in letters at least as big as those on Mr Maskelyne's speculative stand next door to him in St Paul's Churchyard, which proclaimed, 'In Every Heart One Prayer: God Save Victoria'. They certainly dwarfed the figure of Field-Marshal Lord Roberts, V.C., known as 'Bobs', who so tragically soon afterwards was to be repairing the disasters of less-successful generals fighting the Boers in South Africa, but was now, mounted on a white Arab pony, commanding the Colonial troops at the Jubilee.

It is known that a great quantity of Mr Maskelyne's money performed an unplanned vanishing trick as a result of his effort to pack in the carriage trade at St Paul's. One may hope that another of his Diamond Jubilee ventures, a more historic one, had better financial luck. This was his filming of the Queen 'by the new cinematograph process' at the steps of St Paul's. His grandson, Jasper Maskelyne, credits him with thus making the first-ever newsreel. The Queen had been filmed before in the previous year, moving about on the terrace at Balmoral with four generations of her family, including the Tsar of Russia and the Tsarina, the Prince of Wales (afterwards Edward VII), the Duke of York (afterwards George V) and the Duke's son, David (afterwards Edward VIII and then Duke of Windsor). She liked new mechanical devices, and had taken a child-like delight in using a phonograph cylinder to send a message in her own voice, and his own Amharic language, to the Emperor of Ethiopia. She indulged this predilection on her Jubilee Day, pressing an electrifying button, just before she left Buckingham Palace in her procession, to send winging round the world by telegraph her Jubilee Message to the Empire: 'From my heart I thank my beloved people. May God bless them!'

As if it, too, were being operated by some new scientific device, the sun emerged from a dull sky at the precise moment —a quarter-past eleven—when the first gun of the Royal Salute boomed from Hyde Park to announce that the Queen was leaving the Palace; and the rest of the day was fine. Everyone knew, of course, that the British Empire had a special arrangement with the sun; so there was no astonishment. Lord Ronald Sutherland Gower watched from a house in Piccadilly, and recalled in his memoirs, 'It was 11.30 when the Queen passed, looking delightfully bright, happy and interested; the only jarring note in that wonderful scene was when a German general rode by, for the crowd groaned at him.'

The first part of the procession had left two hours before, and it was this section that was intended to stamp the day with an unmistakably Imperial character. There were Canadian hussars and dragoons and, of course, the famous Mounted Police, already known to every schoolboy in the crowds for their habit of 'always getting their man'. They preceded a carriage containing the Premier of Canada. So, as the procession continued, each contingent marched ahead of its own political leader. There were mounted troops from several states of Australia, and some, including huge Maoris, from New Zealand. There were troops from the Cape Colony, Trinidad Mounted Rifles, Zaptiehs from Cyprus, Sikhs, Malays, Dyaks, Hong Kong Chinese, very black Hausas, white men, yellow men, brown men. The crowd clearly loved them all, and some felt, too, that in a way they owned them all, a feeling that some of the newspapers, not least Mr Harmsworth's popular *Daily Mail*, had certainly not discouraged.

After an interval came the Royal Procession, headed by an officer with whom, no doubt, many a man in the crowd sought, as we say nowadays, 'to identify'. This was Captain Oswald Ames, of the 2nd Life Guards, the tallest officer in the British Army, six feet eight inches, moustached and very handsome in exactly the Ouida fashion of the day. The women certainly had special feelings about him, too. Next was a Royal Navy gun detachment, and then came Life Guards, Dragoon Guards, Lancers and batteries of the superb Royal Horse Artillery. Carriages with the old Queen's great-grandchildren brought 'oohs' and 'ahs' and frantic clapping. Princes and what the contemporary reports called 'other illustrious persons', representing almost every kingdom and republic in the world, rode in threes immediately before the Dublin-born Commander-in-Chief of the Army, Lord ('It's all Sir Garnet') Wolseley, given place of honour just ahead of the Queen's carriage.

Once again the Queen was in an open landau—her favourite one, known in Royal Mews lists as 'Number One Plain Posting Landau', which generally met her at the station when she came to London by train. It, too, had been refurbished—to look a little grander than usual. A trifle of gilding and some vermilion had been added discreetly to embellish the basic colouring of dark claret common to all royal plain carriages, and there was additional brass beading. The landau was drawn by eight cream horses of a Hanoverian stock bred at Hampton Court since 1837. They were named Occo, King George, Emperor, Amerongen, Monarch, Majestic, Sovereign and Middachten.

The Queen carried a white lace parasol given to her by the oldest Member of her House of Commons, Mr Villiers. She wore a black silk dress and mantle, embroidered with steel and silver, and a bonnet of black lace trimmed with diamonds and a wreath of white acacia. Opposite to her sat the Princess of Wales and the Queen's third daughter, Princess Christian. On her way to St Paul's, Victoria made the halt at Temple Bar, customary when a Sovereign enters the City of London, to be formally presented with the ancient sword of the City by the Lord Mayor.

The Queen's Thanksgiving was made in a short service in front of the cathedral, with bands and 500 choristers massed on the steps. It started with the *Te Deum*. The 'Old Hundredth' was sung and the National Anthem. The Archbishop of Canterbury gave a blessing. Then the Queen made the return journey to the Palace, crossing London Bridge, to go by way of the poorer districts of Southwark and Lambeth.

When night fell, 2,500 beacons were lighted on the hills of Britain—more than three times as many as at the Golden Jubilee.

As to the staggering, overwhelming success of the great Diamond Jubilee there was hardly a dissenting voice. The *Illustrated London News* struck a note of satisfaction that represented the average Press reaction, when it said, 'As an abstract and brief chronicle, not only of the most glorious reign, but also of the growth of the greatest Empire the world has ever known, Queen's Day, 1897, stands unique.' The old Queen, moved to tears at times, so that the Princess of Wales leaned forward to press her hand, looked delighted throughout most of the procession.

One peevish response came from the novelist, Ouida, who said loftily, 'The Jubilee has been the apotheosis of Philistia, and was, I think, a crime as well as a vulgarity. . . . The long reign of Victoria R and I has been a long triumph of the mediocrities, the hypocrisies and the shams.' But then Ouida sometimes was ungracious—for instance, when she accepted a Civil List pension of £150 a year, but complained that the amount was 'only fit for superannuated butlers'.

The Diamond Jubilee was surely the personal peak of Victoria's reign. It bore stunningly-spectacular witness to her genuine achievement in transforming the meaning of the Monarchy, developing it from something that had declined into a mere institution in some disrepute, until it had become broad-based upon the people's will and held strongly in their affections. By her personal prestige and popularity she had killed the English republican movement which had shown signs of growth in the Sixties, and she had developed, to pass down to her successors on the throne, a new technique of Monarchy.

This new style of constitutional Monarchy was to be maintained and consolidated during the less than ten years in which Victoria's son, Edward VII, reigned. He restored some of the personal glamour of the Sovereign, which had declined during Victoria's long widowhood; and although there had been times when, as Prince of Wales, he had been out of favour with much of the public, he was immensely successful as King and enormously popular. He represented change which reflected changes in the people and in the times. As Elizabeth Longford says, 'Kingship may assume different forms without losing its hold upon men's inconstant minds.'

Edward was so much loved, if not exactly esteemed, by the time of his last illness that he would be a difficult man for his heir to follow. He had great dignity, and as he said himself, '*Mon métier à moi c'est d'être roi.*' But he had also a 'real-toff', 'sporting-gent', man-of-the-world affability that made him endearingly 'Teddy' to the ordinary people of his realm, and was something typical of his period. There is a touching suitability in the fact that possibly the last piece of news he was given on the day he died was that his horse Witch of the Air had won at Kempton Park that afternoon. He was told this by his son, George, Prince of Wales, who at a quarter of an hour before midnight on that day, 6th May 1910, himself became the King, as George V.

George, then Duke of York, had been present with his wife, Mary of Teck, at Victoria's great Diamond Jubilee celebration. Aged thirty-two in the Jubilee year, he was a product of the Victorian age and of a kind that Victoria approved. He was a family man as well as a naval officer who had held command, with an insistent sense of duty; meticulous in all things, sometimes irritatingly so. He was known to be blameless in his private life, as his father had not been, modest, good-natured, frank and honest; but as the *Daily Chronicle* said about the time of his accession: 'If he has seen and travelled more than King Edward he has a less intimate and less extensive acquaintance with the world of men and affairs; and to his own subjects he is somewhat of an unknown quantity.' To pare closer to the point of truth, the paper might have added that to many, even most of them, he seemed, frankly, dull. When King George and Queen Mary visited south Yorkshire early in the reign, the Archbishop of York overheard this dialogue:

'Na then, which is t' King?'

'It's t' little chap i' the front wi' a billycock hat.'

'Nay, he ain't seech a fine man as Teddy.'

There is a less kindly—and distastefully-patronising—upper-class echo of this exchange in some verses Max Beerbohm wrote a good many years later about both King and Queen. Beerbohm conceives this conversation between a Lady-in-Waiting and a Lord-in-Waiting at Windsor Castle:

SHE: Slow pass the hours, ah, passing slow;
My doom is worse than anything
Conceived by Edgar Allan Poe:
The Queen is duller than the King.
HE: Lady, your mind is wandering,
You babble what you do not mean;
Remember, to your heartening,
The King is duller than the Queen.

There is a good deal more of the same sort of thing, and then the Lord stabs the Lady, for whom, as he says, Death 'shall have no sting', and himself takes poison, muttering at the last:

Nevertheless, sweet friend strychnine,
The King—is—duller than—the Queen.

By the time these verses had been written a good many years of George V's reign had passed; and for that vast mass of the nation who—to their loss, certainly—had probably never heard of Max Beerbohm, the King, though he might still seem less exciting than old 'Teddy', had become a deeply-beloved figure both as a person and as the focus for their love of their own country.

The reign lasted nearly twenty-six years; so George V, nine months before he died, was the next monarch after Victoria, and the last before the present Queen, to occupy the throne long enough to celebrate a Jubilee. There were thirty-eight years between Victoria's Diamond Jubilee and the Silver

Jubilee of George V in 1935; and between that, of course, and the Silver Jubilee of his granddaughter, Queen Elizabeth II, in 1977, there have been forty-two years. Although change seems more gradual in one's own lifetime than it does in the pages of history, I am convinced that the Britain of George V's Jubilee year was much more like the Britain of today than it was like that of Victoria's Diamond Jubilee. Ample signs of coming change there most certainly were at the end of Victoria's reign and during that of Edward; but it was in the time of George V that the floodgates opened and the world was engulfed in a deluge of change the effects of which are with us yet. Could it really have been a dull, uninspiring and uninspired little man who through all that tumult maintained and renewed for new times the ancient institution of the British monarchy, not simply for its own sake or as a sentimental survival, but as an essential, evidently functioning, and beneficial part of the British system?

When George V took part in his father's funeral procession, eight other kings accompanied him. By the time of his Silver Jubilee, all but two of these kings or their successors had been toppled from their thrones. The greatest war in the history of mankind had been fought. The two most powerful of George's cousins among the crowned heads of Europe, the German Kaiser and the Tsar of Russia, had been swept away in revolution.

The Kaiser at the time of Edward's funeral was ruler of the greatest military power in Europe. In the Jubilee year he was a half-forgotten exile at Doorn in the Netherlands; Hitler's Nazis had been in power for three years in Germany, and only a few months before the Jubilee celebrations, George V had told the German Ambassador bluntly that Germany was once again the peril of the world, and that if she continued to re-arm at her present rate there was bound to be war. Early in the Jubilee year, Hitler ordered conscription in breach of Germany's treaty obligations. In the month in which Britain was celebrating the Jubilee, Hitler, under a secret Defence Law, appointed a Plenipotentiary-General for War Economy, Dr Schacht, and authorised him to 'direct the economic preparations for war'.

Tsar Nicholas of Russia, so like his cousin George in appearance as to seem almost his double, had by the Jubilee year been seventeen years dead—presumed murdered by the Communists, as were his wife and all but, possibly, one of his children. The Tsar's Empire was now a totalitarian Communist state under the dictatorship of a Georgian, known as Stalin, who was also the leader of the world Communist movement. His régime was punctiliously represented at King George's Jubilee celebrations by Marshal Tukachevsky, the man who had led the Soviet invasion of Poland in 1920 and developed the doctrine of spreading socialist revolution by force of Soviet arms. Stalin had him shot in 1937 with five other generals. In August of the Jubilee year, the Eighth Congress of the Communist International, meeting in Moscow, adopted its 'Trojan Horse' policy, of which one effect was that in the following April, a party of over a hundred Spaniards and pseudo-Spaniards who had been living in Moscow were forwarded to Spain by way of Paris.

There were a number of journeys to Germany and Italy by Spanish military men and leaders of the Falange. The stage was set for the Spanish Civil War. Italy in the Jubilee year was also busy preparing a war of her own, building up overwhelming forces in her colonies in Eritrea and Somaliland to launch an invasion of Ethiopia, which she did, in October.

A year then of international violence, murder, intrigue, war and plotting for war, lying, spying, bad faith and the breaking of treaties, tyranny, conspiracy, persecution and fraud: as I have said, very much more like the present time than like that cosy, confident, safe-seeming Diamond Jubilee year of 1897. Indeed, some years before King George's Jubilee, the people of Britain had already started to look back wistfully, almost disbelievingly, as if across centuries rather than relatively few years, at the golden time before the Great War changed everything. Noel Coward's *Cavalcade*, in which the action starts in 1899, and includes a scene with Victoria's funeral—'Five kings riding behind her.' 'Mum, she must have been a very little lady.'—filled the theatre with sodden handkerchiefs and male, stiff upper-lips, as the smash-hit play of 1931; and friends told Coward they were sure he would get a peerage from a grateful monarch. The screen version won an award as the best film of 1933, and as I remember, it had something of the same effect on people as the recent television series, *Upstairs, Downstairs*; also by coincidence, it had among its characters a dedicated upper-servant named Mrs Bridges. People were certainly remembering *Cavalcade* in George V's Jubilee year, and no doubt some cinemas were still showing it. It expressed to a nicety the mood of the time.

It seems incredible, looking back, that people were not more preoccupied with the real, utterly evil and terrifying facts of the times in which they were living, than they were with this already almost mythical past. It is true, of course, that not everything was known. The full inwardness and extent of the horror and menace of Germany and Russia is something we have discovered in the years since, and so far as Russia is concerned, are still discovering. Yet echoes of the violence, fanaticism, cruelty and injustice of those places—which seemed much further away than they do nowadays—were reaching Britain and having some effect there. Londoners old enough to remember may have seen something of the mob violence—some of it very shocking indeed in an English context—that accompanied the activities of Sir Oswald Mosley's Blackshirts: their Jew-baiting and beating up of hecklers; their clashes with Communists in the East End of London and in Hyde Park; their strutting, posturing and parading in emulation of Mussolini and Hitler, who appeared to the bulk of the population as a couple of shoddy, if vaguely sinister, comedians. The horrifying old monster in the Kremlin was having considerably more success. It was one thing to see him presented as a new Redeemer amid all the pictures of tractors in the copies of *Russia Today* sold by earnest young women outside Victoria Station; it was quite another to have him accepted at his own valuation by people of eminence who must surely have had access to sources of information that told a different story.

Yet in the Jubilee year of 1935, there was published in Britain a book entitled *Soviet Communism: A New Civilization?* Its authors were Beatrice and Sidney Webb, two of the most respected social historians of their age, who had been among the founders of the London School of Economics and of the *New Statesman.* Sidney, ennobled in 1929 as Baron Passfield, held a variety of Government ministries at various times. Beatrice was an ardent advocate of Royal Commissions, and sat on a great many of them. Sidney's greatest achievement, we are told, was 'the placing of the British Socialist movement in its historical setting'. He and his wife failed with remarkable thoroughness in their attempt, if that is what it was, to perform a similar service for Stalin's 'socialism'. It is perhaps fanciful to discern something sinister in the Webbs. They were, no doubt, earnest and well-meaning, though possibly tinged with that intellectual arrogance that can destroy souls. Yet there is a macabre 'Arsenic-and-Old-Lace' quality about William Nicholson's famous picture of the pair. Sitting by their fireside, the hearth-rug littered with White Papers, statistics and reports, they could well be discussing in highly-bred voices the best way to tidy up the bodies in the cellar. That is exactly what they did do in their book about Russia. It is hard to imagine that this solemn parade of half-truths, downright lies and statistics that were worse than lies, can really be in even the smallest degree based on actual experience of the Soviet Union; yet the Webbs paid two visits there and must have believed, those two trained observers, that what they were shown was all they needed to see.

Another apparently deceived at the time was E. M. Forster, the novelist, from whose collection of short pieces, *Abinger Harvest,* I selected a quotation for the beginning of this book, which expresses rather well part of what I am trying to say about the British Monarchy. But I also chose it for fun, because it comes from an address that Forster made to an international writer's congress in Paris in George V's Jubilee year, and in it, he also says, 'I am not a Communist, though perhaps I might be one if I was a younger and a braver man, for in Communism I can see hope.'

There was also that man of God, Hewlett Johnson, Dean of Canterbury, who would believe no evil of the Soviet Union. A friend of mine, an English Communist, who foolishly became a Soviet citizen, and so, in Stalin's good time, a citizen of the Gulag Archipelago, nearly lost his life because of a statement by this clergyman that there were no prison camps in the Soviet Union. When this was reported in the Soviet Press, my friend was set upon by his fellow prisoners as the only available compatriot of the Dean on whom they could vent their fury.

With these examples before them, it is not astonishing that many of the intelligent young men at Oxford and Cambridge about that time took on various shades of Marxist hue from palest pink to deepest red. The former British Communist, Douglas Hyde, an ardent activist at that time, tells in his book,

I Believed, how all this fitted in with the Kremlin's 'Trojan Horse' decision of the Jubilee year. 'It resulted in the tactic of the Popular Front, the decision to enlist the aid of the middle class, the intellectuals . . . The new tactic was to soft-pedal in public whilst sticking to everything as before in private.' He says that books which stated the Communist position with frankness, such as the English version of *The A.B.C. of Communism*, were withdrawn or destroyed. In the Soviet Union, more thorough in such matters, the authors of the book were liquidated.

To revert to comparison of such things with the Diamond Jubilee Year, one recalls the well-known comment of the Victorian lady on a performance of *Hamlet*: 'So unlike the home life of our own dear Queen!' Much else in George's Jubilee year was also utterly different from anything in the dear Queen's time but, like the Communist Trojan Horse, very similar to much that is happening today. For example, some of the books that came out in the Jubilee year of 1935, and were being read by that vast majority of the reading public who would never have thought of picking up *The A.B.C. of Communism*, have a remarkably up-to-date flavour. That was the year of Christopher Isherwood's *Mr. Norris Changes Trains* and Cyril Connolly's *The Rock Pool*, both novels of the Jubilee year rich in sexual variety. Of course, there were a lot of people in that year, and more than there would be now, who would disapprove of such matters being written about at all; and they might have picked instead from the 1935 crop Enid Bagnold's *National Velvet*, which is about a girl who trains a horse for the Grand National and herself rides it to victory. I don't know if George V ever read this book, though it is likely that one of his great-grandchildren has done so.

George V is reputed to have said on one occasion. 'I won't knight buggers.' It seems fairly certain that he did say, when told that a nobleman of his acquaintance was rumoured to be homosexual, 'I thought men like that shot themselves.' In this innocent and forthright opinion, George V was, as in so much else, in step with the broad mass of his people, although in some things a pace, or half a pace, behind. That was one of his characteristics that many people especially liked, because it made him a link with the past as well as someone to revere in the present. It was notorious that he could be explosively-conservative about small matters, such as niceties of dress; but the general impression he had created during an unprecedentedly-turbulent reign, which had started with a constitutional crisis, was of a large tolerance in major change. He was suspicious about socialism—after all, the men who butchered his relatives in Russia called themselves socialists—but he was the first British monarch to have a Labour Government, and it may be said that he reconciled it to the British Constitution. It is charmingly typical that when he first received Ramsay MacDonald as Prime Minister, the King put on a red tie for the occasion. MacDonald acquired a liking for Court dress. The King noted in his diary on the evening Labour took office, 'To-day 23 years ago dear Grand-mama died. I wonder what she would have thought of a Labour Government!' In his reign a large part of Ireland became a free state. Women gained the vote on equal terms with men, making Britain genuinely and completely a democracy for the first time.

The crowds who celebrated the Jubilee were aware of these things, and conscious that in all this great change he had played a vital role, sometimes as a steadying influence, most often as a conciliator. As they put up the flags for his great day, not unaware that the clouds of a new war might be gathering, many remembered him in the Great War visiting his troops in France each year, once suffering serious injury when his horse reared and fell upon him, fracturing his pelvis. He had been the focus of the nation in the high fervour of the war's beginning and during the ecstatic joy and relief of its ending. A great many would have known that as the Sovereign of a civilised people he had fought hard to keep it civilised in spite of the brutalising pressures of the first total war, resisting tendencies to popular hysteria and calls for harsh treatment of conscientious objectors and retaliation against prisoners; that he had always used his great personal influence on the side of humanity and moderation. Many may have sensed what has now become the verdict of history, that he was the first great constitutional Monarch.

Of course, people were remembering little, rather endearing things that were known about him: for instance that, appropriately for a story-book sailor, he had made a favourite pet of a parrot named Charlotte, carrying her on his wrist, and in defiance of his own firm rules of domestic decorum, allowing her to walk about the table as he took his breakfast; that he observed a fashion strange in 1935, and dating from his naval days, of wearing his trousers creased at the sides instead of at front and back; that deeply English in his capacity to be absorbed by a hobby, he collected stamps; that he could lose his temper suddenly, and let out a quarter-deck bellow; that he was astonishingly and genuinely a democrat, on *their* side, and had proved it in some very difficult political situations; and though he was manifestly a very posh and proper King, he was also a very nice old gentleman. He had certainly come to terms with his times, and yet somehow, in the process, he had added to, rather than diminished, the glamour, majesty and magic of the Crown. He was better known to his people than any Monarch in history. They had seen him on the cinema screen, usually doing rather grand and ceremonial things, but sometimes rather homely things, such as riding with the Queen on the scenic railway at the British Empire Exhibition, grimly holding in place his grey bowler hat, but still looking absolutely the King. They associated him importantly with sport, and though his own sports were shooting and yachting, at both of which he was expert, this for the ordinary man meant that his presence was a vital part of the Cup Final at Wembley every year. Above all, he was the first Monarch whose voice was known to all his people, broadcasting a message to them on Christmas Day, establishing a custom that by 1935 had become as much an expected part of the festivities as the plum-pudding.

It would be hard to exaggerate the extent of George V's popularity at the time of his Jubilee; and it could be that, in spite of his kingliness, his upbringing, his complex network of foreign family connections and the long royal line of his ancestry, the British people loved him because they felt he was deeply like them. An anecdote that perhaps shows that this instinct was at least partly correct concerns the friendship he formed with that Grand Old Man of Labour, George Lansbury, a product of elementary schools in the London East End, a family man of the working classes and the embodiment of working-class virtues. When under the first Labour Government Lansbury became First Commissioner of Works, he had frequent audiences with the King because of his responsibilities for parks and palaces. The audiences grew longer and longer. A courtier compelled to interrupt one of them tells how he crept in to find the two old men sitting gossiping 'like charwomen'. The King was saying, 'But they called it a *minor* operation, Mr Lansbury, and they opened me from *here* to *here*.'

So for the King of what was still one of the world's most powerful nations, and for the Emperor of what was still 'the greatest empire the world had ever known', and for old George Lansbury's friend, they put out the flags and cheered. A sixth-form grammar-school boy at the time, living in North London, I remember it all very well: the poorer streets decorated with great invention and trouble; the long tables for children's parties in the open, with tea in urns and jugs, and men leading each other off, all winks and nudges, to where there was also a store of booze; the pianos hauled out into the roadway from the front parlours, where there was still many an aspidistra, for 'Knees Up, Mother Brown!' far into the night. I also went with friends up to town to see the illuminations and flood-lighting and something of the formalities; stood in the crowd to see the carriages go by; heard the 'oohs' and 'ahs' for the passage of the one that held the two little princesses, Elizabeth and Margaret Rose, with their father and mother, then Duke and Duchess of York; and the deafening cheers for the King and Queen themselves. I listened to the King's Jubilee broadcast.

The central event, once again, was a drive by the Sovereign to St Paul's Cathedral for a service of thanksgiving. But celebrations of one kind or another went on in glorious weather for nearly a month, and there were several unheralded drives by the King and Queen into the London suburbs. After a tumultuous reception in the East End, the King remarked with wonder, 'I'd no idea they felt like that about me. I am beginning to think they must like me for myself.'

Not long afterwards he was dead. One of his young subalterns from the Great War, Edmund Blunden, who had also written of the horrors of the trenches, wrote a poem about him.

An honest King's the noblest work of God—
    Now passes one whom all the world termed so.
Some terrified the highest with their nod,
    This Monarch held no subject high or low.
Whatever passion raged, it shall be known,
He but appeared or spoke: that storm was overblown.

QUEEN VICTORIA'S DIAMOND JUBILEE, 1897

The scene at St Paul's. 'In Every Heart One Prayer', but the dentist had an eye for an opportunity

London Clubland proclaims Victoria's sixty years as Queen. Very expensive decorations in St James's Street

King George V and Queen Mary with a preoccupied granddaughter—the next Sovereign to celebrate a Silver Jubilee

Dudley Street, Paddington, puts out the flags for George V's Silver Jubilee. He said, 'I am beginning to think they must like me for myself.'

Whatever Party claimed as right or wrong,
   That he was wise and kind offended none;
Therefore our love shall be his evensong;
   All dwellers in the dark and in the sun,
In the most populous, the most lonely places
Shall set a King among their old familiar faces.

3. How the Queen Reigns

Laying the foundation stone of the Engineering College in Delhi in 1959, the Duke of Edinburgh confessed that he had been in two minds about accepting the invitation to do so. He said: 'You see, there is a sort of myth that members of the royal family do nothing else but open things and lay foundation stones, and I don't want to add any substance to that idea. I may say I have not laid a foundation stone for several years, so you must forgive me if I don't do it very expertly.'

The myth certainly does exist, and this is, to some extent, understandable; for it is in the gracing of public events, in lending a special dignity and air of occasion to them, that the most publicly active of the royal family's members are generally likely to be seen in person by the people. The demands made on the Queen for her presence at an enormous number of varied happenings throughout the country of at least local importance are far greater than she could possibly satisfy; and yet, they are, so to speak, no more than part of the icing on the cake, and something remote from the Queen's constitutional duties.

Following the Queen about the country on regional tours or for some special event, I have sometimes taken the opportunity to ask schoolchildren, who are always much in evidence for a royal visit, just what they know about the work of their Sovereign. I ask such questions as 'What does she really do? What is she for?' I would hardly venture to claim that the children I spoke to were a representative cross-section in any scientific sense; but for what it is worth, I have found a consistent pattern in their answers which leads me to suspect that children in Britain are not taught much at school about their country's Constitution, and that few, if any, schools make such instruction a regular feature of school life, as it seems to be, for example, in schools in the United States. After the wide-eyed and irrelevant first answers from the most easily impressed and effervescent small girls—'I think she's *lovely*!' and so on—I usually find two opposite and extreme conceptions of the Queen are offered with most conviction. There are the blindingly-ignorant romantics, who think she has absolute power—'She could chop your head off!'—like the Queen of Hearts in *Alice in Wonderland*; and there are the self-consciously knowing cynics—'She doesn't do anything really it's all the Prime Minister, isn't it?'—who believe her to be purely decorative. The majority of the children seemed to be among the most truly representative citizens in a democracy, the mighty army of the 'Don't-Knows'. But they liked having a Queen, and without conveying any impression of having thought much about the matter, seemed quite convinced that a president, for example, would be boring by comparison.

That, then, is how children seem to view the British Monarchy, but it may perhaps be useful here to recall what the Queen's constitutional position really is.

The Queen traces her descent very far back, to Egbert, who was sovereign of all England in 829. As Queen of Scotland, she can claim descent through James VI of Scotland (James I of England) in the enormously-long Scottish royal line, which was founded by an Irish chieftain, Fergus MacErc, who established himself in Argyll at the beginning of the sixth century. There used to be a time when at all Scottish Coronations the Sovereign's pedigree had to be recited complete in Gaelic right back to King Fergus, but eventually the Lords Lyon decided only the reigning Monarch and the six predecessors need be named, and perhaps this is just as well. At all events, the Queen's ancient lineage clearly makes the Monarchy Britain's oldest secular institution. Only once—during Cromwell's 'Commonwealth' from 1649 to 1660—has the continuity of the Monarchy been broken in eleven centuries, and even then, it could be held, and was by very many, that Charles II continued to reign in exile. Though there have, of course, been interruptions in the direct line of succession, the hereditary principle has always been maintained.

Much of British domestic history is, as we all know, made up of the series of confrontations which gradually modified the power of the Sovereign to change it from the supreme legislative, executive and judicial power, which it was in the most real sense for several centuries, to the limited, constitutional Monarchy we have today. But precisely what is that? It cannot be simply defined, partly because the United Kingdom has no written Constitution, and there is, indeed, no official document which gives a definitive ruling on what the Queen today may or may not do. Those who attempt simplification usually find themselves writing a great deal more than they intended, or going back to the irreplaceable work of Walter Bagehot who, in *The English Constitution*, first published in 1867, made what is still the best attempt to get the whole thing down on paper in a manner which is intelligible, very readable and, in parts, even entertaining. In practice, of course, the working of the British Constitution, and the Queen's position in it, are well understood. What is more, it amounts to a system that still on the whole works well, and continues—though some might argue about this—to preserve the ancient and hard-won liberties of the British people, expressing their will and translating it into action. It is a system in which political decisions are taken by responsible ministers answerable through Parliament to the people, while the Queen acts as an impartial Head of State.

Inevitably oversimplifying, it is possible to describe the essential workings of the Constitution in a sequence which recurs at least every five years. In a general election, the people elect members to represent them in Parliament; and the Queen invites the leader of the largest party to form a Government. At the State Opening of Parliament, she reads her Speech from the Throne in the House of Lords, outlining the Government's programme. Thereafter, in the House of Commons, consisting essentially of the Speaker, the Prime Minister with his supporters and the Opposition, and in the House of Lords, consisting essentially of the Lord Chancellor, the Leader of the House, Government supporters and Opposition, legislation is introduced, debated, and approved or rejected by vote, and questions are asked and answered, so that Government can govern in the name of the Queen and Parliament. Then, after five years, or less if the Government is defeated on a major issue, or if the Queen consents to its resignation for whatever reason, Parliament is dissolved—although the Lords, as a non-elected chamber, retain their seats. There is another general election, in which the people can vote to bring the same party back into power, or to make a change.

All this accords substantially with Bagehot's analysis, although since his time, the collective responsibility of the Cabinet for government has been modified by the transfer of power from the floor of the House of Commons to the great party machines, the bureaucracy in Whitehall, and most recently, as some would assert, to the trades unions. The five-year rule for the maximum length of a Parliament has also come into being since Bagehot's time, when Parliaments could survive seven years. This was brought about by the Parliament Act of 1911 which, with other later legislation, also reduced the power of the Lords, mainly their capacity to delay measures the Commons had approved.

In this truncated account of the functioning of the British Constitution the Queen does, indeed, seem to play only a purely formal part, opening Parliament as she might open a new town hall or launch a ship; giving her blessing to the scene of deliberations in which she will have no real part; making the signal to start a machine of which she will not be the pilot and which will not have her hand at the controls; making a speech which she has not herself composed, announcing policies and proposals which do not necessarily have her approval as a person, although as a constitutional Monarch she must approve them. Is there, in fact, no more than this to the Queen's constitutional role?

For the greater part of the answer we can again consult Bagehot, and we can do so the more easily because there is available an admirable summary of the relevant part of his book, prepared twenty-seven years after its first appearance by a young man of twenty-nine who was one day himself to be the King of England, and who would, as his official biographer says, apply 'with consistent faithfulness' Bagehot's 'conceptions of the function and duties of a constitutional monarch'. This was George V, at the time Duke of York, who in 1894 was receiving instruction from the Cambridge authority on constitutional history, J. R. Tanner, and summarised Bagehot in careful handwriting in a notebook still kept at Windsor. Part of what he wrote under the heading, 'Monarchy', was as follows:

'The Crown is no longer an "Estate of the Realm" or itself the executive, but the Queen nevertheless retains an immense unexhausted *influence* which goes some way to compensate for the formal *powers* which have been lost; this influence can be exercised in various ways: a) In the *formation* of Ministries; especially in choosing between the Statesmen who have a claim to lead party. b) During the *continuance* of Ministries. The Crown possesses *first* the right to be consulted, *second* the right to encourage and *third* the right to warn. And these rights may lead to a very important influence on the course of politics, especially as under a system of party government, the Monarch alone possesses a *continuous political experience*.'

Later in his notes the future King wrote, 'Thus, though it would be possible to construct a system of political machinery in which there was no monarchy, yet in a State where a monarchy of the English type already exists, it is still a great political force and offers a splendid career to an able monarch; he is independent of parties and therefore impartial, his position ensures that his advice would be received with respect; and he is the only statesman in the country whose political experience is continuous.'

George V's official biographer, Sir Harold Nicolson, says of him, 'His faith in the principle of Monarchy was simple, devout even; but selfless. All that he aspired to do was to serve that principle with rectitude; to represent all that was most straightforward in the national character; to give the world an example of personal probity; to advise, to encourage and to warn. To few men has it been granted to fulfil their aspirations with such completeness.'

The unrestricted access to the Royal Archives afforded by the Queen to John Wheeler-Bennett when he was writing the official life of her father, George VI, has made available to the public facts to demonstrate how he, in his much shorter reign, followed the example of George V in fulfilling his constitutional role—during times of great drama, difficulty and danger for his country—with devotion, rectitude and commonsense, and also with courage, maintaining the efficacy and usefulness of the Monarchy in the midst of profound social change, encouraging and warning his ministers, a focus for the patriotic endeavour and sacrifice of a people at war. By the dedicated manner in which she fulfils her publicly more apparent duties, and by what can be inferred from statements of several of her Prime Ministers, it is not difficult to judge that the Queen herself, already on the throne more than ten years longer than was her father, has in her performance of those functions central to her constitutional role acted, as he did, in what, as one contemplates the promise of Prince Charles, is beginning to emerge as a recognisable Windsor style, constitutional Monarchy *par excellence*.

Bagehot notwithstanding, it has to be stressed that there are still grey areas in the unwritten British Constitution concerning the circumstances in which the Monarch can and should act independently; and they are likely to continue to give great scope for argument among constitutional lawyers. Two of the grey areas relate to the Monarch's powers in the granting of a dissolution of Parliament and in the appointment of a Prime Minister; and in this century, these have caused controversy.

For example, in 1913, George V was made the centre of a major row about dissolution during the trouble over Irish Home Rule. The Lords had twice rejected the Liberal Government's Bill to grant Home Rule, but it was presented to Parliament for a third time, as it could be under legislation passed two years previously. The Unionists maintained that the King should dissolve Parliament, even though the Prime Minister, Mr Asquith, did not want him to do so, to enable the people in a general election to express their will in this controversial matter. In their view, the King retained the right to dissolve Parliament at his discretion, especially when government policies produced the threat of civil rebellion. Others argued, on the contrary, that the Monarch's right to dissolve Parliament on his own initiative had perished from disuse, and in any case, it was not practical politics. It was a splendid rumpus in days when there were more serious newspapers than there are now ready to devote many packed columns to such weighty stuff, and it continued to reverberate until the outbreak of World War I gave everybody other things to think about. There was a somewhat less wordy dispute when the war ended in 1918. The Prime Minister, Lloyd George, wanted a dissolution, so that he could continue his coalition Government in peace-time with the backing of the electorate in the making of the peace. The King took the view that the Government was pledged to make the peace treaty before there was an election, and that because of problems involving soldiers serving abroad, other service voters, and newly-enfranchised women, the election result was unpredictable. Lloyd George had his way, the election was held, and his Government romped home with a big majority.

The matter of appointing Prime Ministers involved the Queen in controversy in 1963, when Harold Macmillan was compelled to step down because of the state of his health. On Mr Macmillan's advice, the Queen very properly named the Earl of Home (later Sir Alec Douglas-Home, on the renunciation of his peerage) who, he informed her, commanded the greatest overall support in the Conservative Party. Later there was a fuss, because some Tories believed this advice to the Queen had been incorrect. What really happened must remain a mystery until the relevant papers become available from the Royal Archives and elsewhere. In the meantime, the Tories have decided to follow Labour's example and elect their Leader; so a precisely similar situation is unlikely to occur again. But the Monarch could still be required to play something more than a purely formal role in naming her Prime Minister; for instance, when there is a minority government, a coalition, or when it is unclear what party or balance of parties would be capable of forming a Government. A striking Liberal revival, presenting the country with a three-party system, could well give the Queen no obvious choice.

Another situation, though one without precedent, in which the Queen might have to play a crucial constitutional role, could arise in the (one hopes) unlikely event of a government's refusing to resign after losing the confidence of the Commons on a major issue. There is, in fact, no constitutional machinery for throwing out such a government, other than the dissolution of Parliament on the Monarch's initiative, or eventually the refusal of Supply by the Commons. Constitutional historians tend to regard such a development as being too unlikely to be worth much thought. According to R. M. Punnett, of the University of Strathclyde, '. . . it is venturing into the realms of Constitutional fiction to see the Monarch achieving today what could not otherwise be achieved by the pressure of public opinion or the threat of civil revolt.' In his view, the practical significance of the Monarch's constitutional functions is slight.

He was writing in 1968. Eight years later, it became evident that there were some politicians in the Labour Party who did not entirely agree with him; at all events, if they were with him in regarding the practical significance of the Monarch's constitutional functions as slight, they also clearly felt that it was not slight enough. This emerged when, in March 1976, the party's Home Policy Committee, of which Mr Wedgwood Benn was the chairman, put forward a document containing proposals aimed at removing the Sovereign's power to dissolve Parliament and to call on a party leader to form a government. The purpose, it was stated, was to take the Crown out of politics. A Conservative Member of Parliament, Mr Nicholas Ridley, questioned the wisdom of this. He thought it was a sensible, democratic safeguard that the Monarch should retain the power to dissolve Parliament and order a general election. 'Taking the Crown out of Politics' meant, in his view, that there would be no one to force a government to go to the country when it could no longer govern. 'In other words,' he said, 'knock out the referee in case he catches you doing a foul.' In an age when increasingly it seems safest to assume that what can happen will happen, and take precautions accordingly, Mr Ridley could well be right. But it would be a grave mistake to assume that the Queen would ever wish to be placed in a situation where the use of her remaining powers was unavoidably necessary. She, like her predecessors back to, and including her grandfather, George V, has never used these powers, and it has been held that they are valuable precisely because it is unlikely that they ever would be used. Clearly, Prime Ministers have a duty to avoid putting the Sovereign in a difficult position, and to use imagination and commonsense to this end. However, this aspect of the Queen's work does throw into relief the fact that she is far from being a mere figurehead, even though, in the Windsor tradition, she would always remain above party politics. She is, indeed, the custodian for the nation of their constitutional processes, the ultimate guardian of their freedoms; and it would be hard to imagine one more disinterested.

The Queen's constitutional role means, in practice, a great deal of sustained hard work, not to say drudgery. She has, as I have said, the right to be consulted, which implies, of course, the right to be informed. Indeed, were she not informed, she could hardly exercise effectively her other rights, to encourage and to warn. This means that every day, wherever she may be, at home or abroad, documents arrive for her scrutiny from her Ministers in the United Kingdom and from her representatives in the Commonwealth and in foreign countries—informative telegrams, despatches and letters; and Submissions for her to approve and sign. I am told that on the average, 120 letters are received for the Queen's attention each day. Each morning and evening, boxes come carrying the Foreign Office telegrams, consisting of the reports of Ambassadors and Ministers and instructions or answers given by the Foreign Office. The Queen also receives details of all Cabinet meetings, accounts of parliamentary proceedings, and indeed, the best of the information available in every government department, not only in the United Kingdom, but also in those Commonwealth countries of which she is Head of State. As Dorothy Laird puts it, 'The Queen has passing before her all the information needed for making her, increasingly as her reign lengthens, the most fully informed person in the world.'

Information comes to the Queen also from the numerous meetings she has with people of importance from all over the world, such as visiting heads of State, Ministers from Commonwealth countries, Ambassadors and High Commissioners, distinguished people from all walks of life in Britain and abroad, and diplomatic representatives of foreign countries. As a matter of routine, the Queen has regular meetings with the Prime Minister and with other Ministers when necessary. Many of them have borne witness to the Queen's ample possession of that 'continuous political experience' which her grandfather carefully underlined when he made his conscientious notes out of Bagehot, and to her capacity for absorbing, marshalling and retaining in her mind the fruit of what her uncle, Edward VIII, in the few months he reigned before abdicating, had vilified as 'this interminable amount of desk work'. Harold Macmillan, recalling his relations with the Queen as Prime Minister, said she was 'not only very charming, but incredibly well informed'; and he praised her memory, telling of how she reminded him at an audience of what he had said to her six years before. Harold Wilson noted that she was a voracious reader of all state documents, and said that if she quoted one he hadn't read, he 'felt like a schoolboy who hadn't done his homework'. Lord Home (as he is now) also once told me in conversation how valuable he had often found the unbroken continuity of the Queen's acquaintance with public affairs, especially in seeking to view them in proper perspective.

Many of the royal functions continue to be exercised through the Privy Council. This has its roots in the *curia regis*, which was the court or council of the Monarch in Norman times, and itself, in some respects, the successor of the even more ancient Saxon *witan*. The Council's chief function today is almost entirely formal, that is, to meet when the approval of the Queen in Council is required to be given to executive acts; but a Committee of the Council can be set up to deal usefully with all kinds of affairs—for example, its Judicial Committee still acts as a final court of appeal for some Commonwealth countries. The Queen summons about twenty meetings of this Council every year. In addition, she gives audiences or holds meetings for all manner of purposes, receives the Lord Chamberlain and the Vice-Chamberlain of the Household when they come at intervals to present addresses from the Lords and Commons respectively, holds fourteen investitures a year, and is the central figure of a great variety of State functions and public occasions.

Far more than any of her predecessors, the Queen has sought to bring the Monarchy closer to the people by seeing as much as she can of all sections of the community; so she takes every opportunity to fit in to her overburdened programme visits all over the country to universities, schools, hospitals, factories, service establishments, and celebrations and events of local importance; and for her, such engagements no longer mean simply shaking hands with the most important people; for she likes to meet and talk with others representative of the workaday activity of the place she is in. Gone are the days of the perfunctory smiling word from the royal visitor. I remember once talking to a warehouse manager with whom the Queen seemed to be chatting with considerable animation when she attended the official opening of the new Covent Garden, the vast market for fruit and vegetables at Nine Elms in South London. When I asked him what the Queen had talked about, he looked at me in genuine wonder, and said, 'Do you know what? She really wanted to *know*. So I told her. And she really *listened*.'

The Queen also represents the nation as its most exalted hostess and its most welcomed ambassador. Her hospitality to visiting Heads of State, with all the attendant grand, but exhausting banquets, receptions and ceremonial, has been regarded by successive Governments as of the utmost importance in the conduct of Britain's foreign relations, as have been the immense number of tours abroad that she has carried out since the beginning of her reign.

In Britain nowadays it is often forgotten—or, at least, not often remembered—that the Queen is Queen not only of the United Kingdom and its remaining dependencies, but also of eleven independent countries of the Commonwealth. These are Australia, the Bahamas, Barbados, Canada, Fiji, Grenada, Jamaica, Mauritius, New Zealand, Papua–New Guinea, and Trinidad and Tobago. Of the other countries which are full members of the Commonwealth, eighteen are republics, with a President as Head of State; four are monarchies with their own monarchs; and one has a Paramount Chief as its elected Head of State. But all these countries accept the Queen as the Head of the Commonwealth, the symbol of the free association of its members. The Queen views her Commonwealth role with high seriousness and great devotion; and of course, it adds a good deal to her preoccupations, even though, as the *Commonwealth Year Book* says, 'No functions attach to the title of Head of the Commonwealth and it has no strict constitutional significance.' That the Commonwealth is something very difficult for those outside it to understand was a fact that King George VI fully acknowledged at a time when it was not quite such a bewildering anomaly as it appears to many today. According to John Wheeler-Bennett, the King used to say that the reaction of the outsider must surely be that of the man who, on first seeing a giraffe, exclaimed, 'There ain't no such animal!' It has to be said also that nowadays there are citizens of countries inside it, including Britain, who do not regard its usefulness as beyond question. The British doubters wonder if what Britain gets out can be commensurate with what she puts in, and take the view that she has useful influence in it only with those nations of which the Queen is Head of State; and that otherwise, her membership of the European Community and of the United Nations is more valuable to her, and should take precedence. However this may be, in Whitehall and at Buckingham Palace much importance was attached during 1976 to the plans to hold a meeting of Commonwealth Heads of Government in London in mid-1977 at the time of the celebrations of the Queen's Silver Jubilee, which it was pointed out was also the Jubilee of her accession as Head of the Commonwealth.

In those countries of the Commonwealth which still have the Queen as Head of State, the Queen is represented by Governors-General appointed by her on the advice of the ministers of the countries concerned. In the exercise of the powers of the Crown in the country to which he is appointed, the Governor-General acts in accordance with that country's constitutional practice, and is wholly independent of the United Kingdom Government.

The astonishingly large amount of her time that the Queen gives to her Commonwealth duties, and particularly to the long periods of exhausting travel that are involved, shows that she remains determined to fulfil the promise she made when, in the Christmas message broadcast from New Zealand in 1953, she said:

'The Commonwealth bears no resemblance to the empires of the past. It is an entirely new concept, built on the highest qualities of the spirit of man: friendship, loyalty and the desire for freedom and peace. To that new conception of an equal partnership of nations and races I shall give myself heart and soul every day of my life.'

Three other high functions involve the Queen in duties which occupy many hours of her working life—her position in relation to the armed forces, her role as the Fount of Honour, and her governorship of the Church of England.

One of the Queen's titles in the United Kingdom—as well as in Canada and New Zealand, though it was dropped fairly recently in Australia—is *Fidei Defensor*, Defender of the Faith. It is commonly assumed nowadays that this relates in some way to the Queen's function as Governor of the Established Church, the Church of England; but though it is in fact a title awarded by Pope Leo X to Henry VIII, in acknowledgment of his book against Luther's anti-papal teachings, *Assertio Septem Sacramentorum*, and scholars may detect some anomaly in its retention by a Royal House compelled by law to be Protestant, even the Queen's loyal Roman Catholic subjects seem ready, in these ecumenical times, to let the title stand for her undoubted, staunch championship of Christianity in general, Christian morals, Christian culture and Christian family life, in a largely post-Christian era. Christianity is a matter on which she is prepared to speak her mind as near publicly as makes little difference; and she made this evident in September 1976, when she replied through her Press Secretary to about 150 letters, some of them petitions signed by many people, which objected to a much-publicised proposal by a Dane to make a film in Britain about what he called 'the sex life' of Jesus. The Queen's reply said she found this proposal 'quite as obnoxious as most of her subjects do'. Buckingham Palace did not publish the reply, which it regarded as a private letter, but several of its recipients did, causing *The Times* to remark stiffly, 'It is rare for a constitutional monarch to express a personal opinion on a matter of controversy'—a stricture which might be held to debar the Queen from taking part in public prayer if it was of a nature to indicate a belief in God and in the unsullied virtue of His Divine Son. Since this is the belief of Protestants—as well as of most other religious groups which regard themselves as Christian—the Queen is legally required to hold it, and so by extension legally required also to regard any attack on it as 'obnoxious'—that is to say, according to the *Oxford Dictionary*, as 'offensive' and 'objectionable'.

The Sovereign, then, as the supreme head 'in earth' of the Church of England, must be a communicant of that Church. Interestingly, this is not legally required of the husband or wife of the Sovereign, although a quaint and almost unique survival of the laws which for centuries kept Catholics and Noncomformists out of public life, still lays it down that the Sovereign's consort must *not* be Roman Catholic. The Queen, acting on the advice of the Prime Minister, appoints the chief clergy of the Church of England, the Archbishops, Bishops, Deans of all Cathedrals, and some Canons, as well as the incumbents of certain livings. She receives English Diocesan Bishops when, on appointment, they do her homage.

As the Fount of Honour, the Queen approves all awards of British honours, and personally presents about two thousand decorations each year. The Order of the Garter, the Order of the Thistle, the Royal Victorian Order and the Order of Merit are bestowed by the Queen's personal decision. Others are conferred on the recommendation of the Prime Minister or of a Commonwealth Prime Minister.

The Queen is head of all three armed services, and she spends much time in her annual schedule visiting service establishments, and has a special relationship with those Army regiments of which she is the Colonel-in-Chief. She has frequent personal contact with the Royal Navy through her travels in the royal yacht, and with a grandfather, father, husband and son who were all serving, sea-going officers, she no doubt feels it part of her family. Her use of the Queen's Flight also frequently puts her connection with the Royal Air Force on a more personal level.

It can easily be seen, then, that the Queen must surely be one of the world's busiest women, and even the anti-royalist Court Jester, the tedious but likeable Mr Willie Hamilton, has conceded more than once that she is 'truly professional' in carrying out her duties. Her former Private Secretary, Sir Michael Adeane, wrote of her, 'Nobody who does not carry such a burden of responsibility is in a position to appreciate the strain it imposes. The Queen is never absolutely free to do as she likes in the way that ordinary men and women are, or to take a complete holiday. Her job is continuous and she cannot, like other hard-worked people, look forward to a period of retirement at the end of her life.' Sir Michael also pointed out that as well as carrying the exceptional burdens of Sovereignty, the Queen carried also those common to all wives and mothers, devoting time and energy to the upbringing and education of her children and to the care and domestic management of the Royal houses.

Sir Michael held, as Private Secretary, a vital post in the highly-efficient organisation that is obviously needed to enable the Queen to get through her heavy programme, to plan the meticulously-timed State functions and ceremonies, to work out the complex arrangements for visits and tours at home and abroad, and carry out the Queen's wishes in the running of Buckingham Palace, Windsor Castle, the Palace of Holyrood House, and the Sandringham and Balmoral estates, as well as countless other tasks that are necessary to keep the apparatus of the Monarchy running smoothly. The present Private Secretary, Sir Martin Charteris, an Assistant Private Secretary under Sir Michael Adeane, was formerly Private Secretary to the Queen when she was Princess Elizabeth. A tall, authoritative, but notably humorous and courteous man, now aged sixty-two, he served with the King's Royal Rifle Corps in World War II, and was one of the few survivors when the troopship *Yorkshire* was torpedoed in the Atlantic in 1940. He is a talented sculptor, and a bust by him is in Norwich Cathedral.

The Private Secretary can properly be described as the right-hand man of the Queen, her closest assistant, and his post is as a rule filled by the Sovereign's personal choice. Helped by a deputy and an Assistant Private Secretary, he deals with all the correspondence between the Queen and her Ministers in both British and Commonwealth Governments. Government appointments for which the Queen's approval is needed are sent to her through her Private Secretary. He is also responsible for the Queen's speeches, messages and private papers, as well as for her engagements at home and overseas, for the office of the Press Secretary, and for the royal archives. All letters addressed to the Queen go first of all to her. She selects some of them, and returns the remainder to the Private Secretaries for further selection. Besides the weighty matters of State, many letters arrive from individuals with all sorts of requests; sometimes there are letters from children; or there are letters asking for telegrams of congratulation to be sent for diamond weddings and centenaries, and about fifteen hundred such telegrams go out every year. Hardly any letters that reach the Palace remain unanswered, and this calls for a high degree of clerical efficiency by a relatively small staff which is, fortunately, very dedicated and prepared to take long hours for granted when they are necessary. The Queen's desk work is voluminous and exacting; if she ever needed to choose some new symbolic object to incorporate in armorial bearings, it might appropriately be a pen.

The senior officer of the household is the Lord Chamberlain, Lord Maclean, who is approaching his sixtieth year, and gives the impression of being a relaxed, even breezy, out-of-doors kind of man; and that could seem out of key with his chief function, which is the organisation of all Court ceremonial, including that connected with State visits and royal tours in Commonwealth countries, the State Opening of Parliament, even the relatively informal royal garden parties. Such events as Princess Anne's wedding ceremony and the lying-in-state of the late Duke of Windsor were arranged by him. He is Chairman of the Household Committee and Chairman of the Committee of Royal Warrants of Appointments; and precedence, uniforms, styles and titles, the flying of flags, and all manner of out-of-the-way matters are his concern, such as the regalia, the Queen's swans and her rights over sturgeon off the British coasts. He is responsible for the most important household appointments, for the Royal Library and art collections, the Chapels Royal

Senior officer of the Royal Household, the Lord Chamberlain, Lord Maclean

The Queen's right-hand man: Sir Martin Charteris, Private Secretary since 1972

The Crown Equerry, Sir John Miller, looks after the Queen's carriage horses, carriages and cars. He is also a gold-medallist in world coach-driving championships

The first State occasion for an Heir Apparent. Prince Charles at the Queen's side in a Coronation Day family picture

Prince Charles at school in Australia. 'I absolutely adored it . . . The most wonderful experience.'

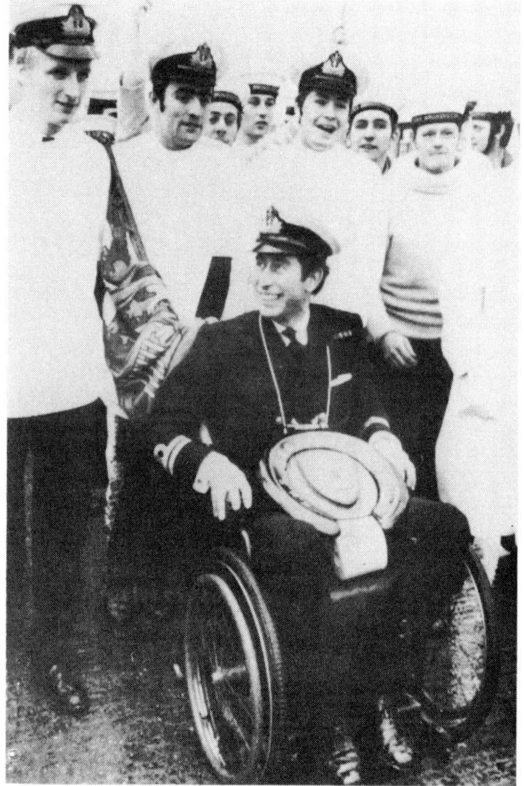

Brother officers contrived their own special departure ceremonies when Prince Charles ended his service with the Royal Navy

Individuality, forthrightness, a sort of innocence. Lord Snowdon's nineteenth-birthday portrait of Princess Anne

and the Windsor State Apartments. Lord Maclean lives in an apartment at St James's Palace, but he also has a family home, Duart Castle, on the island of Mull, and he is an enthusiastic cattle-breeder. He used to be the Chief Scout.

The officer who looks after day-to-day household affairs for the Queen, the Master of the Household, is a man very much used to detail and its exact ordering; his entire career up to about three years ago was with the Royal Navy. This is Vice-Admiral Sir Peter Ashmore, who organises the domestic economy of the Queen's five great houses with much the same kind of efficiency as might reasonably be expected aboard a like number of battleships. He is responsible for the supply of food and drink, not just for the royal family, for State banquets and the entertainment of guests, but also for the entire household staff. He engages and manages all the domestic staff, such as cooks, housekeepers, footmen, pages and maids. His job is not unlike that of the manager of several very large and good hotels.

The payment of salaries and wages to the Queen's household officers and servants is made by the Keeper of the Privy Purse and Treasurer, Major Sir Rennie Maudslay, a retired Army officer of sixty, who has the Palace accounting at his finger-tips after seventeen years' experience in handling it. As Keeper of the Privy Purse, he is responsible for personal payments made from the Queen's private resources. His department consists of the Privy Purse Office, the Treasurer's Office and the Royal Almonry, at the head of which is the High Almoner—an ecclesiastical appointment, at present held by the Bishop of Rochester—who in earlier times was responsible for the almsgiving of the Sovereign. One can be constantly charmed—or annoyed, if your predilections so dispose you—by the way in which the great antiquity of the Monarchy causes the past to reach out into the present in the workings of the Royal Household. For instance, although Major Maudslay's department is crammed with modern accounting gadgets, there really is a Privy Purse. It is about the size of a large handbag, and the Major would have to carry it if he were in attendance on the Queen at a great ceremony.

The Master of the Horse is the third dignitary at Court, and in days gone by this was an office of great power in the realm. Today it carries the charge of the Queen's stables, and the responsibility for providing horses, carriages and motor cars for processions and for the daily needs of the royal family. In State processions, the Master of the Horse, at present the Duke of Beaufort, rides immediately behind the Queen. His main duties are carried out day by day by his deputy, the Chief or Crown Equerry, Lieutenant-Colonel Sir John Miller, a 56-year-old bachelor, who led the British team to a gold medal in the world coach-driving championships. It was he who encouraged the Duke of Edinburgh to take up the sport when he had to give up polo on the orders of his doctor. Among Sir John's charges are the four state Rolls-Royces, the cars the Queen normally travels in. They are without registration plates. They, with the other royal cars, are housed in the Royal Mews, behind Buckingham Palace, together with the magnificent ceremonial coaches and other carriages which make up one of the finest collections in the world. Also in the Mews, of course, are the horses. The Mews is opened to the public on two afternoons in the week.

These officers, then, with others subordinate to them and clerks and secretaries, make up the permanently employed staff on which the organisation of the Queen's life and work mainly depends; and they are relatively few in number, less than a hundred people. Domestic staff of various kinds, chauffeurs and grooms and others doing a variety of jobs in serving the Family and the Household and in various specialist tasks probably bring the total of the people working full time in the Queen's Household to rather less than 340. The figure does not remain constant. Sometimes extra people are employed for special occasions. There are always efforts to economise. Since the beginning of her reign the Queen has reduced her Household by 58.

Of course, when one looks through the official list of the Household and its officers issued by the Lord Chamberlain's Office, one finds a long string of appointments that do not employ the full time of their holders, or which are honorary; and again, there is much that reaches into the past. For example, some of the medical advisers, eminent men in their professions, are listed as 'Apothecary' to the Household. The Captain General, Adjutant and Secretary of the Royal Company of Archers are listed. So is the Poet Laureate, Sir John Betjeman, and the Master of the Queen's Musick, Malcolm Williamson.

There are four Women of the Bedchamber and two Extra Women of the Bedchamber, and these are in fact the Ladies in Waiting. They do not live at the Palace, as they were required to do in the past, but one, at least, is on duty each day, accompanying the Queen when she goes out in public and generally acting as a Personal Assistant, dealing with private correspondence and helping in various ways. There are romantic-sounding titles, such as Gentleman Usher to the Sword of State; Gold Stick; Hereditary Standard Bearer of Scotland; Keeper of the Tower of London Jewel House; Mistress of the Robes (a very important lady); Clerk and Deputy Clerk of the Closet (clerical appointments, one a Bishop); and the Captain, Lieutenant and Clerk of the Cheque and Adjutant of the Yeomen of the Guard. Not astonishingly, Her Majesty's Representative, Ascot, is listed, as are the Racing Manager, the Manager of the Thoroughbred Stud and the Veterinary Surgeon. As I've said, you find it all charming and interesting, or boring and irrelevant, according to the way you are made.

Not in this reign alone, but probably in every reign far back into history, and especially in Parliament and in the newspapers, the question has frequently and properly been put: What does all this cost and is it worth it? The straight answer nowadays is that it costs as little as is necessary and unavoidable if the Monarchy is to be maintained in the style at present required of it. As to whether it is worth it, the answer is, No, if you do not approve of Monarchy anyway; it is, Yes, if you do approve of it.

Debating the cost of Monarchy puts one in mind of the man who was contemplating the purchase of a yacht, and was told, 'If you have to ask the price, you can't afford it.' Better still, perhaps, is the down-to-earth comment of that great patriot and man of the people, Emmanuel Shinwell, who said, 'We can't have the royal family going about in rags.' My own view, after having read, heard, written and talked a great deal on this subject, is that we pay comparatively little for what we get. What is quite certain is that none of the money provided by Parliament for the upkeep of the apparatus of Monarchy, and to ensure its functioning in the style the Government (and so, presumably, the people) demand, is wasted, either through inefficient costing, needlessly lavish spending, or any other form of bad management. In this matter, the Monarchy would certainly come out the easy winner if compared with any government department.

More than three-quarters of all expenditure arising from the official duties of the royal family is met by public departments, and this includes, for example, the costs of the royal yacht, *Britannia*, the Queen's Flight, travel by train and the upkeep of the royal palaces. Apart from this, the Queen's public expenditure is financed from the Civil List, a payment from public funds authorised by Parliament. The greater part of this provision is required to meet the salaries of staff dealing with State papers and correspondence, the organising of State occasions, visits and other public engagements in the United Kingdom and overseas, and arrangements for the many interviews and investitures undertaken by the Queen. The Queen herself receives no cash whatsoever from the State, and has not done so since 1972. In fact, when inflation affected the costs that the Civil List was supposed to meet, and a larger sum had to be voted early in 1975, the Queen contributed £150,000 of her own money so that the State would need to find less, and in addition, she has herself agreed to meet the official expenses of some members of the royal family which had previously been paid by the State. Nevertheless, when in 1975 the Government announced—having leaked it to some of the newsmen in advance—that the Civil List provision was to be increased from £980,000 to £1,400,000, an astonishingly large number of newspapers came out with some such headline as 'Queen Gets Pay Rise'. Even the B.B.C. in one news bulletin said something to this effect, in spite of warnings I had circulated well ahead in the hope of averting precisely this error.

There seemed to be a disposition to regard £1,400,000 as very large for the Civil List among the same people who had not turned a hair at an expenditure of £3,000,000 *a day* on the development of the Concorde aircraft. The only way to try to convince them that the sum involved in the Civil List was really relatively small for what it produced was to seek valid comparisons, although something that can be compared exactly, point for point, is hard to find. An interesting discovery was that the amount of the Civil List would be rather less than enough to buy one cup of railway station tea for everyone in the kingdom. It was only about a quarter of the cost of the diplomatic element alone of the British Embassy in Washington. Comparison with an executive presidency like that of the United States was laughable; for the cost of the mere security arrangements for protecting President Nixon were about ten times more than the entire Civil List provision. A closer comparison might be with a non-executive president of a European State of much the same size as Britain, which makes the West German President a reasonable choice; and he apparently gets rather more than £2,000,000, compared with the £1,400,000 of the Civil List. However, I never heard that his residence in Bonn attracted hard-currency tourists like flies, and admirable man though he is, I feel sure he would not lay claim to much in the way of regal splendour and charm to make him prominent in the world's headlines.

However all this may be, it does seem that the costs of the Monarchy could be really drastically reduced only by making the whole style of it utterly different. There would have to be an end, for example, to such things as the State processions, with a saving of rather more than £90,000 a year, which is at least what it costs to maintain the thirty official horses. There would probably have to be an end also to the four annual royal garden parties, which give pleasure and acceptable recognition to about 30,000 people of all sections of the population at a cost of more than £60,000. This would amount to replacing the 'gold filling in a mouth of decay'—John Osborne's elegant view of the Monarchy—with a set of National Health plastic gnashers. I doubt if such a course would have wide national appeal, and it would lead to a big loss in foreign currency.

Though the Monarchy is in no way specially designed to attract tourists, any more than the Pyramids were, or the Vatican, there is no doubt at all that, like them, it does do this—which is one of the reasons why many people say that the Monarchy pays for itself. Another is the fact that the Civil List provision was originally given to George III in exchange for hereditary revenues, mainly income from Crown lands, which until 1760 the King had used to pay all expenses of government, including the salaries of judges, ambassadors, civil servants, and the expenses of the royal palaces and households, but which he now found inadequate for these purposes. The argument is that these hereditary revenues are now worth immensely more than they were when first handed over, and certainly more than the amount of the Civil List.

However, there are all sorts of imponderables involved when one attempts to consider royal finances. One springs from the fact that the Queen does not pay income tax or investment tax or death duties. What this means to her financially has never become known to the public, because the size of her personal fortune is not disclosed. The only other members of the royal family who receive government allowances are the Duke of Edinburgh, who gets £65,000; Queen Elizabeth the Queen Mother, who gets £95,000; and Princess Anne and Princess Margaret, who each get £35,000. All of these sums are taxed. The Prince of Wales gets no allowance from the State, but he has the revenues of the estate of the Duchy of Cornwall, comprising extensive property in south-west England and various parts of London, and all this is exempt from taxation. However, he undertook voluntarily to surrender one-half of the net revenues to the Consolidated Fund, with the proviso that this was subject to review should he marry or have some other change of circumstance. The income from the estate of the financial year 1975–6 was £129,208.

Any informed discussion of the cost of Monarchy almost invariably leads to attempts to make guesses about the Queen's personal wealth. It is a frustrating game to play, because there are too many unknown factors, and because it is not easy to determine precisely which of the Queen's possessions are really her own and which are, so to speak, held in trust for her successors on the throne, and so, in effect, the property of the State. What belongs to the Queen as a person and what to the Monarchy as an institution? The royal palaces are clearly in practice regarded as state property, in the sense that while they technically belong to the Queen, she could not sell them. But there seems to be some doubt about the status of the Duchy of Lancaster lands owned by the Queen. Balmoral and Sandringham are undoubtedly her own personal possessions. But what of the royal art collections, the furniture, the jewellery, the Royal Library, of which the total value must be many millions of pounds? Of course, there is no serious suggestion that the Queen would ever disperse them; she means them to be handed on to future British Monarchs. It is no wonder, perhaps, that the question, 'How rich is the Queen?' gets an even colder and more tight-lipped response at the Palace than questions about Prince Charles's possible wedding plans. Its officials are certainly wise in maintaining this attitude; for to change it would undoubtedly raise further clamour for the Queen to be taxed. As Elizabeth Longford says: 'What is taxation for? If the answer is, to promote equality by redistributing wealth, the question follows, is that what Monarchy is for? Clearly not.'

4. The Heir Apparent

Prince Charles was cheered by large crowds in the streets of London within a few minutes of his being born. Thereafter, by the wise decision of his parents, he spent several years learning to be modest. So well did he learn that on a private social occasion twenty years later he looked embarrassed when a man older than himself asked, 'Would you like something to drink, Sir?' Seeing this reaction, the man added, 'Or aren't you allowed to drink?' The Prince said: 'No, it's not that; it's just that I'm not used to being called Sir!'

In this then, his deeply-ingrained sense of propriety, good manners and the respect due to others as well as to himself, he might have to plead guilty to the charge sometimes levelled by critics of the royal family that he has too little in common with his contemporaries, is not up-to-date, not 'with it'. He is aware of this kind of criticism, unworried by it, and quite ready with his answer, which is that he doesn't care what people think about him, provided that he himself can go on believing in what seems to him to be true, right, decent and honourable. On television and in magazine interviews, he has explained that having been brought up mostly with older people and having met vast numbers, he has had a 'chance to see what the world is all about' earlier than most. 'That, perhaps, makes me more square,' he said. Whether one agrees with these views or not, they do seem to show that acquiring the habit of modesty at an early age does not necessarily soften the will or weaken the capacity for making up one's mind.

To discover how the Queen's son and heir apparent, Charles, Prince of Wales and Duke of Cornwall, has become so modest and unfashionable, and yet at the same time so self-assured, one has to look first of all at the way he was educated. That process, for all of us, begins of course in the cradle. Charles had the one that had been his mother's. He was the first male born in direct line of succession since the birth fifty-four years earlier of the Duke of Windsor. Even before his arrival he had been the cause of two changes in royal custom to bring it more into line with the spirit of the times. Firstly, putting aside the Victorian prudery which through several reigns had made the subject of pregnancy unmentionable, King George VI had insisted that it be made known in advance that his daughter was expecting a baby. He also decided to put an end to an old-established and genuinely distasteful practice, that of having the Home Secretary present at the births of royal heirs. According to John Wheeler-Bennett, the custom had no constitutional basis anyway, and did not even date, as generally believed, from the celebrated Warming-pan Incident of 1688, when it was suggested by the Whigs that a baby born to James II's Queen had been substituted by another smuggled into the Palace in a warming-pan. At the start then, Charles was the cause of the disappearance of two bits of royal nonsense which had never been pleasing.

It was because the birth was expected by the nation at large that crowds were flocking around Buckingham Palace from dawn. When it was officially announced to have taken place on Sunday night, 14th November 1948, the cheering could be heard all over the West End. The fountains in Trafalgar Square were switched to blue (for a boy) and kept blue for a week. Mr Robert Menzies, soon to be Australia's Prime Minister for the second time, was in London with his family, and they joined the jubilant multitude outside the Palace. The noise continued for so long that somehow an appeal had to be conveyed for the people to disperse so that Princess Elizabeth could get some sleep. Prince Philip's Private Secretary, Michael Parker, went to the forecourt railings to find someone intelligent-looking to start relaying this message. The man he chose turned out to be David Niven. Queen Mary, eighty-two years old, who called at the Palace and stayed until nearly midnight, said she was delighted to be a great-grandmother. A week later, the baby was christened by the Archbishop of Canterbury, Dr Fisher. Princess Margaret, the youngest godparent, held him at the font and announced his names, Charles Philip Arthur George. She is reported to have said afterwards, 'That makes me Charlie's Aunt.'

The nationwide rejoicing—a rather striking expression of the fact that the British people still liked living under a Monarchy—was not something that was ever likely to turn Charles's head, because it was a very long time before he even heard about it. He disclosed twenty years or so later, in a B.B.C. radio interview with Jack de Manio, that the realisation that he was anyone special came upon him only gradually and slowly. Asked at what moment he had taken in the fact that he was heir to the throne, he said, 'It's something that dawns upon you with the most ghastly inexorable sense.' All this may properly be regarded as part of the process of his education.

His earliest memory, he told Dermot Morrah, was an impression of the great size of his pram. This was, in fact, his mother's old pram re-upholstered, for he was a little boy living in the period of Britain's post-war austerity; and indeed, shortly after he was born, a Palace official had gone down to the Westminster Food Office to collect the Prince's ration book for free cod-liver oil and orange juice. Education at this time meant principally the attention he received from two Scots nannies, Helen Lightbody and Mabel Anderson, but also from his mother who, even after she had become Queen, set aside some of her morning hours for playing with him and the lively young sister, Anne, that he acquired when he was nearly two years old. The Queen often saw her children again at tea-time, helped to bathe them and put them to bed. Prince Charles was present at the Coronation, though informally, watching from the royal gallery in the care of Queen Elizabeth the Queen Mother and Princess Margaret. He was fascinated by the gold plate on the altar, and eagerly questioned his grandmother about it. He had stayed with his grandparents before the death of the King, and says he remembers this, as well as visits to his great-grandmother, Queen Mary.

Gradually Charles began to have glimpses of State ceremony on occasions such as Trooping the Colour. Photographers used to keep watch for him when he was taken for a drive. He was told that they probably wanted to take pictures of the car.

Deliberations about the method of his formal education began at the Palace very early on; and there was no lack of suggestions from outside it. An astonishing number of people thought they knew the right formula for the education of the future King of a modern democracy, and in a democracy, it was entirely proper that they should publicise them or seek to do so. It may be taken for granted that the Queen and Prince Philip, in the deep consideration they were giving to so important a matter, were also bearing in mind what they saw, or knew, or sensed instinctively, about the gradually-emerging character of their eldest son. They were, after all, modern parents in the sense that in spite of very full and busy professional lives, which involved frequent absence, they were always closely and lovingly involved in a personal way in his upbringing, in an atmosphere which was that of a genuine family even if it had to be an extraordinary family, a family that formed part of the apparatus of the State. They contrived for him and for his sister an easy, happy way of life, in which a feeling of affection and security was not so much balanced against as intermingled with known rules of good behaviour; and if that sounds boringly-worthy and dull, the evidence is that the Prince's own recollection is of a happy childhood. His own words on the subject, in an interview in 1975, were these, 'I'm very lucky, because I have very wise and incredibly sensible parents who have created a marvellous, secure, happy home.'

Just what Charles's emerging character was is a little difficult to assess from the quite astonishing amount that has been written or said on the subject. Allowances have to be made for a natural and not unpleasing inclination towards effusive praise by those who really did know him as a child, as well as for the same thing coming less pleasingly from people who refuse to have a word said or written against royalty. I select from a variety of sources the following adjectives and phrases which have been applied to him in attempts to describe what he was like as a child: biddable, tractable, undemanding, sensitive, already somewhat self-contained, sweet-natured, quietly-grave in his reception of visitors, amenable, shy but inherently aware of what was required of him, dependent on people and companionship. Of course, if all that list were exactly truthful and unalloyed, one would be compelled to add to it the words, 'tedious and priggish'; but judging by what I have seen and heard of the grown-up Prince Charles, I am quite certain that those adjectives can seldom, if ever, have been justly applied to him. Probably most of what is in the quoted list may be taken as mostly true most of the time, if due weight is also given to his own declaration, 'I know I needed discipline. If I hadn't had it I'd have been abominably spoiled and a miserable sort of youth.' It is a matter of record that he was occasionally, though not very often, spanked.

Education continued, of course, while its eventual form continued to be debated publicly and privately. Charles learned to ride, firstly at Balmoral on an old Shetland pony called Fum, then on a Welsh mountain pony named William. It seems that he quite likes horses, but they are not one of the great interests of his private life as they are for the Queen, and certainly not the absorbing passion that they represent for Princess Anne. Miss Vacani, from a celebrated London dancing school, came to the Palace to teach him to dance. At the age of five, when English children become by law subject to compulsory education, a qualified governess, Miss Peebles, from Glasgow, gave him his lessons in a schoolroom fitted up in the Palace. However, Prince Philip had come to the conclusion that, whatever might be decided on later, it was important for Charles to experience the kind of discipline imposed if one is educated in the company of others, to learn to live with children of his own age; so when he was eight, he was sent to Hill House, a pre-prep day school in Kensington. His first school report said he was above average in subjects such as art, scripture and history which called for imagination, but he was not good at sums. Miss Peebles had come to similar conclusions.

Under her tuition he had already started learning French. Indeed, early in life he had mastered two useful French words, so that he could say '*Bon jour*' to President Auriol of France and his wife when they came to England on a State visit and took great pleasure in joining him for a nursery tea of sponge cake and banana sandwiches. A recommendation by Lord Altrincham that he should also be taught Russian and Hindi seems never to have been adopted, just as it was also decided not to fall in with suggestions that he should go to a State primary school near the Palace rather than to Hill House; but it is by no means certain that no consideration at all was given to these ideas. Lord Altrincham, who renounced his peerage when the law enabled him to do so in 1963 wrote six years later, as the political journalist John Grigg, that it had been reported to him that Prince Philip saw at once that his criticism —which also concerned other royal matters—should be taken seriously. I shall be referring in a later chapter to the public fuss that the Altrincham criticisms caused, but a national opinion poll, published by the *Daily Mail*, showed that thirty-three per cent of those questioned in it supported what he had to say about Prince Charles's education. While there is nothing conclusive about such figures, one must agree with Mr Grigg that they cannot be lightly dismissed. After all, there was nothing so very revolutionary, and certainly nothing disloyal, subversive or silly, in his suggestions about the Prince's education. It should also be noted that their author has described himself as 'a pretty ardent monarchist', and has explained that his purpose was to do 'a small service to a great institution in which I believe'.

While at Hill House, Charles played his first team football, volley-ball, and cricket, at which he was quite good, carried out gymnastic exercises, had swimming instruction in the Chelsea baths, and also did some lessons in the usual preparatory school subjects, including Latin and French. Prince Philip formed the opinion that Charles benefited from working and playing with boys of his own age. He was happy at Hill House and seemed more self-assured. At the school, the Prince was treated exactly as were the other boys. For the first time ever, a son of the Monarch, indeed the heir to the throne, was attending a day school; also he was going out into the world for part of his education ten years younger than any of his predecessors for the past five hundred years. Even though he was getting a kind of education at the start which was not available to everybody, and so left some of the critics unappeased, the Queen was certainly breaking with tradition.

The success of his schooling at Hill House confirmed the Queen and the Duke in their opinion that Charles should continue with school education, and that there should be no reversion to the royal custom of being tutored at home. Before a decision was made about his next school, the Queen devised occasions for visiting a number of possible places and talking to their headmasters. In the meantime, during the summer holiday at Balmoral, both Charles and Anne were given extra teaching in French by Mlle Bibiane de Roujoux, who had been recommended by Mme Untermeyer, the French tutor of the Queen and Princess Margaret. The school for which Charles was eventually entered was his father's old preparatory school, Cheam, near Newbury, in Berkshire, which is probably the oldest establishment of its kind in England, dating back at least to the reign of Charles I.

By this time, it must have been evident to Charles that there was something special about him. The growing attentions of Press photographers surely made some impression. But it seems he was still unaware of his precise status; and the Queen was determined that this knowledge should come to him only gradually. The time for it was not yet. When Charles went to Cheam in September 1957, stringent conditions had been laid down by the Queen to make sure that he would live exactly the same kind of life as the other boys there. For instance, as far as was possible, his studies at Cheam were not to be interrupted to enable him to attend royal occasions, and he was to be shown no favour. The attention showed to him by the Press did not abate. All manner of hearsay stories got into print, some of them possibly true. A very popular one told of Charles's running short of his strictly-rationed pocket money and selling off some possessions to buy chocolate fudge for a dormitory feast. This led to what might be seen as a late stirring of that generous spirit which promoted the American 'Bundles for Britain' campaign in the War. A convention of American confectionery manufacturers sent a large consignment of sweets and other goodies to Cheam School. Their President explained, 'We were told the Prince was short of candy, so our committee unanimously passed a resolution to the effect that we ought to pitch in and help him out of a jam.'

By 1958, Charles certainly did know that he was heir to the throne, and considerable pains had been taken to ensure that this knowledge was very much in the context of the responsibilities that awaited him, although I cannot find any record of his ever having said anything very precise about the kind of feeling, the trepidation possibly, that this may have aroused in him. He was good at history and interested in it; so his reaction, as the truth crept in on him, was probably mixed. In that year, anyway, during a week-end break at home in the summer, a positive event brought the fact of his inheritance to the fore; the Queen told him that she had decided to make him Prince of Wales, though he was to keep this secret for the time being. Later in the month, Charles and some of his friends were called into their Headmaster's study to listen to a radio broadcast. A slight illness had prevented the Queen from carrying out a planned tour of Wales, during which she had meant to proclaim Charles as Prince of Wales when she attended the British Empire and Commonwealth Games at Cardiff Arms Park. Instead, she tape-recorded the message, and after words of introduction from Prince Philip, the recording was played to the crowd at the Games and was, of course, also broadcast by the B.B.C.

The message said, 'I want to take this opportunity of speaking to all the Welsh people, not only in this arena but wherever they may be. The British Empire and Commonwealth Games in the capital, together with all the activities of the Festival of Wales, have made this a memorable year for the Principality. I have therefore decided to mark it further by an act which will, I hope, give as much pleasure to all Welshmen as it does to me. I intend to create my son Charles Prince of Wales today. When he is grown up I will present him to you at Caernarvon.'

The great tide of cheering that greeted this announcement came roaring over the radio from Cardiff Arms Park and into the study at Cheam. So did the enormous sound of thirty thousand voices—a melodious sound, because they were Welsh voices—singing 'God Bless the Prince of Wales'. The boys round the radio-set cheered, too, and clapped—all except one of them, who was now Prince of Wales, Duke of Cornwall and Duke of Rothesay, Earl of Chester, Earl of Carrick and Baron of Renfrew, Lord of the Isles and Prince and Great Steward of Scotland. According to one of his friends who was watching him, he looked overwhelmingly embarrassed. By his own account, he was experiencing something more than mere embarrassment; at the age of nine years and eight months, a sensation of loneliness had come over him, a realisation of 'an awful fate' awaiting him in the future.

This initial shock—and that is probably not too strong a word for what the small boy felt—did not, fortunately, last very long. Charles was so very happy and busy at Cheam and in his holidays with his family. His first day or two at the school had not been pleasant because his special circumstances made acceptance by his fellows on equal terms even more of an ordeal than it is for most new boys at school. During the holidays a letter from the school had told parents of boys there of the Prince's pending arrival. It said the Queen and Prince Philip wished that there should be no alteration in the running of the school and that the Prince should be treated the same as other boys, and given the same education and upbringing. It would be a great help if the parents would explain this to their sons. No doubt they did. At all events, at the beginning, a naturally-diffident Charles hesitated to push his way into acceptance. Other boys were shy in their approaches to him for fear they should be thought sycophants. However, the barriers were overcome. Later, the Headmaster felt able to describe Charles as 'a very good mixer who was popular with all the boys'.

There were other problems, some of which lasted throughout the Prince's time at Cheam, such as the prying of snoopers, who included people prompted by sheer curiosity, others who had a pathetic attraction to royalty which was not wholly sane, and a good many who were hunting snippets for the newspapers. Naturally there were unobtrusive security arrangements for Charles's protection, and it seems that practice at Cheam helped with the development of some techniques that were of future use to the Special Branch. Press intrusion became a very real embarrassment. So many stories about the Prince were appearing in the papers that people in the school or connected with it began to suspect each other of leaking gossip to reporters and the social atmosphere became soured. In the end, London editors were asked to call at Buckingham Palace where they were told of the real distress that the Press persecution was causing; and that it had become so intolerable that, if it did not stop, the Queen would be compelled, much against her wishes, to take Charles from school and have him educated privately, not for his sake alone but for that of others who were involved. The response of the editors was sympathetic, and thereafter, in general, only real and significant news about the Prince was reported.

This incident became fairly widely known. Possibly some of those who had so earnestly urged that the Prince should be given the ordinary State education, available to all, now began to see at least some of the difficulties this would have entailed. If the Prince and his schoolfellows and people connected with them could be so persecuted at a relatively-sheltered private school such as Cheam, what would have been the situation had the Prince been sent to a State day school, and what would have been the extent of the resultant security problems? No

Nail-biting anxiety as the Queen, with Prince Andrew, watches Princess Anne ride in the 1976 Olympic Games in Montreal

Understudy to the Heir Apparent. Prince Andrew, 'a blend of Charles and Anne', gains his proficiency wings as a glider pilot, after a solo flight, at the age of sixteen

Prince Edward, a cheerful small boy growing up. 'The quietest of my children,' said the Queen

Stricken East London saw much of Queen Elizabeth, now the Queen Mother, in the war years. East-enders cheered her again on a victory tour with the King in 1945

21st March 1974. Police search The Mall, London, for bullets on the morning after the attempted kidnapping of Princess Anne

doubt some of these questions did occur to certain of the host of experts on the education of princes who were still very vociferous. The fashion now was to look beyond Cheam and into the future.

One distinguished man who had made his views known could be regarded as a genuine expert, at least to the extent that he had published writings on the subject of Monarchy —was the official biographer of George V, who was deeply informed about the education of princes in the past. This was Sir Harold Nicolson, who said in a lecture which attracted some publicity that the heir to the throne should be sent to private school, public school and Oxford. To support this opinion, he contended that George V had been brought up 'in a most ridiculous way', and so had his father, Edward VII. As for Edward VIII and George VI, they were 'hardly educated at all', and he could not think what their teachers had been up to. Now that Charles was at Cheam, and probably launched on some such educational voyage as that suggested by Sir Harold, many were the voices that protested against his being given an 'upper-class' training which would inevitably cut him off from ordinary people. Several peers thought he should go not to a public school but to a grammar school, for these schools were not yet themselves being abused as promoters of class division to the extent that they are nowadays. Lord Kilbracken, however, did think that a State comprehensive was the kind of place for Charles's next step. Rumours that the Prince might go on to Eton seemed to cause the most agonised howls of protest, for that was not merely quite hopelessly upper-class, but a place where he might make friends with future Cabinet Ministers who could one day be his advisers; and they would almost certainly be Conservatives. It is true, of course, that Eton has produced a very high proportion of Prime Ministers and others of Cabinet rank, including some famous Conservatives; but might not Charles at a State school find himself making friends with some future Bevin, or Bevan, or Herbert Morrison, or at a grammar school with some as yet mute and inglorious Harold Wilson? At this distance of time the fuss seems a trifle silly—but perhaps not to everyone, even yet.

Eventually, the Queen pressed on with what, though it can be seen as a middle course, was most certainly an enormous departure from previous royal practice and also capable of equipping the Prince, as Lord Altrincham had advocated, with all the knowledge he could absorb without injury to his health, and enabling him to mix during his formative years 'not merely with future stockbrokers and land-owners'.

Charles apparently enjoyed himself at Cheam, the second stage of his education out in the world. He took up fencing and photography. He began to show a degree of musical talent, first of all at the piano, though over the years since he has experimented with a good many other instruments. He continued to shine most in those imaginative and creative subjects that had interested him as a very small boy, particularly art and history. He took part in all the outdoor activities and games, of which there were a great many, was only moderately successful at team sports, seldom got into the first eleven at cricket, preferred soccer to rugby, and was best at swimming. But at Cheam he was given his first real opportunities as an actor, developing another talent that he has continued to nourish, and which in the age of mass communication has already been of use to him in public life.

Dermot Morrah, in his book about the Prince, *To Be a King*, ends his account of the Cheam period with two quotations from the school magazine, the *Cheam School Chronicle*. The dramatic critic wrote of Charles's stage performance as Richard III: 'Prince Charles played the traditional Gloucester with competence and depth: he had a good voice and excellent elocution, and very well conveyed the ambition and bitterness of the twisted hunchback.' But the same issue of the magazine also had to notice the performance of the soccer team that season, when under Prince Charles's captaincy, Cheam scored only four goals and had eighty-two scored against them. The football correspondent wrote: 'At half-back, Prince Charles seldom drove himself as hard as his ability and position demanded.' From all of that, one may suppose, Prince Charles, at that stage of his life, could be judged to be either 'an individualist' or 'not a team man', according to one's own temperament.

At about this time, while the British papers continued on the whole to stick to their self-denying ordinance, and give the young Prince and his friends peace and quiet, the United States was showing a remarkable interest in him. His hair-style was copied there, admired by young women, and for unstated reasons called 'the Cambridge cut'. A replica of the kind of bicycle he used was reported the best-seller of the cycle stand of the British Exhibition in New York in the summer of 1960, another instance of the royal family's being good for trade.

When the time came to move on from Cheam, a public school was in fact decided upon for the next educational phase, but it was one very different from most. Once again, the Queen enquired about and considered several schools before deciding that the Prince should go to Gordonstoun. Even though this meant that once again, as at Cheam, Charles would be following in his father's footsteps, the choice of Gordonstoun was relatively daring. The Queen is said to have made it not simply because Prince Philip favoured it, but also because she had formed her own opinions about the general state of the British public schools at that time. She saw that to a great extent they had remained rigid in the mould cast by the famous Dr Arnold, of Rugby School, an excellent innovation in its own day but inadequate for the special needs of the mid-twentieth century. Gordonstoun was seen as a school which looked to the future rather than to the past. It is an establishment difficult for an outsider to judge. From what one hears, it clearly takes a good deal from Dr Arnold in its emphasis on what the British talk about as 'character-moulding', something more often commended than defined. With this, whatever it may be, Gordonstoun combined a great deal of spartan outdoor endeavour, much emphasis on qualities of leadership, whatever *they* may be, team spirit, self-discipline, social responsibility, service to others. To one who never experienced its rigours it all sounds very well-meaning, over-earnest perhaps, rather theoretical, rather German. Its origins were in fact German. Its founder was a German Jew, Kurt Hahn, once an Oxford student, later private secretary to the last Chancellor of the Kaiser's Germany, Prince Max of Baden. Pondering the possible reasons for the defeat of that Germany in the First World War, he decided that something could be learned from the victors—team spirit and what he saw as the British public school tradition. He set up at Salem Castle in South Germany, the property of Prince Max, a 'school for leaders' which was to incorporate some of these ideas. Hahn, firmly and outspokenly anti-Nazi, left Hitler's Germany, and re-instituted his school at Gordonstoun, in Morayshire, which he had explored in his student days.

Looking back, and remembering all the earlier rumpus about Prince Charles's schooling, it is mildly astonishing to note the muted reaction at this time of the newspapers, and of those contributors to them whom one was accustomed to see jumping up and down in a frenzy of criticism and advice whenever the royal family made any move of importance. They all accepted Gordonstoun like lambs. Benignly, not to say patronisingly, the *Daily Mail* gave its positive approval. 'It is a good choice,' concluded its leader-writer. 'The rather more rigorous disciplines of a school which is in some ways less conventional than others will do the young Prince no harm.'

Less unctuously, and more practically, the paper also pointed out that the Prince would 'find less public distraction in Scotland than ever he would nearer London'. If it meant that there he would be less the prey of snoopers, it was making a good point. In fact, once again, the Palace took a hand to fend off the reporters, and the editors agreed to be good, though there were some lapses.

What did Prince Charles think about it all? This matter was not much touched upon in the papers, but there is some evidence that although he was not compelled to go to Gordonstoun, he agreed to go with some reluctance. Dermot Morrah says the Prince thought the publicity for the place 'sounded pretty gruesome'. Prince Philip's view, speaking from experience, must be given full weight. He told Basil Boothroyd, 'It's somehow got the reputation of being a spartan, tough, rigorous, generally body-bending sort of organisation. In fact it isn't at all, and never has been. It's a misunderstanding of what it's all about. I think it rationalises the whole of the physical activities.' He said Gordonstoun had a great many more activities than what he called the 'standard' public school 'obsession with games'—the idea that one had to be good at football or cricket to get anywhere. But the alternatives were not necessarily absolutes. Not everybody did everything. Charles has said he is glad he went there, and that the toughness of the place is much exaggerated.

The truth is, probably, that like most schools, and certainly experimental schools, Gordonstoun suits some people but not others. It suited Prince Philip. Prince Charles put up with it, and became, as his father had done, head boy, or Guardian as they call it there. Perhaps this exercise in self-conquest may even be seen as a victory for Gordonstoun, a fulfilment of its motto, *Plus est en vous*. In a sense he did even better there than had Prince Philip, who on his own admission enjoyed it.

One breach by the newspapers of their agreement about stories on Prince Charles in his Gordonstoun days was the way some of them reported what happened to him on a school cruise to Stornoway, when he took refuge in a hotel bar to escape sightseers. Rather at a loss, and quite probably ignorant of the laws against selling alcoholic drinks to minors, he ordered a cherry brandy. Some of the papers could not have made more than they did of this if he had been found sprawled under a railway arch with a group of meths drinkers. I have been told on good authority that the scar left by this Press treatment is still with him. He was given further cause to mistrust newspapers when he lost an exercise book containing essays, including some thoughts on democracy. The West German magazine *Stern* paid someone £1,000 for it and published extracts.

If Charles's feelings about Gordonstoun are not entirely enthusiastic, he leaves no doubt at all that he thoroughly enjoyed the two terms he spent at Timbertop, which forms an outlying part of the Geelong Church of England Grammar School in Victoria, Australia. He said, 'I absolutely adored it. . . . The most wonderful experience.'

This recollection is interesting, because Timbertop was in many ways a much tougher place than Gordonstoun. The Prince has described the twice-weekly cross-country run 'at ninety in the shade, with flies everywhere, dust and everything dry and brown'. There were three-day walks of from sixty to seventy miles with peaks to climb on the way. But his studies also continued. He apparently worked hard in the room he shared with a senior boy, Stuart Macgregor, a sheep-farmer's son. There was an interlude when he went to meet Queen Elizabeth the Queen Mother who was visiting Australia for an arts festival. He visited sheep-stations, attempted some unsuccessful panning for gold, went on long fishing trips. But it seems to have been the Australians even more than Australia that made this period of his life one of his brightest memories. He was deeply impressed and delighted by the informal friendliness and good-natured lack of reserve with which he was treated.

It was contrived by the Australians that his period under their care should include a visit with the Headmaster and thirty other boys to missionary stations in Papua–New Guinea, which was then still a dependent territory of Australia. The news that the Prince was with the party had gone ahead, and thousands of people were lining the beach to greet him when he arrived, after a journey by air to Port Moresby and in an Anglican mission launch to Dogura. The days at these missions were a mixture of secular and religious activity. The Prince saw all aspects of the missionary work. He also went to feasts, to plays and to dances. The religious aspects of his stay seem to have made the deepest impression. He wrote later, 'How fresh and sincere I found the Ministry. . . . Everyone was so eager to take part, the singing was almost deafening. One felt that it might almost be the original Church. Where Christianity is new it must be much easier to enter into the whole spirit of it whole-heartedly.'

Charles, at his urgent request, was given a second term at Timbertop, and altogether his stay in Australia lasted about a year. He was now seventeen, which meant that he was a couple of years older than most of the boys who were with him there; and apparently this, after a few days only of breaking the social ice, was the only thing that in any way set him apart from them. He was never made to feel self-conscious about his rank, nor did it make the Australian boys self-conscious. This made life easier for him and must also be seen as an important part of his education. The Australians responded to him as a person and not as a prince. He was able to pay visits with a feeling of freedom and uncomplicated acceptance to the homes of people connected with the school and townspeople. This was a new experience. His academic work gained a fresh impetus. He was studying for 'A' level in French and History, and was left to get on with this largely on his own, with an occasional visit to a tutor to talk or read an essay, as if he were a university undergraduate rather than a schoolboy. The method seemed to suit him. Some people close to the Prince have said that his Australian interlude completed for him the process of growing up.

On 14th November 1966 Charles was eighteen, and this automatically brought about certain changes in his legal position. On accession to the throne he would be able to reign without a Regent, and he would himself become Regent in the event of the Queen's total disablement. More practically, he became the first of the four adults nearest to the throne who, in the Queen's absence from the country, act for her as Counsellors of State. This situation arose in July 1967, when the Queen visited Canada for a week. But he was not called upon to do anything, which was just as well, because he was at the peak of his 'A' level studies at Gordonstoun. He obtained passes in History and French of the sort, it was said, 'expected of a good average candidate'. He gained distinction in an optional special History paper, and the Secretary of the Oxford and Cambridge Schools Examination Board said, when this was reported, that only just over 6 per cent of history candidates normally achieved this.

Charles had already been told that it was the opinion of the Queen and Prince Philip that he should go on to a university before training in the Services. After a good deal of deliberation and enquiry, it was decided that he would go up to Trinity College, Cambridge, where three-quarters of the students came from grammar schools, and he would have a further chance to widen the range of his acquaintance.

After a preliminary visit early in 1967, Charles went up to Cambridge as a freshman in October of that year, taking over rooms on staircase E in New Court at Trinity. Lord Butler, the Conservative politician, who had been Chancellor of the Exchequer in the early Fifties and holder of other Cabinet posts, had become Master of Trinity after his retirement from politics, when the Conservatives were defeated at the polls in 1964. Charles had met him at Buckingham Palace to talk about his Cambridge plans. He had also met during his earlier visit to Cambridge Denis Marrian, who was to be his tutor. A close friend of Charles, Edward Woods, son of the Dean of Windsor, lived on the next staircase.

Partly because of its centuries of familiarity with very important people of rank, or attainment, or both, and partly because of the good manners of town and gown, Cambridge enabled Charles to feel that he very nearly was just like any other undergraduate, able to cycle about the place, go shopping, explore bookshops, call on his friends and acquaintances, without fuss or unwanted attentions. His detective used to be somewhere about, of course, to perform the usual security tasks, and was given the nickname 'Odd Job' by the Prince's fellow students. During his years at Cambridge, he managed to find time to practise on his various musical instruments, live a fairly active social life, cook for his own dinner parties, contribute to the magazine *Varsity*, indulge in some acting and clowning, and also do at least as much work as was necessary most of the time and, at intervals, a great deal of work in desperate bursts. Briefly, had he not been the Prince of Wales, one could say that he had a pretty normal Cambridge career. But he did have that exalted title, and increasingly he was being asked to accept some of the responsibilities and duties that went with it. There were times when this involved him in happenings that were not wholly agreeable, faced him with hostility that he did not feel he deserved and did not understand, and that hurtfully repulsed his own genuine good will. These, too, of course, were part of his education.

One of the first of these troubles came when he used part of his summer vacation to learn something at first hand about the workings of a number of government offices and various national projects. He made his first journey down a coal mine at Welbeck Colliery; saw work in the tunnels of the London Underground Victoria Line, then still under construction; flew out by helicopter to a North Sea oil rig; saw the workings of an Edinburgh newspaper; met an acquaintance from Trinity doing a vacation job with the Central Electricity Board when he was visiting Bankside Power Station. All these trips were happy affairs. Less happy was an encounter he had outside the Welsh Office in Cardiff when he was touring regional offices of the Department of Employment and Productivity. Some Welsh Nationalists of the more militant sort jeered at him and threw smoke-bombs and eggs. The Prince left his entourage, and quietly asked one of the demonstrators the meaning of the slogan in Welsh on a banner he was carrying. He was answered with abuse and a shout of 'Go home, Charlie'. That part of the crowd which had come to welcome him had been cheering all the time and now cheered even louder.

At this time the Prince had learned only a little Welsh. It had already been decided that as Prince of Wales he should acquire more of the language before his Investiture. Students at the University College of Wales, Aberystwyth, had petitioned the Queen for Charles to be sent there to study; so in April 1969 he was enrolled for a nine-weeks crash course in Welsh history, language and culture. There were demonstrations by some students and members of the Welsh Language Society. There were counter-demonstrations. When the Prince arrived to begin his course in May, extremists of the Welsh Nationalist movement felt that the extra attention this drew to Wales was something they could share. The police found dumps of explosives and machine-guns, and a time-bomb blew up a Royal Air Force radio post. Charles himself at his student hostel was treated with courtesy and allowed to get on with his work. His next-door neighbour, a Welsh Nationalist, was friendly to him. He went shopping unmolested in the town, practised his Welsh on anyone who would let him, including the college cleaners, and spent five hours a day in the language laboratory. Making his first public speech in Welsh six weeks later at an eisteddfod, he said that after all those hours of studying the language, he would certainly 'never let it die without offering stout resistance'. As Basil Boothroyd says in his informal biography of Prince Philip, 'If Prince Charles hasn't quite mastered Welsh to bardic standards he doesn't make the fool of himself in it that most of us would.'

Playing a fuller part now in the official life of the royal family, Charles had ceremonial duties to perform from time to time. He was invested with the Order of the Garter; and on 1st July 1969 he was at the centre of the most spectacular event of the Queen's reign since her Coronation. This was the ceremony in which, at Caernarvon Castle, she formally invested him as Prince of Wales, as she had promised she would in her address to the Welsh people, when the crowds in Cardiff Arms Park had cheered so enthusiastically, a sound which a small boy listening to a radio had heard with an inward tremor and a certain awe.

Four thousand people watched the ceremony inside Caernarvon Castle. An estimated 500 million all over the world watched it on television. It was beautifully stage-managed, and in that Charles took an almost professional interest. He confessed that he even rather liked the dressing up, differing in this from the last Prince of Wales, later King Edward VIII and then Duke of Windsor, who had asked plaintively: 'What would my Navy friends say if they saw me in this preposterous rig?' At Edward's Investiture, which was the first for three hundred years, the costume designed for the occasion had included white satin breeches and a mantle and surcoat of purple velvet edged with ermine. Charles retained a modified form of the mantle, which he wore over the Number One blue regimental uniform of the Royal Regiment of Wales, of which he is Colonel-in-Chief. The ceremony was organised by the late Duke of Norfolk, Earl Marshal of England, who had also planned the Queen's Coronation and that of her father. Lord Snowdon, Princess Margaret's husband, also had a part to play as Constable of Caernarvon Castle. The Investiture clearly gave pleasure to a great many people, not least in Wales itself. Some newspapers ran special supplements about it. But it also caused controversy. There were many who thought it an obsolete ceremony not sufficiently significant to warrant the cost. Others questioned its advisability at a time when Nationalist dissent in Wales was making its presence so evident. A magazine printed a cartoon in which, as the Queen placed the coronet on Charles's head, he was represented as saying, 'Mother, I think it's ticking!'

The climate of opinion in Wales was certainly not entirely as it had been eleven years before in Cardiff Arms Park. But a three-day 'progress through Wales' which the Prince made after his investiture indicated beyond question that he was held in great affection. He travelled hundreds of miles through Wales, using motor-car, ferry boat and helicopter, met hundreds of people and was cheered by thousands, and according to those with him, was plainly moved by the warmth of his reception.

He returned to Cambridge for his final year, during which he celebrated his twenty-first birthday, joining the royal family for a concert and a party at Buckingham Palace, after an early morning visit to the Chapel Royal in the Tower of London, where he made an Act of Thanksgiving and Dedication. He was successful in his final examinations at Cambridge, taking a reasonably good honours degree, and making history as the first heir to the throne ever to do so.

That success may be said to have completed the Prince's formal education. What kind of young man has it produced? Firstly, it is beyond question that he is extremely popular throughout the country, and it does not need to be said that this is important for an heir apparent. His popularity, though, is not of the kind that was accorded, particularly after

World War I, to his predecessor as Prince of Wales, the late King Edward VIII and Duke of Windsor, who as Hector Bolitho points out in a rather waspish book, 'became a public hero and a lion . . . a romantic figure, like a prince of old'. We may be thankful that no journalist today would be likely to write about Charles the embarrassing kind of eulogy that was often written about Edward. Take this, for instance, in a description of that unfortunate young man's investiture. 'Now out of the tower came the Prince himself. He appeared before us now as a young knight, a white flower of chivalry. Tall and slim he looked, with a short surcoat of purple velvet above his white silk breeches and stockings. Round his left knee was a jewelled garter. He was bareheaded, and the sun glinted upon his fair hair.' I will not recall the name of the author of that little cameo, because it might make him squirm even in his grave. People who remember those times tell me that even sicklier stuff about Edward appeared frequently without producing any apparent public demand that there should be an interval for nausea.

A thoughtful piece about Charles when he was invested was headed 'Heir Unpresumptive'. More than seven years and many more public appearances later this still seems a fair, though incomplete, summing up of the Prince's apparent character. What it leaves out is a fact that must be evident to anyone who has met him: that he would almost certainly make a mark in life and very probably become a public figure, even if he were not a member of the royal family, and even if, at the start, he had been a person of no particular status and without unusual opportunities and advantages. For example, if I may be considered a judge of my own trade, he seems to me to have all the talents—some natural, some acquired and cultivated—that he would need to become an outstanding professional on radio or television, particularly the latter. He has made an impact on television, of course, with a number of appearances by himself or as the subject of an interview. He seemed to me to be an interesting person in himself and not simply as the Prince of Wales, naturally modest but at the same time highly articulate, and in a quiet way impressive, partly, I think, because he gave no sign of trying to impress. In one appearance fairly recently—a kind of guided tour of Canterbury Cathedral, in connection with its Appeal Fund—he produced, apparently without effort, a few touches that professionals might have recognised as rather difficult tricks of the trade. I mentioned them the next day to one rather well-known professional, suggesting that they had resulted from sheer instinct and not training. My hard-working colleague said, 'Yes, I thought so, too. Doesn't it make you *sick*!' I later learned that the script of this performance, which was a sound, workmanlike job, had been written mainly by the Prince.

What else might the Prince do, if he were not the Prince? One of his teachers in the past thought that he had all the natural qualities needed for a good schoolmaster; but that was rather a long time ago. More recently, that distinguished historical biographer, Elizabeth Longford, seemed to be assessing his possibilities in her own profession, and judged that a foreword he wrote for John Brooke's *King George III* was 'a model of persuasiveness and good sense'. In her book, *The Royal House of Windsor*, she is enthusiastic about him in more general terms also. She describes him as 'the miracle come true' of which Walter Bagehot despaired: a Prince of Wales who, despite his not coming to the throne in early youth, was not a 'pleasure-loving lounger' but high spirited, not a wastrel but a graduate with an excellent record at Cambridge, and with talents ranging from an introduction to the *Goon Show Scripts* to history. She could have added to the list that he drives a car well, can pilot an aeroplane, and a helicopter, plays several musical instruments, is not a bad amateur painter, can ride well enough to be a good polo player, is a pretty good actor, with a bent towards clowning, and also a keen archaeologist, and has a knowledge of several languages.

These abilities have all been noted by one person or another who knows the Prince; lumped together, they make him sound too good to be true, so perhaps they had best be regarded soberly as not necessarily indicating a great deal more than the wide range of his interests. However, even if this caution is observed, the Prince conveys when observed at close hand an image of genuine sensitivity, character and ability. I have heard him holding his own well in a conversation with a group of very hard-headed businessmen after a City dinner, and they were not discussing trivialities. Would he have been a good businessman? He has always been notoriously bad at sums. I have also noticed on several occasions how skilful he can be at making others talk about their own expertise and special knowledge. One such was when he opened the British Museum exhibition on the American War of Independence; and of course there was a certain poignancy in seeing such a task being performed by the great-great-great-great-great-grandson of the King in whose reign the American Colonies were lost. So would he have made a skilled diplomatist? That is something, of course, that his position in life will always compel him to try to be.

In the meantime, he has completed a career as an officer in the Royal Navy. This was the profession he chose to take up in the footsteps of his father, his grandfather, his great-grandfather, and his great-uncle, Earl Mountbatten. He did so after a spell with the Royal Air Force, during which he received his wings after a telescoped training course of five months. His report from Cranwell said he would make an excellent fighter pilot at supersonic speeds, that he had a natural aptitude for flying, that he excelled at acrobatics in jets, and that he had all-round ability. That report simply has to be true. You cannot play the fool over the matter of whether or not someone can be allowed to fly a jet aircraft, especially if he is the heir to the throne.

The Prince joined the Royal Navy by signing on for three to five years under a Graduate Entry scheme in the rank of sub-lieutenant. His pay and allowances were given, at his wish, to King George's Fund for Sailors. He did an initial course of six weeks' basic training, and came out top in navigation and seamanship. Since then he has seen service in a variety of ships, including the guided missile destroyer *Norfolk*, the Fleet Air Arm frigate *Hermione*, the coastal minesweeper *Glasserton*, and the frigates *Minerva* and *Jupiter*. He has been on training courses at various shore establishments, qualified as a pilot of naval helicopters, and taken part in NATO naval exercises in the Mediterranean. Voyages on naval duty have taken him to the West Indies and the South Pacific and other areas. Various other official and private visits to various countries in addition to his sea-going service with the Royal Navy have made him one of the world's best-travelled young men. Early in 1976 he was given his first naval command, a tiny vessel, the mine-hunter *Bronington*.

Intermingled with this busy naval career, Prince Charles

somehow contrived to fit in a schedule of royal duties and other activities so large that keeping track of it was difficult. For instance, and to select almost at random, he has taken his place in the House of Lords and made a speech there in a debate on community service, a subject on which he felt he had some expertise to offer. He made an unexpected appearance at Bart's Hospital in London to talk to people injured in the Moorgate tube crash. Men of the Welsh Guards badly hurt in a pub bombing had the Prince, their Colonel-in-Chief, among their first visitors. Prince Philip's expressed opinion of his son has a note of almost wondering satisfaction that rings true. He said, 'What a great relief it is when you find you've actually brought up a reasonable and civilised human being.'

The Prince nowadays is not hounded by the Press quite so much as when he was younger and offered an easy subject for conjecture. But on one matter concerning him speculation has been recurrent at intervals since even before his Cambridge days. When and whom will he marry? The names of a large number of young women, some of them in the meantime married to other young men than Charles, have been bandied about in the newspapers, usually on no stronger ground than that he has been seen with them in public. It could well be that the Prince has someone particularly in mind; but on few subjects is Buckingham Palace more tight-lipped than on this. During the Jubilee Year of 1977 he will be in his twenty-eighth year; and he will have ended his naval tour of duty, enabling him to play his full role in support of the Queen at the celebrations. Especially, he will have a time-consuming task as Chairman of the Queen's Silver Jubilee Appeal, which is to be concerned with fund-raising for youth work. 'I personally feel,' he is reported to have said, 'that a good age for a man to get married is around thirty.' He also hinted that he would be unlikely to consider marriage while he was still pursuing his naval career. But in fact, the career ended in hilarious naval style in the middle of December 1976, when he relinquished his command of *Bronington*, and brother officers at Rosyth base in Scotland pushed him along the dock in a wheel chair, an inscribed lavatory seat, with a roll of lavatory paper attached, hanging from his neck like some strange and immense order of chivalry. Journalists anxious to be convinced were told that this was a modern variation of a custom of Lord Nelson's time.

Bronington's medical assistant waved a stethoscope and a cardboard banner which read 'Command has aged me.'

Not unnaturally, speculation about possible marriage plans redoubled as the Jubilee Year approached; and a good deal was made of the fact that a country house of his own, which he could well make a family home, was awaiting him. This is Chevening House, near Sevenoaks in Kent, which was for 250 years the home of the Earls Stanhope, of whom the last died childless in 1967. It became available to the Prince, in accordance with the wishes of the last Earl, and he accepted it.

The Prince has more than once made public his clearly strongly-felt views on marriage, and has expressed some dismay about the publicity directed upon girls known to be his friends. This he thought more unfair to them than to him. He is very sure that for him marriage must be considered with great care, and that falling in love is not necessarily the starting point. For him there could be no question of divorce. He has stressed in a number of interviews that in his view marriage must be rooted in friendship and mutual respect as well as love, and that love can grow from deep friendship; and that he sees the essential purpose of marriage as the creation of a secure family unit in which to bring up children. Even if these opinions are level-headed and serious rather than romantic, most young women would probably agree that he is likely to be a good husband. A more important question is: Would he make a good King? Has he the character and ability to succeed as the centre of a spiritual, social and political structure that is changing and must go on changing with the changing times, if it is to continue to perform its ancient and historic function usefully? On the evidence, the answer seems to be that if anyone can do it, he can.

5. Two Princes and a Princess

The two least-known members of the royal family are the Queen's youngest children, her sons, Prince Andrew and Prince Edward; and yet, of course, they come next in line of succession to the throne after the Prince of Wales until such time as he may have children of his own, and before their elder sister, Princess Anne.

Prince Andrew Albert Christian Edward, born in 1960, has been variously described by the few people who have written articles about him as 'the toughie' of the royal family, 'puckish', 'bright', 'blunt and forthright', 'a bit of a handful', and by more than one writer— for graphic phrases are reborn, though not always with acknowledgement of their parentage—as 'one heartbeat away from the throne'. All these descriptions, judging from what Palace people say, seem entirely applicable to him, and the last of them, of which, I think, Audrey Whiting, of the *Sunday Mirror*, was the original begetter, does, indeed, express the most important truth about him for the British people at present. That any misadventure should keep so promising a prince as Charles from the succession is something only unwillingly contemplated, but he has been in a dangerous profession, and while he is not foolhardy, he most certainly does not shun necessary risk, and he has a taste for adventure. While the Palace do not talk about this, they are compelled to think about it. Both his great-grandfather, George V, and his grandfather, George VI, were younger sons who succeeded to the throne, the one because the Heir Apparent died, the other because his older brother abdicated. This is why, as is entirely evident, Prince Andrew is being trained and educated as someone who could some day be King.

So far, in its outline, the formal education he has been given appears very like that of his older brother. In fact, there are important differences in detail, not so much as the result of any very deliberate new policy, but partly because, like most parents with several children, the Queen and the Duke have learned something more about rearing them as they have watched the development of each child, and they have made certain adjustments.

Both of the younger boys of the royal family have been far less bothered as children by the spotlight of publicity than was Prince Charles. The Queen, remembering his gruelling experiences, determined that, literally from the moment of their birth, everything possible would be done to shield them from such persecution. With Andrew, it might be said that perhaps too much was done at first. For instance, no photographs of his christening were issued from Buckingham Palace, and the Palace was so unresponsive to enquiries from the papers about the baby, that some editorial staffs began to toy with the idea that something about him was causing concern and being concealed. Nothing could have been further from the truth. Prince Andrew was a sturdy and even too-active child and he has grown up into a very striking and obviously balanced and self-possessed young man. At sixteen, he was already taller than the Prince of Wales, and seemed, partly in consequence of that, rather older than his age. He is athletic and lively.

His education started much as Prince Charles's had done when he was at home, still too young to go to school; but the Queen made sure that he had other small boys to play with. Then, when he was eight, he went to the Heatherdown Preparatory School, at Ascot, in Berkshire. It was a school with about eighty boarders of ages from eight to thirteen, the usual sports amenities in about thirty acres of grounds, and a conventional programme of studies, including Latin and some Greek. Andrew, when he was driven there on his first day, in the company of the Queen and the Duke of Edinburgh, after travelling overnight from Balmoral, was, perhaps, better equipped than Charles had been for the rigours of his first school. Prince Philip had insisted that this second son should be given every chance from the earliest years to acquire physical and athletic skills and a degree of toughness. He had his first swimming and riding lessons at the age of three. That was the age at which he received his own coat of arms, a variation of the Royal Arms with the addition of anchors in the design. 'He needs them,' was the comment of a member of the Household staff who remembers his talent for creative mischief at that age and for some time afterwards.

From early on he seems to have been seeking for answers to questions beginning, 'What would happen if . . .?' This started with pure enquiry as, for example, when a guard commander at Balmoral made the formal request for permission to 'march off the old colours', and the Queen indicated her assent, the small Prince Andrew asked loudly, 'What would happen if Mummy said, "No"?' And he added: 'I do wish she would sometimes!' Judging from a whole range of stories, some of which may be apocryphal, though apparently representative of a general truth, he moved rapidly from oral questioning to practical experiment, and in this phase, is regarded by many as the hidden hand behind such mysteries as the well-remembered case of the switched signs at a garden party, which sent guests scurrying in confusion to the wrong places; that of the nameless froth which appeared suddenly in the Windsor Castle swimming pool and was traced to the secret introduction of a large quantity of bath essence; and the still unsolved riddle of the altered television aerials at Buckingham Palace. Now that the Prince is of an age to be above such diversions it is, perhaps, unfair to record reports that suspicion of his involvement was strengthened by his known relatively large expenditure at that period of his career on stink bombs, hairy hands, rubber masks and whoopee cushions.

Though he was originally put down for Eton, Prince Andrew was sent on from his preparatory school to follow his father and his brother at Gordonstoun. The Queen's choice of this experimental and unusual school rather than one more orthodox had, as I have said, been quite daring when Prince Charles was sent there. It could be regarded as being even more so when Prince Andrew's turn came, because in the meantime there had been an important development. The school had become co-educational with the introduction of a hundred or so girls. As a place of education for a British royal prince it represents a new departure though one, like so many others in the changing style of the Monarchy, that is in keeping with the spirit of the times. It seems the school retains some of its more spartan characteristics, but they are less evident than when Prince Charles was there, and it is luxurious compared with what it was in the Duke of Edinburgh's schooldays. By all accounts, Prince Andrew finds the place suits him, just as it suited his father, and he plays a full, rather extrovert part in its life. He is 'Andie' to his friends there, who include a good many of the girls; he joins in the usual kinds of rowdiness and ragging, as a result of which, when he was fourteen, he was slightly hurt by a bang on the head, and had to spend a night in a nearby hospital.

A few months earlier, Prince Andrew was one of fifteen pupils from Gordonstoun who spent three weeks studying at a school in France, the Caousou Jesuit College in Toulouse. His identity was kept secret to all but a few, and Scotland Yard and the French police cooperated in his unobtrusive protection. On an official form he was required to complete he gave his name as Andrew Edwards, his father's occupation as 'gentleman farmer', and stated that his mother did not 'go out to work'. The college's report on him was that he was a bright student, who got along well with his French classmates, enjoyed his stay, showed real interest in visiting the region and learning its history, and certainly improved his French. The Prefect of Studies described him diplomatically as 'a lively boy with the same good points and bad points as any boy of his age'. Another teacher added, 'He was a bit of a handful.'

Two of the people who knew his real identity were the doctor and his wife in whose home he stayed, in Balma, a residential suburb of Toulouse. Journalists who knew of his presence agreed to keep quiet about it, and this enabled him to visit south-west France as he pleased, and to play football against a French college team. He scored a goal, but Gordonstoun lost the match.

That a prince of the British royal family, a possible heir to the throne, should have anything to do with the Jesuits, and especially receive any education from them, would have provoked widespread and angry reaction from extreme Protestants well within the lifetime of people who are middle-aged today, and perhaps even more recently than that. But the announcement in the British papers that Andrew had studied at Caousou produced, so far as I can see, no published comment at all. The Palace had apparently judged accurately the extent to which attitudes have changed. The bigotry which made the word 'jesuitical' synonymous with 'crafty' and 'deceitful', so that it retains these secondary definitions in standard dictionaries, is, one may gladly assume, no longer thought influential.

Prince Andrew is said to be good at games, including cricket, rugby and soccer, which was one of his early enthusiasms, and he used to be proud of a Bolton Wanderers club scarf sent him by someone who had heard he admired the team. He is a strong swimmer and knows how to handle a sailing-boat. He can ski, rides a horse well, and plays tennis and squash. The Duke of Edinburgh has seen to it that he has had some good coaching. He himself taught him how to sail at Cowes, and arranged for Graham Hill to give the Prince driving lessons on the roads of the royal estates, for his cricket to be coached at Lords and his tennis by the former Wimbledon champion, Dan Maskell. In July 1976 Prince Andrew, as a corporal in the Gordonstoun School Air Training Corps, gained his first proficiency badge as a glider pilot by flying three four-minute circuits alone over the A.T.C. gliding school at Milltown, near the R.A.F. Lossiemouth base, in Morayshire.

It is understood that Prince Andrew will stay at Gordonstoun until he is eighteen, taking the usual public examinations; and nothing has been said about what may be planned for him after that. However, his Gordonstoun career was to be given an interlude abroad by a spell of two terms at Lakefield College, Ontario, Canada, which is linked with Gordonstoun, from the beginning of 1977. Buckingham Palace has continued to be very reticent indeed in issuing news about him, adhering understandably to the firm policy that he must be allowed to get on with his schooling in peace. His public appearances have been few, though he is being edged gently towards the busy schedule of royal engagements. He has presented trophies at the Royal Windsor Horse Show, and has stood beside his father when the Duke was taking the salute at a Scouts' march-past. I saw him playing a public role for the first time when he accompanied the Queen to Aberdeen for the ceremonial start of the flow of North Sea oil. Tall, spruce and poised, with an expressive face that conveyed enthusiasm and amiability, he had an easy manner with the dignitaries who were presented to him, and gave the impression that this type of royal activity would never for him pose any difficulty. It is said that his family see him as 'a blend of Charles and Anne'. As understudy of the heir apparent, he could find that a very useful qualification.

The youngest child of the Queen and the Duke of Edinburgh, Prince Edward Antony Richard Louis, born in 1964, followed his brother to Heatherdown, and was his fellow-pupil there for a year, before the older prince started at Gordonstoun. Soon it will have to be decided whether or not this school will also be the next for Edward. It is certainly not a foregone conclusion that he will go there. Probably the Duke of Edinburgh would favour his doing so, but the Prince himself will have his say. Whatever changes there have been over the years in the methods adopted by the Queen and the Duke in bringing up their family, the children themselves have always been consulted when important new stages in their lives had to be considered. Edward, although he has been described by the Queen as 'the quietest of my children', is also seen by those close to him as a small boy who usually knows what he wants and can be determined, even obstinate, about it. He is gentler and more self-contained than was Andrew, it is said, and though he can be lively enough when this is called for, an almost grave absorption in whatever activity he may be pursuing is rather more characteristic of him. The Queen Mother, who likes to have him in her company quite often, has said she is impressed by his ability, rare in a child, to sit still. It could be that he will decide that Gordonstoun is not for him, and, indeed, the Queen might also feel this.

It is said that he mixes well in the rough and tumble of school life, and he showed this as a little boy, when he spent a couple of terms at a day school in London before going on to Heatherdown. Earlier than that, he had been given plenty of juvenile company at home, where his principal playmates were Princess Margaret's daughter, Lady Sarah Armstrong-Jones, and the son of Princess Alexandra, James Ogilvy, who became his fellow pupil at boarding school.

He seems to have done pretty well in his studies, and like his eldest brother, the Prince of Wales, he has a capacity for sustained hard work. In this, in his quietness, and also somewhat in his appearance, people see resemblances to his grandfather King George VI. He has his enthusiasms. Soccer is one of them and photography another. Since he was about eleven years old he has been an ardent fly-fisher, encouraged by the Queen

Mother, who is herself devoted to this sport and years ago initiated into it her oldest grandchild, Prince Charles. But it is early days yet to make solemn assessments about the character and abilities of Prince Edward, who is essentially, at the moment, a cheerful small boy growing up; and that is the way in which he impressed himself on millions over television when for once he was under the fierce light of publicity from which the Queen has so firmly shielded him. That was when he was page to his sister, Princess Anne, at her wedding in November 1973.

Princess Anne has always made news and, because of her prowess as a horsewoman, unquestionably would have done so even had she not been the daughter of the Queen. As a child, she was never as much pestered by the pressmen as was Charles, her senior by two years; but because for quite a while she was the only little girl in the royal scene, she was made the subject, not to say the victim, of some of the most nauseatingly-mawkish rubbish that writers about royalty have ever inflicted on the long-suffering public. Looking today at some of these slim volumes of pretty pictures and a modicum of sickly text, which are only too easy to find in five-penny throw-away trays outside second-hand bookshops, it is hard to believe that there was ever a market for them. They all strike the same fair-haired, blue-eyed, fairy-tale princess note, and beyond that, there is little in them except boring and pointless anecdotes about American love-birds, corgis and ponies. I note this with a certain feeling of frustration, because I have not found it easy to obtain a clear impression of what Princess Anne was really like as a small girl, although I am convinced that she cannot in any way have resembled the pink-fudge character that these books dimly evoke. It is impossible that the strikingly-positive, confident, assertive and relaxed young woman that we see today, as a Princess highly active and competent in her public duties, and as a rider of Olympic standard, did not as a child demonstrate similar, rather tough qualities. The pretty pictures do show something of this, perhaps—for instance, that she seems to be feeling more herself in jodhpurs and a shirt, saddling her pony—the Welsh-bred strawberry roan, Greensleeves—or messing about in a boat on the lake at Frogmore, than she does posed sweetly in a charming little dress. I would suspect that she was, in fact, self-willed, affectionate, exhaustingly-active, frequently naughty, and if one dare say it, sometimes a trifle spoiled, probably by her father, all of which amounts to a much nicer child than the one that seems to simper through the dreadful, sycophantic, contemporary accounts of her.

All that, however, is largely guesswork. To state the undoubted facts, she was born at Clarence House on 15th August 1950; she began having regular instruction from Prince Charles's governess, Miss Peebles, when she was five; continued having lessons at the Palace, but now together with two other little girls, Susan Babington-Smith and Caroline Hamilton, when she was seven; and when she was twelve, stayed for a couple of weeks in France as the guest of the Marquis de St Genys to improve her French, before going off to boarding school. The French visit was not her first journey abroad, because she went out in the Royal yacht *Britannia* when she was four to meet the Queen and the Duke of Edinburgh at Tobruk when they were completing a Commonwealth tour, and there were stops at Malta on both the outward and homecoming passages.

When the Queen and the Duke of Edinburgh decided, after consulting Princess Anne's own wishes, to send her to a boarding school when she was thirteen, they were once again adapting the royal way of life to the changing times. The decision was positively revolutionary; for never before had the daughter of a British sovereign gone to school for her education, mixing in, and conforming to the same rules, the same programmes of activity and study, and the same living conditions as the other pupils. All of them, including the Queen herself, had been educated at home by governesses and tutors and, in previous reigns, anything else would have been unthinkable. For a complex of reasons the choice of the right school was not easy. Not the least of them was the need that the Princess's fellow pupils should not themselves be put out of their stride because of her presence among them, but be able to work alongside her without being hampered by either sycophancy or social unease, accepting the person rather than the princess. I think it is true to say—at the risk of offending ardent feminists—that this is, or was at that time, a greater difficulty in a girls' school than in one for boys. However this may be, I understand that the choice did present problems. The school finally selected was Benenden, near the village in Kent of that name, forty-five miles or so from London. The nucleus of the school is a large, mid-Victorian country house, and other buildings have been set up round it since the foundation in 1924. When Princess Anne was there, the school had rather more than 300 pupils.

The Princess was absolutely at liberty to make any friends she chose at Benenden, and she did so, fairly quickly. Judith Campbell, in her book, *Anne: Portrait of a Princess*, suggests, interestingly, that far from feeling herself restricted at the school, Princess Anne, because of her unique circumstances, found a freedom there that she had never known before, because it enabled her to be simply herself, a teenage girl who was just one in a crowd of others. Academically, she seems not to have been greatly concerned about examination results, but she obtained six 'O' levels, without apparent difficulty, and then 'A' levels in History and Geography, gaining a Merit grade in an extra, optional, special History paper. She passed an examination in the use of English which is required for Oxford or Cambridge entry. But the school's verdict was that she had worked at her studies only as hard as was strictly necessary, and that she was capable of having done better.

Serious consideration was given to the question of whether or not she should go to a British university—probably one of the newer ones—but she decided she did not want to do so. Her main interests at school were athletic and social. She had some talent for tennis, spurred by early training from Dan Maskell, as well as for lacrosse. She sang in the school choir, played the piano and, for a time, the oboe, and was a highly-active member of the Dancing Club. She was in demand as an actress, too, showing something of Princess Margaret's flair for mimicry and reproduction of dialects. She liked pop music, and played the percussion instruments in the school orchestra. In all this then she was a fairly average schoolgirl, and also, as she confesses, rather lazy about her studies.

However, in one matter at least, Princess Anne was quite certainly much above the average, and can certainly never have been lazy, or lacking in determination and application. That, of course, was in her devotion to horses, managing them, training them, riding them. You cannot ask much more of anyone who takes up any sporting activity than the achievement of the highest standard required for international competition. Princess Anne has achieved it, which means she is the only member of the royal family to attain recognition as one of the world's greatest practitioners in a chosen discipline, the only one to put it beyond question that she is able to get to the very top, by her own ability and hard work, in something in which her high rank is in no way involved and cannot have helped her. That she has been able to do this while carrying out to the full the duties that rank imposes, as she certainly has, is astonishing and admirable.

I know nothing at all about horses or riding so I am quite unable to assess what qualities in the Princess's performance make her a champion; and I cannot with honesty report the comments of the experts, because I would not understand them. But I can set down, for the record, what I am told are the most important stages of her riding career so far. She had her first lessons in riding when she was only two years and six months old; so obviously it pays to start straight out of the cradle. Her teacher at that time was the Queen. Later, she had more advanced instruction at Windsor from the daughter of the man who taught the Queen as a child, Miss Sybil Smith. When the Princess was twelve, she and Prince Charles had successes as members of the Garth Pony Club in Berkshire. She had more training between 1963 and 1968, while she was at Benenden, from Mrs Hatton Hall, and then she started schooling for Eventing with Mrs Alan Oliver, the wife of the famous show jumper. In 1969, she won the Windsor Horse Trials, and by the end of that year had qualified for Badminton. In 1971, after winning the European Three-Day Event, she gained four different nominations as sports personality and sportswoman of the year. In 1973, she won the Combined Championship at Hickstead. She has also been runner-up in the European Three-Day Event, and later said on television that she was prouder of this than of her 1971 victory, because she had been riding a horse other than her famous Doublet, which proved that those who said a woman could only be successful on one horse were wrong.

In the summer of 1976, Princess Anne won a place in the British team for the Three-Day Event at the Olympic Games at Montreal. British teams had won gold medals in this part of the Olympic competition in 1968 in Mexico and in 1972 in

Munich. They were unlucky in Montreal; but even someone totally ignorant of equestrian skills, as well as those who know all about them, is unlikely to forget the drama of Princess Anne's fall, which to the uninitiated looked appalling, when her horse, Goodwill, took one obstacle on the cross-country course. She remounted with what appeared to be total unconcern; but she was, in fact, concussed, so that her memory was affected, and although she finished the course, had later no recollection of her ride after the fall. In spite of that, and an injured arm, she continued undeterred in the further stages of the competition. This incident, many people think, produced one of the best, though also one of the least flattering, photographs ever taken of the Queen, as she watched, her face a concentrated mask of nail-biting anxiety. Millions of television viewers were sharing her distress, concerned at the same time for her and for the unshakeable Princess.

From a woman in Denmark Hill, a South London suburb, the London *Evening News* received a letter which said, 'The concern that haunted the face of the Queen at Montreal as Princess Anne and Goodwill took that disastrous tumble is familiar to mothers the world over. Garden swing or Olympic fence—it makes no difference where they fall. Thank heavens we are grown up enough nowadays not to make this an excuse for trying to stop Princess Anne from enjoying her favourite sport.'

The writer of this, Mrs Margaret Williams, was expressing a human reaction. But she was also stating one of the demands of modern times to which the Monarchy has already adapted itself. Lady Longford has identified what she calls 'cotton-wooling' as one enemy of a modern Monarchy which our own royal family has overcome. She says, 'We have seen how the youthful House of Windsor, as represented by Prince Edward and Prince Albert [later George VI], battered itself sick against George V and his Government in an effort to reach the danger zones of the First World War. Prince Albert alone fully succeeded, at the battle of Jutland. Today the physical restrictions have been relaxed. Prince Albert's daughter got to Ghana and Prince Albert's eldest grandson has jumped from a parachute into the sea and piloted a supersonic jet solo.' As the cameras whirred in Montreal, the Queen and Mrs Williams suffered but approved when Prince Albert's granddaughter was allowed to take her chances, too.

If Princess Anne has given the Queen and the Queen's subjects some anxious moments in her cheerful efforts to 'do her own thing', so far as she can within the inescapable limitations of her station, she has also provided a good deal of fun, and quite often, some genuine glamour. Many fathers of daughters must have found her endearing when she first emerged on the social scene in her late teens, obviously being allowed a pretty free hand to experiment with the trendy clothes of her age-group. She was as fond of wearing different and striking hats as the late Sir Winston Churchill, who would, I think, have liked her very much had he lived long enough to know her at this stage of her growing-up. She hit the bull's-eye with some of the hats. Some others were preposterous, but she still looked attractive in them, because she was young, and because she obviously felt she had made a good choice, and because, of course, any reasonably-presentable young woman in her teens can put almost anything on her head and look charming, provided she does it with style and confidence; and these are qualities Princess Anne seems always to have possessed.

However, it was no sweet young thing who, round about the spring of 1969, began carrying out royal duties and honouring public functions in her own right. At nineteen, Princess Anne was no more a fairy-tale princess than she had been as a little girl, although Lord Snowdon did succeed in conveying a large measure of some such quality in his enchanting nineteenth-birthday photograph of her, together with a democratic hint of the prettiest girl in the tennis club. The real Princess was, and is, an entirely new kind of article, a modern princess, of whom the outstanding characteristics seem to be individuality, forthrightness and knowing her own mind, even though she does also radiate freshness and youth, with a sort of innocence, and is easy on the eye. The forthrightness can, and sometimes does, bruise feelings, particularly of news-cameramen. I have seen it happen. For instance, at a horse show that I remember, she had a brush with cameramen when she was making a preliminary inspection of part of the course. They had gathered at a water obstacle where they thought the setting would provide a good picture of her. When she arrived, she said aloud, 'Ah, the goons gathered at the water-hole!' I think her intention was humorous, and that she did not mean to give offence; but some feathers were ruffled. The reason for this, which she could not have known, was that some of these cameramen had heard that the Princess had been upset during the dressage by a very loudly-whirring camera which she thought was disturbing her horse; so they had deliberately chosen to get their pictures while she was merely looking at the course, thus making sure that her performance would be in no way affected. Judith Campbell recalls the Princess saying of her fellow pupils at Benenden, 'They were a caustic lot who knew exactly what they thought about other people.' Especially where her riding is concerned, she does sometimes reflect this fashion from her schooldays, and there are countless Fleet Street stories about this aspect of her, which occasionally get into the papers.

Throughout the first years of the Seventies, as the papers and magazines assiduously followed the activities of the Princess, social, official and equestrian, and speculated from time to time as to whether or not she would marry this or that young man with whom she had been seen, a retaliatory harsh or mocking note did sometimes creep into what was printed about her. It seems that she was quite unconcerned about this, giving substance to a wistful remark made (to Andrew Duncan) by Princess Margaret, 'Anne's much more positive than I was, so I think she'll be all right. She's much tougher, too, and has been brought up in a different atmosphere, and went to school.'

Then, on 29th May, 1973, Fleet Street decided joyously that it could and would let bygones be bygones for the next few months, for it had been given a great story about the Princess together with the prospect of an even bigger one to follow, and felt wholly justified in sprinkling stardust lavishly, and even brushing-up on the fairy-tale routine. The reason for this was, of course, that the Court Circular had put an end to all the guessing games by announcing, 'It is with the greatest pleasure that The Queen and The Duke of Edinburgh announce the betrothal of their beloved daughter The Princess Anne to Lieutenant Mark Phillips, The Queen's Dragoon Guards, son of Mr and Mrs Peter Phillips.'

At the time of their engagement, the Princess was twenty-two and Lieutenant Phillips twenty-four. Their growing friendship had been watched and reported on for months, and had given rise to repeated denials of any more important relationship by Buckingham Palace and, as recently as March, by firstly the Princess and then the Lieutenant. Buckingham

Palace explained that all these denials had been true at the time they were made. They had become engaged only at Easter over the weekend after the Badminton Horse Trials. They had been frequently in each other's company since their meeting following the Mexico Olympics, five years previously. It was decided that the engagement would be announced during the spring holiday, when all the royal family would be at Balmoral, because the Prince of Wales would be able to fly home from the West Indies, and Prince Andrew and Prince Edward would be on holiday from school. Lieutenant Phillips joined this Balmoral gathering, having been given nine days privilege leave from his regiment, with whom he was serving as Assistant Adjutant, at Hohne, in West Germany.

Lieutenant Mark Phillips was a well-connected young man, belonging essentially to what used to be called the squirearchy, but linked to the aristocracy on both sides of his family, and with successful soldiers, Midlands mining-engineers, professional men and bankers in his ancestry, as well as, in the remoter past, on his mother's side, German merchants. His maternal grandfather was aide-de-camp to King George VI, the maternal grandfather of the Princess; but a detailed family tree published by Debrett's showed an actual blood relationship in the maternal ancestry of the young couple. According to this, they are thirteenth cousins, three times removed, through the two marriages of Sir William Griffith, who lived at Penrhyn Castle, Caernarvonshire, in Henry VIII's reign. Debrett's say Sir William's daughter by his first wife was an ancestor of Queen Elizabeth the Queen Mother; and his daughter by his second wife was an ancestor of Captain Phillips's mother.

Lieutenant Phillips's home background had the atmosphere of soldiering and horses, hounds and sporting dogs, from his earliest childhood. His first years were spent on the family farm at Tewkesbury, Gloucestershire, where his father, Major Peter Phillips, and his mother, Mrs Anne Phillips, were members of the Ledbury Hunt. He was riding his first pony at an even earlier age than had Princess Anne, before his second birthday. When he was nine, the family moved to Great Somerford, in Wiltshire, where the 400-year-old manor house became their home. It is by no means one of the stately homes of England, but a fairly modest gentleman's house, with six bedrooms, looking from the outside mellow, pleasant and appropriate in its setting—a rural community, not great at all in size, in spite of its name, with a small population of people who have become Princess Anne's ardent admirers and regard her as one of themselves.

Mark Phillips's father was a major in the Queen's Dragoon Guards, in which his own father had been a brigadier and which his son was to join. Major Phillips later became a director of the Walls food firm which is probably best known for the sausages it makes. Mark was sent to a preparatory school, Stouts Hill, in Gloucestershire, and then to Marlborough College, where he was celebrated as a sporting all-rounder, becoming captain of athletics in his last year, though academically he was, in the opinion of his housemaster, 'quite good but not noteworthy'. However this may be, he certainly fitted the bill at Sandhurst, where he went next, because he was runner-up for the Sword of Honour. By the time he received his commission, he was already a leading Three-Day Event rider, and soon he found himself occasionally competing against Princess Anne, notably at the 1971 Badminton Trials, which he won on his horse Great Ovation, although the Princess, on Doublet, was in the lead at one stage. He has appeared as rather shy and certainly unassertive when he has been interviewed on television with Princess Anne. I suspect that while wanting to be amiable and helpful, he was at the same time wishing that the interview had simply never been thought of. I have met him, and found him just as amiable, though less shy and much more articulate, probably because we were not on television but at a drinks party in the wardroom of one of Her Majesty's Australian destroyers. The Australian officers said they liked him, too, and they certainly would not have been disposed to do so on the sole ground that he was married to Princess Anne. He also had to overcome the initial disadvantage of being both a pommy and a pongo, which is no mean achievement on a couple of gins in only about an hour.

In the six months or so between the announcement of the Princess's engagement and the day chosen for the wedding, 14th November, there were plenty of developments to retain public interest as preparations went ahead for what, it had been decreed, must be a great national occasion—though this was something the Princess suffered rather than sought: for it seems she would have preferred a much smaller family ceremony in

St George's Chapel, Windsor, rather than the magnificence and pageantry planned for Westminster Abbey.

In his professional life, the Lieutenant became a Captain. In his all-too-public private life, the papers were speculating about whether, like Princess Margaret's husband, his marriage would lead to his being given a title; but the Palace spokesmen simply said they had no knowledge of any such plan. He was appointed a personal aide-de-camp to the Queen, which might be seen as an acknowledgement of his new status; for it has been common since Victoria's day for the Sovereign to honour in this way members of the royal family who are serving officers.

Wedding programmes, less formal in appearance than such things had been in the past, with a sprinkling of photographs and a biographical sketch of Princess Anne by Lady Longford, went on sale in October at thirty pence each, the proceeds going to King George's Jubilee Trust which helps youth work. The design was made public of a special issue of postage stamps, which consisted almost entirely of a close-up photograph of the bride and bridegroom; but as is customary, a small silhouette was also included, and the manner in which it was done prompted the facetious in London clubs to say, 'The Queen seems to have got into Anne's hair.'

It was made known, and duly communicated in the papers under large headlines, that the Princess would adhere to the normal Wedding Service and undertake to *obey* her husband; and, indeed, a few days before the wedding, she had declared herself to be 'a rather old-fashioned girl'. This happened when she and Captain Mark Phillips responded bravely to streams of searching questions in a long television interview. It was not as bad a performance as it became the smart thing to say that it was, in spite of several instances of a silly question deserving, and getting, a silly answer; but undoubtedly its most lasting result was to acquaint the public with the fact that the couple shared an intriguing habit of speaking in the third person. It was not long before Alf Garnett's daughter in the television series *'Til Death Do Us Part* was asking her appalling father, 'Is one going to one's pub?'

The Princess was genuinely moved as she expressed her appreciation of the goodwill that she and Captain Phillips had evoked. She said, 'We've really been struck by people's generosity. We've had some marvellous presents. We've also had some presents from people we've no idea who they are. Just tiny little things. We got one toffee from a small girl.'

Captain Phillips said, 'But I think also that the intense interest which the Press and television have shown in the wedding, and the people all over the world who would appear to be interested in the wedding, reflect a little bit the state of the world at the moment, in that every day people pick up the paper and read about some disaster or some new scandal, and I think they are really rather relieved to read about something that is genuinely happy and good.'

That observation of Captain Phillips was far and away the best thing said in that interview, and it hit the nail on the head. The year 1973 had been nasty, brutish and far too long. It had been the year of Watergate in the United States, where the Vice President had resigned, and been fined and given three years' probation for tax evasion. In Britain there had been the Poulson affair and the stink of corruption in local government. There had been resignations of ministers from Her Majesty's Government over scandals involving a call girl and what were called 'casual affairs'. The whole economic future had become a frightening mystery because the oil sheiks were holding the industrial world to ransom. Industrial relations in Britain seemed to be approaching an unprecedented crisis. With only about six weeks of the year to go, the Royal Wedding came as a tonic, exemplifying splendidly the famous pronouncement of the greatest of the analysts of Monarchy, Walter Bagehot, years before, 'All but a few cynics like to see a pretty novel touching for a moment the dry scenes of the grave world. A princely marriage is the brilliant edition of a universal fact, and as such, it rivets mankind. . . . Just so a royal family sweetens politics by the seasonable addition of nice and pretty events.' He and Captain Phillips were clearly on the same wave-length.

With millions of people watching it on television, the wedding must have been the most public in history. In matters of timing and the ordered control of large numbers of people, in the nature of much of its spectacular quality, it was something akin to a military operation. In some respects, of course, it was precisely that—not least because the bridegroom was a professional soldier and his regiment had its part to play, and also because, as colonel-in-chief of several regiments, the Princess too had special links with the Army. In fact, the Navy and the

Princess Margaret spends her thirty-ninth birthday happy with her husband and children in the gardens of Kensington Palace

A goodbye kiss from Lord Snowdon as Princess Margaret leaves London for a West Indies holiday in 1969

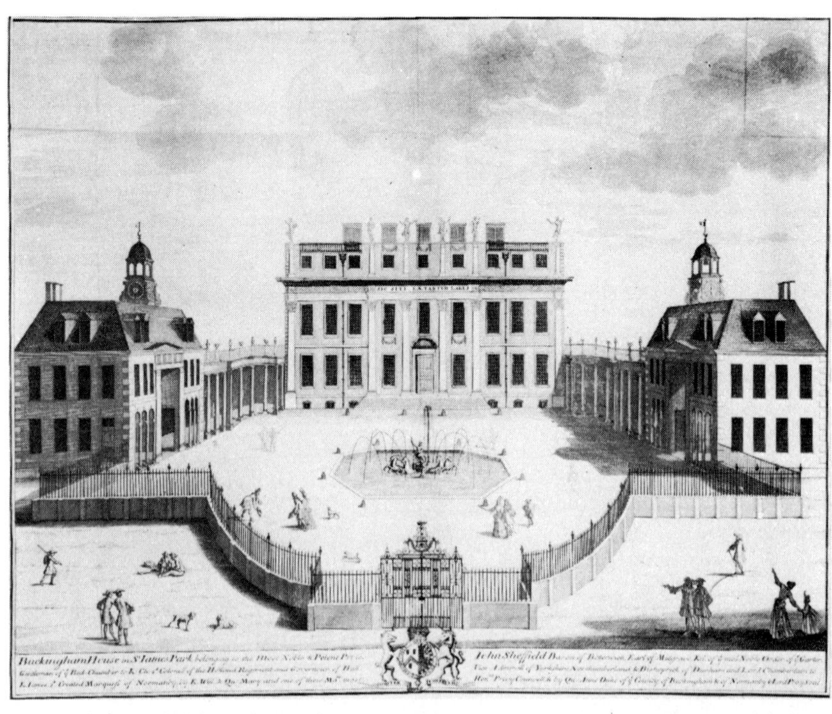

George III bought Buckingham House in 1761. George IV turned it into Buckingham Palace, London home of the Sovereign through eight reigns

Sandringham House in Norfolk was visited by Queen Victoria only twice, but was George V's best-loved home. Queen Elizabeth II thinks it is too big

Air Force did not play proportionally so large a part as they would have done in, for example, a state visit. In the streets along which the wedding processions passed it would not have been noticed that, because of the situation in Northern Ireland, the military force generally was smaller than would have been normal for such an event—about two-thirds of that for Princess Margaret's wedding thirteen years before, smaller even than that for most state visits in recent years.

Inside the Abbey, where I was fortunate enough to have a seat very close to the central happenings, the general atmosphere, in spite of the grandeur and colour provided by military uniforms, clerical vestments, and ladies dressed for an important morning occasion, was happy and relaxed as for a family event. It was on the family that most people in the Abbey kept their gaze, while somewhere outside, Princess Anne was driven in the glass coach through the autumn sunshine, along streets lined with well-wishers, many of whom had waited since the day before. They looked at the Queen, in royal blue, who had taken her place near the altar, with Queen Elizabeth the Queen Mother and the Prince of Wales beside her and other members of the royal family near-by. The bridegroom's parents were opposite them. Captain Mark Phillips and the brother officer who was his best man waited standing at the bottom of the altar steps, occasionally smiling and chatting to each other.

Then a flourish of trumpets signalled the moment all had been waiting for, and eyes turned towards the aisle, as Princess Anne, her hand on the arm of her father, approached the altar. Behind came the only bridesmaid, her then nine-year-old cousin, Lady Sarah Armstrong-Jones, in white, and the kilted page, her youngest brother, Prince Edward, then also nine. For almost everyone in the Abbey this was the first view of the Princess's wedding dress—white, of course; silk; with a high neckline, a widely-flared skirt and a circular train.

All that week at the Palace, in the middle of the excitement usual in any household during the preparations for a wedding, including all the pleasant female bustle that goes on at such times, there had been a good deal of talk about that dress; about the grand, but jolly pre-wedding reception, which was not in essence a State affair, and where a high proportion of the 1500 guests were close friends of the royal family, of Captain Phillips's family, and of the Princess and the Captain, there to have fun and to express their affection and regard for the young couple; and even about such trifles as what might be the 'something old, something new, something borrowed and something blue' that the Princess would wear, in keeping with tradition. Yet one knew that for that family, such things were not the heart of the matter; for in it there was a very deep and genuine sense that all that was going to happen on the great day for Anne had at its centre a Christian ceremony, a sacrament; and that the only really important moment would be the one when the young couple made their vows before the Archbishop.

So it proved detectably to be when, in the Abbey, that moment came. It seemed somehow a decorously private moment in that otherwise so public ceremony. There was an extraordinary hush, in which you thought you could hear the breathing of people near you, just before the Archbishop, at the altar, called on Captain Phillips to make his vows, and the Captain uttered 'I will', firmly and clearly.

Most of the royal family, including the Queen, joined in the singing in the service that followed; and after the signing of the register, Princess Anne—now also Mrs Mark Phillips—left the Abbey smiling on the arm of her husband. It had been a grand, royal, military, national and international event; but I think that anyone present in the Abbey must have sensed how much it was also something very solemn and at the same time a very happy family occasion for which Johann Strauss the elder's Radetsky March—unusual at a wedding—seemed entirely appropriate as it mingled with the clamour of the bells.

On the day of the Royal Wedding a young man named James Wallace Beaton, aged thirty at the time, started a new job. He became Princess Anne's bodyguard. Just eighteen weeks later he was in Westminster Hospital with bullet wounds in his chest, abdomen and right hand, having proved that in times like ours such an assignment is no sinecure. Another policeman, Constable Michael Hills; Princess Anne's driver, Alexander Callender; and a free-lance journalist, Mr John McConnell, were also in hospital with bullet wounds. All had risked their lives in helping, with extraordinary courage and determination, to rescue Princess Anne from an armed, mentally-deranged man who had attempted to kidnap her within a hundred yards of Buckingham Palace.

The full picture of what really happened on that evening of Wednesday, 20th March 1974, did not emerge until the would-be kidnapper, Ian Ball, aged twenty-six, a man with a history of mental illness, was, at the Central Criminal Court, committed to hospital for an indefinite period, after pleading guilty to the attempted kidnapping, to attempting to murder two policemen, and to wounding two other men.

The Princess and her husband may well have narrowly escaped death. They were being driven to Buckingham Palace in the evening after attending a private showing of a documentary film of the Riding for the Disabled organization, one of the great interests of the Princess, who is its Patron. When they were in the darkest part of the Mall a white car swerved in front of theirs and forced it to stop. The white car's driver, a man, approached the royal car just as the Princess's detective had got out to see what was happening, and shot him in the shoulder. Inspector Beaton fired back, in spite of his wound, but missed. Then his gun jammed. The man next attempted to force open one door of the royal car, calling on the Princess to come out to him. There followed a confused struggle, with Captain Phillips striving to keep the door closed, as the wounded Inspector entered the car from the other side, and leaned across the Princess to shield her with his body. The attacker then fired through the rear window, but Inspector Beaton put his hand in the line of fire, and it was wounded by the bullet and by shattered glass. As the man again went for the door, and this time wrenched it open, the Inspector attempted to throw him off balance, but was shot in the stomach and collapsed at the gunman's feet. The Princess's driver also tackled the man, and held on to his arm, but was shot in the chest. At one stage, the man was trying to drag the Princess from the car, while she talked to him, trying to calm him down, and Captain Phillips held her firmly by the waist. The journalist, Mr McConnell, saw what was happening, stopped the taxi he was travelling in, and tried to persuade the gunman to give up his gun, but he, too, was shot in the chest. Constable Hills, coming on the scene from nearby St James's Palace, from which he had heard the noise, made a similar effort, but was shot in the stomach. Nevertheless, he managed to send a clear account of what was happening by his personal radio, and to ask urgently for help, and he even picked up Inspector Beaton's abandoned gun but collapsed before he could attempt to fire it. Two more civilians now joined in, Mr Glenmore Martin, a chauffeur, and Mr Ronald Russell, a company manager. Mr Martin helped Constable Hills, ignoring the danger from the gunman. Mr Russell punched the gunman, who fired at him, but missed; and after some more struggling at the car doors, Mr Russell punched him again. By now police were arriving, and the gunman ran off. One of the policemen, Constable Peter Edmonds, gave chase, and although menaced by the man's gun, brought him down with a rugby tackle. Other policemen then seized and disarmed him.

When I got to the scene, after receiving a telephoned message of something dramatic, but unspecified, happening to Princess Anne, the whole of the Mall was cordoned off. The police in front of the Palace were uncertain if what had happened had been an assassination attempt, an action by some terrorist group, or even that there was only one assailant. Police were searching St James's Park. I entered the Palace with some difficulty, even with my Palace pass. Knowing the state of alarm along the Mall, I was astonished by the real, if rather determined calm, which I found prevailing in the Palace. The first thing that happened was that one of the equerries offered me a drink.

The Queen and the Duke of Edinburgh were away on a visit to Indonesia, and the Queen's Press Secretary, Ronald Allison, was with them. The Assistant Press Secretary, Anne Hawkins (now Mrs Michael Wall), was trying to find out what had happened, so as to give what story she could to me and to my Press Association colleague, Douglas Dumbrell, who had also arrived; and since no one at that moment knew much more than that there had been shooting and violence in the Mall, and that the Princess was involved, a degree of evident alarm would have been pardonable. But it was stiff upper-lips all round. I understand that much later, in the early hours of the following morning, I told the *Today* programme: 'The whole thing was rather like the American notion of how the British behave in a crisis.' Well, it *was* like that—*Mrs Miniver*, *Bridge over the River Kwai*, cups of tea in the blitz, that kind of atmosphere.

We waited. Somebody gave me another drink. Presently we heard that the Princess and her husband were in the Palace, and quite soon, somebody that Miss Hawkins made contact with, a woman's voice, over the Palace intercom, told us that Princess Anne and Captain Phillips were unharmed, and gave us a telescoped, but cool, calm and collected account of what had happened. I asked some questions, and got some clear answers. It was only later that we learned that our informant had been Miss Rowena Brassey, Princess Anne's lady-in-waiting, who had been in the car with the Princess and Captain Phillips and had clearly been in great danger. She did not mention this.

Douglas Dumbrell and I telephoned a story to our news desks. Then we were rather privileged to be taken to one of the private rooms which was next door to where Princess Anne was telephoning to Indonesia to tell the Queen and the Duke of Edinburgh that she was safe, though shaken. Her actual phrase was, 'We are delighted to be in one piece.' She was very distressed about Alec Callender, her wounded Scottish chauffeur, who had been in the Palace service for twenty years, and about Inspector Beaton. With the royal corgis running about our feet, Douglas and I telephoned another story.

All the wounded men recovered, and they, as well as Mr Martin, Mr Russell and Constable Edmonds were awarded honours by the Queen. Inspector Beaton received the highest award for peacetime gallantry, the George Cross. Eventually, Princess Anne herself was made a Dame Grand Cross of the Royal Victorian Order and Captain Phillips a Commander of the Order for their behaviour during the kidnap attempt. In the meantime, the bizarre story behind that attempt had become known. Ian Ball, who was described in court as 'by any standard' mad at the time of the attempt, 'potentially suicidal and homicidal', and in need of treatment, was said to have planned the kidnapping for several years, though he had carried it out on impulse. He sought to gain a ransom of £3 million, and also to draw attention to what he called 'the lack of facilities for treating mental illness under the National Health Service'.

Two days after an experience that would have sent many young women in search of a rest cure, I watched Princess Anne, relaxed and smiling, as she received a wedding present, planted an oak, unveiled a plaque and made a speech, at Great Somerford, Captain Phillips's home village. The day after that, I saw her competing with her horses at the Amberley Horse Show in Cirencester Park and getting cross with photographers. So far as I am concerned, a lady like that can get cross with anyone she pleases, and in the third person if she likes. She is a Princess indeed.

Even when there are no kidnapping attempts or comparable excitements to bring her name into the papers, speculation of one kind or another still keeps it there; and a favourite question is concerned with when she might start a family. Just as it has been suggested that Prince Charles's acquisition of a country house, Chevening, might prompt him to an early marriage, so when the Queen bought the Princess and Captain Phillips a country house and estate—Gatcombe Park, between Minchinhampton and Avening in the Cotswolds—the idea that now there might be a royal grandchild was floated again. The Princess had told an interviewer, Miss Marjorie Proops, early in 1976, that she planned to have children, but she still had to achieve the ambition of taking part in the Olympic Games, and having a family could wait a bit longer. When the Olympic Games were over, therefore, speculation began again.

6. Royal Ladies

Queen Elizabeth the Queen Mother is now nearer eighty than seventy years of age; she has been carrying out royal duties for more than half a century; and yet she is still one of the most active in public life of all the members of the royal family. Her popularity among her daughter's subjects has never diminished. She is also a well-loved figure outside Britain, where the special, personal qualities she has contributed to the glamour that the British Monarchy still retains almost everywhere make her continually interesting and often mentioned and pictured in the Press.

She has played a most important part in that gradual process of change by which the Monarchy has moved with the times to retain its hold on the loyalty and affection of a changing nation. From the start, she represented something new. When, in 1923, she married the Duke of York (later King George VI), it was the first time that a British Prince had legally married a commoner under the provisions of the Royal Marriages Act of 1772, which required the Sovereign's consent for such a marriage. In the fairly remote past marriages between royalty and commoners had not been unusual, but they had been rare since the days of Henry VIII, four of whose six wives, including the two he had beheaded, were not of royal rank at birth. The marriage of George IV, as Prince of Wales, to Maria Fitzherbert, though unquestionably valid sacramentally, was not legally so under British law because of the Royal Marriages Act. So Lady Elizabeth Angela Marguerite Bowes-Lyon, youngest daughter of the 14th Earl of Strathmore, made history at her marriage. She did, in fact, have royal blood, if one wants to enter into niceties; for her family goes back to Sir John Lyon, of Glamis, Chamberlain of Scotland in 1377, who married Princess Jean, daughter of King Robert II; but it is possibly more interesting that her less distant ancestry contains some refreshingly-ordinary British names—Smith, Browne, Webb, Tucker and Carpenter, for instance, back in the late eighteenth and early nineteenth centuries. As a fascinating result of this, our present Sovereign and her children have less royal blood than has the Duke of Edinburgh, in whose family tree you would have to seek very hard to find anything less exalted than a 'High and Well-Born'. Those who enjoy following such tenuous threads may also like to know that through the Queen Mother's descent from the Very Rev. Robert Hodgson, who died in 1844, the royal family is linked with that of one of the most celebrated opponents of the British Crown, the rebel colonist, George Washington, first President of the United States of America.

She became a national figure from the first. The Duke's choice of a British bride had pleased all sections of the population, and the marriage, in Westminster Abbey, was made an occasion of great national rejoicing. As wife of the King's second son, she became 'Her Royal Highness' with the status of a princess, and carried her new rank as if she had been born to it. Those who remember her early days as a member of the royal family say that it was apparent, as she fulfilled her public engagements, that she was bringing a new quality to the job of being royal, a feminine sparkle and genuine warmth that charmed everyone. In ways not easy to define, matters of manner rather than method, she seemed to take some of the starch out of royal occasions in which she was involved. At the beginning, this was partly achieved no doubt by the natural appeal of a young, vivacious and very pretty woman; but rather to the astonishment of the self-consciously hard-boiled Smart Young People of the early Twenties she turned out to be also rather tough, dedicated and indefatigable, and not merely a sweet young thing. In her seventies she still retains a remarkable youthfulness that seems simply to be part of her nature, and she still seems tireless. She continues to fulfil about 150 public engagements each year, although she travels abroad less than she did up to a few years ago. Long walks in the country are among her favourite recreations to this day, and one of her equerries told me that although she often likes to be alone on these walks, he has to keep her just in sight, and frequently finds this very exhausting.

During the thirteen years in which she was Duchess of York, and popularly known as 'the smiling Duchess', her firmness of character and shrewdness made her an invaluable partner and support for her somewhat retiring and shy husband, whose natural diffidence had been increased by a speech defect from which he had suffered since early childhood and which made public speaking an agony for him. The official biographer of King George VI, Sir John Wheeler-Bennett, has indicated that the King as a child was highly-strung, sensitive and easily rebuffed, and his stammer deepened these characteristics; but he did not receive from his parents, especially his father, the kind of sympathy and understanding that he needed more than most children. His marriage changed his life. From his wife he received abundantly all the encouragement and overt affection that his nature demanded. His home life, says Sir John, became from the first days of his marriage his refuge and safeguard against the world, and on the love and companionship of his wife was based his lifelong contentment.

It was his wife's loving persistence that eventually enabled him to overcome his stammer. The treatment and advice of a number of doctors had been unable to help him, and when he was told that a young Australian, Lionel Logue, had been achieving some remarkable successes in a speech-therapy practice he had set up in Harley Street, he was reluctant to make another effort and risk one more disappointment. His wife persuaded him, and accompanied him on his visits to Harley Street; and this time the stammer was eventually almost completely cured. What was more, the future King's self-confidence received a tremendous boost.

At no time in their married life was the support of his wife more vital to him than during the dramatic days of the Abdication crisis that brought him so unexpectedly to the throne. From every kind of record of those days it is evident that for the Duke of York they brought an appalling sense of shock. The abdicating King recalled in the memoirs he wrote as Duke of Windsor his brother's reaction when he told him that he meant to marry Mrs Wallis Simpson even if this meant his giving up the throne. 'Bertie was so taken aback by my news that in his shy way he could not bring himself to express his innermost feelings at the time. This, after all, was not surprising, for next to myself Bertie had most at stake: it was he who would have to wear the crown if I left, and his genuine concern for me was mixed up with the dread of having to assume the responsibilities of kingship.'

It is known now that this unexpected and unwanted accession was not the Duke's only dread as the situation developed. In a letter he expressed the fear that 'the whole fabric' might 'crumble under the shock and strain of it all'. That the Monarchy did survive this crisis was, on the testimony of many who were close to the events, a result to a great extent of the guidance, support, even leadership that the new Queen Consort—the first commoner to attain this eminence for three centuries—gave to the reluctant King, her husband. The King acknowledged the importance of her role in the broadcast he made to the nation on the day of his accession. 'With my wife and helpmeet beside me,' he said, 'I take up the heavy task which lies before me.' Then, two days later, on his forty-first birthday, he showed his gratitude to her by bestowing on her the highest honour the Sovereign can bestow, the Order of the Garter.

Unquestionably loyalties in the country and in the Empire were divided at the time of the Abdication, and this was apparent for some time as the new reign began. But there was a feeling of rightness, of propriety, in the fact of the throne's being occupied by a home-loving family man, the father of two small girls who were themselves immensely popular, and whose Queen was a figure much loved and admired. The country settled down remarkably quickly. An awareness that this family were taking on their new great duty because it was a duty, and very much against their will, became understood instinctively by the people, and caused the new King and Queen to be held in affection and high regard.

It fell to the Queen to tell the two young Princesses about their new status, of the changes this would bring to their lives, and that they would now have to move from their home at 145 Piccadilly and go to Buckingham Palace to live. Princess Elizabeth exclaimed in a shocked voice, 'You mean, for *ever*?' She asked if an underground passage could be dug, so that the family could go back to their old home each night to sleep.

During her first two years as Queen Consort, Elizabeth made visits with the King to Paris, in 1938, and to Canada and the United States, in 1939. Both visits were highly successful. That to the United States was historic, in that it was the first occasion on which a reigning British Sovereign had set foot in the New World. During the visit to Washington, the Queen chatted for a long time to a Senator who was well known as an isolationist. Afterwards the Senator congratulated the King on being 'a very good Queen-picker'.

Soon after the King and Queen had returned to Britain, World War II started. They stayed in London during the worst of the bombing, and sometimes with the King, sometimes alone, the Queen made countless visits to hospitals, military bases and camps, or to places which had been bombed, to talk with and comfort the homeless. The story has often been told of her reaction to a suggestion that the two Princesses would be safer out of the country. She is reported to have said, 'The Princesses cannot go without me, and I cannot possibly go without the King. The King will never go.'

Queen Elizabeth carried out at least one of her wartime visits while an air raid was in progress. It was to an exhibition of work by disabled ex-servicemen, and she arrived and departed driven in an armoured car.

People close to the Queen Mother who remember her in wartime say that if she ever felt fear she certainly never showed it, although she spoke constantly of the courage of the many bombed-out people she had spoken to; and she did once confess to a fear that the Princesses might be captured in some way and held as hostages. She showed very clearly on one bizarre occasion that she could behave with enormous calm and practicality in a situation that would have terrified most women. This was one evening early in the war when she was dressing for dinner at Windsor. She went alone into her bedroom, and a man suddenly sprang out at her from behind a curtain and seized her round the ankles. She had the presence of mind to assume that he was someone far from normal who might seriously harm her if she screamed. Carefully keeping an ordinary and quiet voice, she said, 'Tell me about it.' He told her that he was a deserter whose family had all been killed in the bombings, and while he did so she was able quietly to ring the bell on the other side of the room. It turned out that the man had used false papers to get employment with a firm doing work at the Castle, and he had gained access to the Queen's rooms by telling an inexperienced housemaid, who showed him the way, that he had to go to them to change a light bulb.

The pre-war tour of Canada had been intended as the start of a series of visits to a number of parts of the Commonwealth; so when the war ended this was resumed. For an extensive visit to South Africa and the Rhodesias, the two Princesses accompanied their father and mother. In that same year, 1947, the Queen was made deeply happy by the marriage of Princess Elizabeth to Prince Philip, and in 1948, by the birth of her first grandchild, Prince Charles. By then the King's health was giving cause for anxiety, and although he made a temporary recovery, both the Queen and Princess Elizabeth were often called on to deputise for him. During the final months of his illness, the Queen rarely left the King's side. He died in his sleep early on 6th February 1952. A new phase of Queen Elizabeth's life started. Now she had a new part to play in the royal family, and she has made it one of continued influence and service.

Although George VI did not reign long enough to be able to celebrate a jubilee, there were ceremonies on 26th April 1948 for the Silver Wedding of the King and Queen. They travelled in state for a Thanksgiving Service in St Paul's Cathedral, and later the same day made a less formal drive in an open car through crowds of cheering people along twenty-two miles of London streets. There was a hint of the kind of role that the Queen would later take up as Queen Mother in the theme she selected for the broadcast she made to the nation that evening. She spoke principally of the importance of the family and of family life in the life of the country. She said, 'The world of our day is longing to find the secret of community, and all married lives are, in a sense, communities in miniature. There must be many who feel as we do that the sanctities of married life are in some way the highest form of human fellowship, affording a rock-like foundation on which all the best in the life of a nation is built. Looking back over the last twenty-five years and to my own happy childhood, I realize more and more the wonderful sense of security and happiness which comes from a loved home.'

It seems to be an essential part of the British conception of the Monarchy, something understood rather than frequently expounded, that it should be expressed ideally in a family—

the royal family, the highest family in the land, and so hardly an ordinary family, but nonetheless a counterpart of what is still the basic, natural and stabilising unit of the social system, even though these are days in which the value of the family is being questioned and even attacked by an articulate few who are able to gain publicity for their opinions out of all proportion to their number. Queen Elizabeth the Queen Mother is seen instinctively as an embodiment of the more joyous, natural and humanly-satisfying aspects of family life, a loved and loving, maternal figure, who has nothing whatsoever to do with the gloomy, inward-looking, devouring, 'Dear Octopus' notion of the family, which is fashionable among some adolescents, rather often publicised, but not generally held. This, it seems to me, is the underlying reason why millions all over the world call her, affectionately, 'the Queen Mum'.

She remains, of course, very much a public figure, demonstrating almost daily the talent for public life she has always had, opening public celebrations or official occasions; launching ships; visiting institutions, factories, military units, exhibitions; speaking at dinners; conferring degrees; laying foundation stones. It has always been an obvious fact that she genuinely enjoys meeting people and has the enviable gift of being able to talk to them as if they were the only people in the world she really wanted to hear about at that particular moment. A new element, perhaps a breath from the non-royal world, that she has always seemed to be able to bring to these sometimes pompous occasions, has been a sense of fun. When she was asked a second time for permission to move the foundation stone of the National Theatre which she had solemnly laid a few years before, she suggested, 'Why don't they put it on castors?' Visiting wounded soldiers in a military hospital—which had, of course, as they say in the Army, been 'ponced up to the eyeballs' for the occasion, and was bursting with tension—the Queen Mother almost instantly produced a miraculous relaxation in the atmosphere by signing, with a flourish, 'Elizabeth R.' on the plaster round a young guardsman's arm, and giggling girlishly as she did so. She is a jolly lady.

The Queen Mother has a style all her own; and part of it is her taste in dress, very consistent over the years, with furs and feathers an important constituent. Those who find fault with it, as a good many do nowadays, perhaps pay too little attention to the fact that it expresses very well much in her personality that endears her to the majority; and those interested in such matters may recall that after the magnificently-successful State Visit to France in the summer of 1938, Paris, still regarded then as the world's fashion centre, raved about Queen Elizabeth's wardrobe, and the French papers declared her the best-dressed Queen to visit that city. However this may be, the Queen Mother's way of dressing is as much part of her popular image as is her enchanting smile, in which her whole face lights up; and that smile is one of many things that she has passed on to her daughter, the Queen. Another, of course, is her well-informed, and continuing interest in horse-racing which, in fact, she took up enthusiastically relatively late in life, in the season of 1949/50, when mother and daughter decided to own a steeplechaser in partnership. This was the Irish-bred chaser, Monaveen, which raced under Princess Elizabeth's name and colours, and came fifth in the Grand National. Princess Elizabeth was greatly upset when the next season Monaveen had to be destroyed after breaking a leg in a fall, and thereafter concentrated her interest on the Flat and on breeding. But the Queen Mother persevered, has owned the winners of hundreds of National Hunt races, became Patron of the National Hunt Committee in 1954, and later, with the Queen, a Patron of the Jockey Club, with which the Committee amalgamated.

To her daughter, the Queen, as, indeed, to all the ladies active in the work of the royal family, the Queen Mother has, in many ways, been the outstanding exemplar of professionalism in the modern style of Monarchy. It is known that Queen Elizabeth II often consults the Queen Mother during their frequent meetings and almost daily telephone conversations, not only on family matters but also on their day's public duties. The Queen Mother sees a great deal of her grandchildren and has a very close and affectionate relationship with Prince Charles.

The Queen Mother is a friend, and sometimes a refuge, for all the members of her family, and not least, for her younger daughter, Princess Margaret, who has had so much unhappiness in what, for others, would have been private life, but which for her has been suffered under the spotlight of often cruel publicity.

After Queen Elizabeth II came to the throne, Princess

Margaret was her mother's frequent companion on many of her public duties, and she lived with her at Clarence House. The Princess was then twenty-one years old, an extremely pretty young woman, with much gaiety and charm, who loved dancing and the company of people of her own age. She was obviously the subject of a good deal of Press interest, not least in Commonwealth publications. Most of it was affectionate, and it included all the speculation about a possible marriage that is usually, and sometimes tiresomely, attached to any member of the royal family of marriageable age. She had been carrying out some public engagements alone since her fifteenth year, and at eighteen, she made an official journey abroad, to Amsterdam, for the inauguration of Queen Juliana of the Netherlands, flying her personal standard for the first time in the aircraft of the King's Flight which took her there. Now, with her sister on the throne, she carried out further royal duties abroad, sometimes together with the Queen Mother, sometimes alone, as for instance when, in 1955, she briefly toured the British islands in the Caribbean and, a year later, Commonwealth countries in East Africa.

Everything one reads and hears about the Princess during this period has a happy note about it, which seems a natural enough continuation from the quite extraordinarily sunny childhood she seems to have enjoyed as the inseparable playmate of her older sister. Of course, much of what was written about those two charming little girls seems a trifle sweet on the palate today. Children were more childlike, and most adults preferred them to be so. I am quite old enough to remember that the country's interest in the Princesses, even before Princess Elizabeth became Heir Presumptive, was very real, that they were generally held in great affection, and that the newspapers and magazines which published reams about them as well as innumerable photographs satisfied a genuine demand.

In his thoughtful book about the Nineteen Fifties called *The New Look*, Harry Hopkins has recalled that the Coronation, in 1953, enormously stimulated interest in news about the royal family and, in the Coronation month, the biggest newspaper sales boom of all time, which brought the circulation of the *Daily Mirror*, for example, to 7,000,000, more than 50 per cent above normal. He notes that, thereafter, Princess Margaret, in particular, was 'always news' throughout Europe and America, and quotes a calculation that in the first twenty-nine weeks of 1954, 214 articles and reports about her appeared in London newspapers alone. But Mr Hopkins also suggests that there was an important new element in all this introduced by the profit motive—a mass-produced 'intimacy' in the treatment of the Monarchy in the Press, which was 'machine-made, formula-packaged for market, continuous—and overwhelming'; and the consumer or the audience naturally possessed proprietary rights in the 'Admassian personalities' so created. I think there is much truth in Mr Hopkins's contention, and that it expresses something from which Princess Margaret has, in the long run, suffered.

Firstly, in the early part of her sister's reign, the Princess was given the degree of publicity, and much the same kind, normally afforded to sex-symbol film actresses. While they, for obvious reasons, generally seem to welcome this treatment, in spite of its inevitable, accompanying vulgarities, there was plenty of evidence that she did not. As Andrew Duncan has recorded—in *The Reality of Monarchy*, a book of interest as a possibly unique attempt to write patronisingly about the Queen and her family—the time came when Princess Margaret's 'faults were paraded publicly, exaggerated privately'.

Mr Duncan quotes Princess Margaret as saying: 'When my sister and I were growing up, she was made out to be the goody goody one. That was boring, so the Press tried to make out I was wicked as hell. . . . I used to get appallingly upset, with no way of hitting back. I was an absolute wreck after some of the publicity but, luckily, that's all over.'

It was not all over, of course. Princess Margaret was to continue to be, as in the past, handled by the Admass publicity machine with the maximum degree of insensitivity, sensationalism and sly malice—rich in overtones of circulation-building mock-sympathy—at times of deep and personal distress in her private life.

This kind of thing started, as is well remembered, in the early Fifties, when the world Press, after speculating busily about almost every young man with whom the Princess was seen in public, settled with glee on Group Captain Peter Townsend, a former fighter-pilot, a former member of the royal household and a man of striking good looks who had been the innocent party in a divorce. As Mr Hopkins recalls, the 'Romance of the

Century' was soon occupying vast acreages of newsprint. The hounds really started baying somewhere in the summer of 1953. Looking back on only a relatively small selection of the stories in the British papers, it is easy to find gems that indicate clearly that this was a story that some editors had decided must be kept running at all costs. For instance, there are quite a few examples of that richly-comic class of 'news' story, the negative report, the positive announcement that something has not happened. 'Princess Margaret—No Cabinet Talks About Possible Marriage', was the headline in one popular daily paper. Nothing connected with the Princess was too trivial to mention. 'Princess—A Cold in the Head', became matter for a headline. Sedately, the *Manchester Guardian* (as it was then) noted, 'The "popular" press everywhere is having the time of its life with the affairs of Princess Margaret,' and then went on about them itself for nearly half a column.

From the effects of all this abroad, I myself drew some unexpected benefit. At that time, the B.B.C. had a staff correspondent who bore a quite marked resemblance to Group Captain Townsend. I was having a drink with him and some other journalists in some place in, I think, Strasbourg, and we were all delighted, if a little puzzled, when the proprietor assured us with polite, even fawning, gestures that we must not pay. Everything was 'on the house'. It was only as we were leaving that the mystery was solved by someone in the place who told us, 'Of course, we quite understand that the Group Captain wishes to remain *incognito*.' I wonder if the real Group Captain ever drew any such bonus from what must have been a damnably disagreeable period for him? I hope so.

The editors searched frantically for new angles. The *Daily Mirror* devoted about half a page—including 'Your Voting Form'—to a poll of its readers on whether or not the Princess should 'be allowed' to marry Peter Townsend. No editor, so far as I can see, deduced anything from the fact that what the paper described as 'the greatest poll in newspaper history' drew a response from only 70,142 of the paper's several million readers. The popular papers just went on bashing away at the story, presenting it, to quote Mr Hopkins, 'as a battle not only of eager youth against crabbed old age, but of aristocracy *versus* democracy, of the "stuffed shirts" against the non-stuffed shirts'. There were attacks on the Church of England

Archbishops, hints of Disestablishment, paragraphs about a 'wicked plot' against a young girl's happiness. The highest mark for gratuitous, tasteless impudence should probably go to the *Pictorial* for its headline: 'Come Along, Margaret, Please Make Up Your Mind!' That for fatuity might go to the *Chicago Tribune*, which in a solemn report about what it saw as a threat to 'the future of monarchy in England', declared hilariously, 'British newspapers do not indulge in idle gossip about their royal family.'

British papers continued with their efforts to prove just how wrong about this their American colleagues were. They kept up the pressure, and in the summer of 1955, as the Princess approached her twenty-fifth birthday, some of them tried hard to pump it to bursting point. They did this by expounding a conveniently telescoped version of the Royal Marriages Act of 1772, so as to make it appear that at the age of twenty-five, its provisions would no longer present any barrier to her marrying anyone she pleased. It may well be held that this archaic Act, contrived by George III to prevent his sons from marrying anyone except Protestant royalty, ought to have been repealed long before as something historically un-English, unsuitable in a democracy, and a violation of human rights because of its religious discrimination. However, it had not been repealed; and as the *Daily Telegraph* very properly pointed out, when the Princess became twenty-five years old, the Sovereign's objection to her marriage would, indeed, no longer be enough alone to prevent it, but the Privy Council could still delay it, and the disapproval of both Houses of Parliament, expressed within a year, could stop it. The *Manchester Guardian* gave a similar explanation. Both papers deplored the new outbreak of rumour, and the *Guardian* said, '. . . this sensationalising of the intimate affairs of anybody, even if she be a Princess, is distasteful.' The poor old *News Chronicle*—which still had five years to live as a responsible 'popular' paper before the tornado of catch-penny journalism sunk it with all hands—remarked mildly that it was a pity that a section of the popular press should have forgotten its manners, only to be rounded on by the *New Statesman*, which accused it of pontificating about Princess Margaret 'in an excess of righteous indignation'.

Popular press enthusiasm became frenzy when it was learned that the Princess and the Group Captain—who had returned from what was probably a tactful posting to Brussels—had met each other again after an interval of two years. The Queen's Press Secretary found it necessary to state that no announcement concerning Princess Margaret's personal future was at present contemplated, and to appeal on her behalf that the Press should respect her privacy.

Eventually Princess Margaret issued this personal message from Clarence House:

> I would like it to be known that I have decided not to marry Group Captain Peter Townsend.
>
> I have been aware that subject to my renouncing my rights of succession it might have been possible for me to contract a civil marriage, but mindful of the Church's teaching that Christian marriage is indissoluble and conscious of my duty to the Commonwealth, I have resolved to put these considerations before any others.
>
> I have reached this decision entirely alone and in doing so I have been strengthened by the unfailing support and devotion of Group Captain Townsend. I am deeply grateful for the concern of all those who have constantly prayed for my happiness.

With this statement, it became, for the first time in all the long months of newspaper-generated excitement and manufactured crisis, possible to feel some genuine emotion about it all. The Princess had, it was now clear, undergone a torturing experience, a conflict between her deeply-felt affections and her conscience. She had decided in favour of her duty and the dictates of her religion. I think only the shallower cynics could have been unmoved by this. But it is also true that it would have been far better if she had been permitted to arrive at this agonising, highly personal decision in peace and privacy. It was a section of the world's Press, but especially the Press of the Princess's own country, that made this impossible. It did so almost entirely because her unhappy situation presented the news desks with 'a good, human story' that could be guaranteed to sell newspapers as long as it could be kept going. There was no real crisis of the Monarchy beyond that which they promoted.

I suppose the Princess decided, or was advised, to make a statement in the hope that the papers might now at last let the matter rest. In fact, the Princess's statement was the first real confirmation from either of the two people most concerned that they had ever thought about marriage. Was the statement really necessary? It would, no doubt, have been incumbent on the Princess, as third in succession to the throne at that time, to let the people know if she had decided that she *would* marry the Group Captain. Why did she need to tell anyone but him—and, presumably, the Queen—that she would *not* marry him? It would certainly have been more fun to have left the newspapers with their great story ending in nothing definite, a mountain of conjecture, speculation and shameless circulation-hunting that had failed to bring forth even a ridiculous mouse. As it was, the news hounds continued for a very long time to slaver and snap over the bone they had been thrown. There was yet a good deal of mileage to be made out of taking sides over the question of whether or not the Princess had made the right choice. Admiration and affection for her were, of course, expressed, but some of this was accompanied by suggestions that she had arrived at her decision under pressure of various sinister kinds, and not 'entirely alone', as she had unequivocally stated. But to express admiration and affection for someone and call them a liar in the same paragraph is not beyond the abilities, or the stomach, of many a skilled practitioner in my trade. As I remember, and as Mr Hopkins records, several million Britons were left with 'a vague feeling of bewilderment and even of revulsion'. Many of them might have agreed with the Vatican newspaper, *Osservatore Romano*, which in its single comment on this whole affair said that the reaction of many newspapers and some of the public had been outstanding in this century as an instance of journalistic and moral bankruptcy. As late as May 1958, Buckingham Palace was still having to deny Press reports that the Princess had changed her mind.

Not quite two years later, the royal family, for once, stole a march on the Press when Queen Elizabeth the Queen Mother announced from Clarence House 'with the greatest pleasure' that Princess Margaret had become engaged to Antony Armstrong-Jones, son of a barrister, Ronald Armstrong-Jones, Q.C., and the Countess of Rosse. The young man the Princess was going to marry was a recognised photographer, designer and film-director, and certainly well-known in Fleet Street; but although, as the Queen Mother's Press Secretary disclosed, he had been seeing Princess Margaret continuously since their first meeting at a London party two years before, the news of their engagement was as unexpected by the Press as it was by the people generally. Mr Armstrong-Jones was known to have taken photographs of members of the royal family on a number of occasions, and visits he had made to Sandringham, Balmoral, Clarence House and Royal Lodge, Windsor, where he was a frequent week-end guest, had probably, when they were noticed, been assumed by the vigilant reporters to be concerned with his profession. It was hardly astonishing that those closest to Princess Margaret, especially the Queen Mother, had been determined that she should not again be subjected to the miseries the Press had inflicted on her over her friendship with Group Captain Townsend, and even some members of the royal family did not know of the engagement until it was publicly announced. Bernard Levin is one chronicler of the period who thinks this secrecy was ill-advised. He goes so far as to say that the gossip columnists determined to have their revenge, and that, for this reason, 'paragraphs began to appear which on the face of them were unexceptionable, but which carried an unmistakable flavour of hostility'. Certainly, there were enough mean little barbs in some publications—for example, remarks about the prospective bridegroom's preferring Pimlico to Belgravia—to provoke *The Times* into rebuking, after the royal wedding on 6th May 1960, what it called 'mischief mongers who have done their best to pollute its atmosphere with rumour'.

The wedding was the first great royal occasion of the Sixties, and the bulk of the population ignored, or were unaware of, the sly digs in a section of the Press. It was welcomed in a spirit of national jubilation. Hundreds of people spent all night in the streets in the area of Buckingham Palace, the nucleus of the biggest crowds to assemble in London since the Coronation. It was a sunny day; the Princess looked happy and smiling in the glass coach as the crowds cheered her; the ceremony in Westminster Abbey was splendid and moving. It is estimated that 150,000 people swarmed round Buckingham Palace afterwards, chanting, 'We want Margaret,' and 'We want the Bride,' until the Princess appeared on the balcony with her husband and was presently joined by the Queen, the Duke of Edinburgh and Queen Elizabeth the Queen Mother, who were all greeted with great waves of cheering. When the Princess and her husband drove to Tower Pier to go aboard the royal yacht *Britannia*, which was to take them on their honeymoon in the Caribbean, they arrived nearly an hour late, mainly because of the huge crowds which swarmed round their car.

There can be no doubt of the goodwill of the people generally towards Princess Margaret at that time; but *The Times*, no doubt thinking back to what had happened in the Fifties, sounded a note of warning. 'If the British people mean the cheers they raised on Friday they will by their conduct make public life as welcoming and private life as private for Princess Margaret and her husband as they could wish for themselves. The couple have embarked on a much longer voyage than the cruise of *Britannia*: may it always be a happy one.'

Sadly, this wish was not fulfilled, although the marriage did have some happy years. At least, the gossip writers were constrained to draw in their claws, and this was partly the result of reaction to their efforts to wound at the time of the wedding. Penelope Gilliatt, wife of the surgeon, Roger Gilliatt, who was Antony Armstrong-Jones's best man, wrote an article which exposed some of the gossip writers' methods and characters. This was detailed, searching and devastatingly effective, and quite soon the whole tone of this kind of journalism changed and appeared to be acquiring some sense of decency and respect for the privacy of individuals.

Returned from their honeymoon, the young couple took up residence at Kensington Palace, and in October 1961 the Queen conferred on Mr Armstrong-Jones the title of Earl of Snowdon. The son that was born to them in November was known as Viscount Linley. In the following summer the Princess, accompanied by the Earl of Snowdon, represented the Queen at the Independence celebrations of Jamaica. A daughter, to be known as Lady Sarah Armstrong-Jones, was born in May 1964. Thus far, and for a few years more, the married life of the Snowdons seemed to be going well publicly, and they were known in private life to be devoted parents, as, indeed, they still are. But although the newspapers read by the bulk of the population continued to be reasonably kind, Andrew Duncan is entirely correct in reporting that 'every year, a few blows hit'. He instances the visit made to the United States by the Snowdons in November 1965 as part of a British Week tour, at Foreign Office expense, and recalls that some English newspapers inferred that this was a promotional stunt for Lord Snowdon's professional activities and hinted that most of their time was spent at parties. I was in the United States at that time, and although I was chiefly concerned with United Nations business, I did cover enough of the Snowdon visit to know that it was generally well received there. At the same time it was impossible not to be aware of a critical note, not very specific, but quite real, creeping into the newspaper coverage. Cynicism between the lines in the British newspapers was quite rapidly reflected in those of the United States.

Quite naturally and properly, my own people at home asked me about this. I could find nothing to support suggestions that the Snowdons were not carrying out their official task conscientiously, and I said so. It certainly did not seem to me proper to act as a relay station for a whispering campaign, but the campaign, though not at a very serious level, did exist. When Princess Margaret and the Earl of Snowdon visited the United Nations building I thought they looked tired; but as a correspondent who has followed a great number of royal visits from start to finish, I know that they can be exhausting. Some of us thought that Princess Margaret did not look very happy, and that the royal smile sometimes seemed a trifle strained. However, the United Nations headquarters is a place where most official smiles are understandably strained, and you learn not to read too much into it; and as every serious reporter knows, the middle of a whispering campaign is a time when you must be very careful indeed not to read too much into things.

By the time the marriage was ten years old it became fairly apparent that it was no longer going well; and earlier than that, some newspapers abroad, notably in Germany and France, were speculating that it was about to break up. Lord Snowdon, in New York on business, told reporters, 'It's news to me, and I would be the first to know.' Through 1970, speculation and rumour began to gather momentum. In August, *Private Eye* excelled itself by publishing a photograph, with invented dialogue superimposed, which reflected in terms of the utmost cruelty stories that disagreement between the couple was now sometimes apparent in public. Perhaps it will be possible years ahead to judge this creation simply on its merits as humorous journalism and decide that it was very funny, which it was.

Nearer to the events, one would need to be abnormally insensitive not to be repelled at seeing any couple in such a sad situation so viciously and so casually kicked. The indications were that there were indeed difficulties, but that the couple were trying to repair the marriage. In December 1970, after Clarence House had denied a *Washington Post* story that they had agreed on a separation pending a divorce, the Princess and her husband went on holiday together to the Bahamas. This may have been an exercise in mending fences. If it was, it failed in the long run. The couple spent increasingly lengthy periods apart. Princess Margaret made fairly frequent visits alone to the island of Mustique, where she spent part of her honeymoon, and where she and her husband had a plot of land given them as a wedding present by a close friend of the Princess, Mr Colin Tennant, the island's owner. She once described the island as 'the only place in the world where I can truly relax'. It is one of a chain of small islands, the Grenadines, between Grenada and St Vincent in the Windward Islands. The Princess had built there a three-bedroom villa which was serviced by a permanent staff of three. Lord Snowdon did not go to the island again after the honeymoon visit.

In the early part of the Seventies, although much word-of-mouth rumour continued, the British newspapers, on the whole, treated the affairs of Princess Margaret and Lord Snowdon with fair discretion and decency, although some European publications occasionally, on a dull news day, perhaps, did a little sensational kite-flying. In Britain there was a fairly general assumption that the couple had quietly agreed that they would, without any public breach, to some extent go their own ways; but they still made visits abroad together, or appeared at public functions from time to time. The bond that they shared in their children, many people supposed, if nothing more, made an official separation unlikely. Those who remembered, or really understood, the reasons given by Princess Margaret all those years ago for her renunciation of Group Captain Townsend, would have regarded a divorce as out of the question. Among those of her own age, who recalled with affection the gay, clearly rather independent young woman, who had contributed a certain sparkle of her own to the social scene in the late Forties and in the Fifties, and among their elders for whom, sentimentally, perhaps, she would always be the cheekier one of two small girls whom the British people had loved very much, Princess Margaret was regarded with much sympathy. It is not to be supposed that many people—other than Mr William Hamilton, M.P., the nation's amiable, professional anti-royalist—kept a score to try to prove what was widely reported, that the Princess was carrying out fewer public engagements than in the past; but had they done so, they might charitably have supposed that unhappiness about her marriage could provide an understandable explanation. A Household official told me that, in fact, contrary to the reports, the Princess did not reduce her public work; and that, although it was not always of a nature likely to be reported in the Press, it showed no marked diminution compared with the average over the years.

Matters came to a head in March 1976 when, after some days of rumour, prompted originally by an article in a German paper and later by another in the *News of the World*, there came an announcement from Kensington Palace. It said, 'Her Royal Highness the Princess Margaret, Countess of Snowdon, and the Earl of Snowdon have mutually agreed to live apart. The Princess will carry out her public duties unaccompanied by Lord Snowdon.'

In spite of a great deal of repeated innuendo in most of the newspapers, including the re-publication of a photograph of the Princess having a drink with some friends in a swimsuit on Mustique—a picture about as significant in itself as anybody's family-album snapshot—it is not publicly known precisely why this particular time was chosen to give legal form to a situation that to a great extent already existed, and to announce that this had been done. Foreign newspapers suggested that this picture had provoked Lord Snowdon. I cannot see why it should have done so—except, perhaps, in his professional capacity. Although there was no further statement, I found no disposition among people in the Royal Households or close to them to let it be assumed that the recent resurgence of publicity about the married life of the Snowdons had been the cause of the final break, or that it had influenced the Queen, or the legal advisers, or anyone concerned, in their discussions.

The announcement came at a time when the Press, under various pressures—some internal, some political—was doing some heart-searching about the lengths to which it might properly go in reporting on people's private lives. This may be one reason why it behaved with some restraint in its reactions to it. There was some unkind or ill-mannered comment, and rather more of the knowing, inside-story sort that had a familiar, spurious ring, curiously reminiscent, though it had a different purpose, of some of the stuff that used to appear in the far-off days when lick-spittle writing about royalty was popular with editors, and its writers used to convey a curious impression that they spent a large part of their waking lives lurking, with the greatest respect, under tables at Buckingham Palace, though never under the beds.

The comment dried up in most of the papers in about a week. The *Daily Telegraph* echoed a great deal of general feeling when it wrote, 'The right emotion now is sympathy,' and 'This is a family matter, not a constitutional one.' Princess Margaret showed a determination to play the fullest part demanded of her in the public duties of the royal family, surmounting with courage the physical effects of her recent emotional strain. Those well disposed to her were pleased to see her working through a full engagement list with authority, dedication and charm, as well as with the humour and lightness of touch which are characteristic of her. Her activity continued undiminished in a number of charities that are especially close to her heart and in which she has for years taken a lively, working interest. Most of them are bodies concerned with the welfare of children and young people, such as the Invalid Children's Aid Association, for whom she has done much fund-raising and has attended business meetings; the Girl Guides Association, which has been important to her since she was a child; and the youth and community centre work of the Dockland Settlements.

Looking back through reports of the public activities of Princess Margaret and her husband, I have been struck by the ungenerously small amount of notice given to the sound instinct of Lord Snowdon, born a commoner, for doing royal things in a truly royal way when the occasion offered. His activity at the scene of the Aberfan disaster of October 1966 deserves recall. He was the first member of the royal family to go there, hurrying to the spot on his own initiative as soon as the news came that so many children had lost their lives when a pit-heap collapsed and engulfed their school. The best account of what he did there is in the memoirs of the Prime Minister of the day, Harold Wilson, who says:

> . . . the highest praise was for Lord Snowdon. He had gone spontaneously and, instead of inspecting the site, had made it his job to visit bereaved relatives . . . sitting holding the hands of a distraught father, sitting with the head of a mother on his shoulder for half an hour in silence. In another house he comforted an older couple who had lost 13 grandchildren —in another where they were terribly upset he offered to make a cup of tea, went into the kitchen and returned with a tray of cups for them all. He helped an older man persuade his son, who was clutching something in his tightly-clenched fist, to open his hand. It was a prefect's badge, the only thing by which he had been able to identify his child . . .

To a man of such evident sensitivity, the break-up of his own family life must have been a cause of deep emotional distress.

7. The Queen's Palaces

The Queen has three State residences—Buckingham Palace and Windsor Castle in England; and in Scotland, the Palace of Holyrood House in Edinburgh. She has also private residences at Sandringham in Norfolk and at Balmoral in Aberdeenshire. However, with a British singularity that students of our institutions regard as either perverse or charming according to to taste, the British Court is still called the Court of St James's, and the diplomatic representatives of foreign countries are accredited there, even though no British Sovereign has lived in St James's Palace since 1837 and the office of the Marshal of the Diplomatic Corps moved out of it more than forty years ago. Most people thinking of the Queen 'at home' think of her as being at Buckingham Palace; and she does, in fact, live and work mostly there, although she likes to get to the less urban atmosphere of Windsor whenever she conveniently can, and is customarily there for Easter.

Buckingham Palace has been the London home of the British Sovereign through eight reigns. It was George IV who first set John Nash to work on the reshaping of Buckingham House, a property which had been bought by his father, George III, in 1761, although the site, originally a piece of marsh-land known in remote times as 'Bulunga Fen', seems to have had its earliest royal connection through James I of England and VI of Scotland, who set up a mulberry garden on part of it in an effort to start an English silk industry. The scheme failed because he planted a kind of mulberry tree that does not suit silkworms. George IV was also not entirely lucky with his own plans for the place two centuries or so later. As a child, he had lived for some years in the relatively-modest Buckingham House, deliberately chosen by his home-loving, respectable parents to be an orderly and comfortable dwelling in which they could bring up their large family away from the ceremonial, functions and officialdom of the Court at St James's. Although he was so often and so bitterly at loggerheads with his parents George, by the time he became King, seems to have looked back on his Buckingham House childhood with a degree of affectionate nostalgia.

However this may be, there is evidence that when George IV formulated his first ideas for work on his childhood home it was domesticity, even if a regal domesticity, that he had in mind, rather than an imposing palace, an architectural embodiment of majesty. He is said to have told Nash in the presence of a responsible witness never 'at his peril' to advise him to build a palace. According to Nash, the King said, 'I am too old to build a palace. If the Public wish to have a palace, I have no objection to build one, but I must have a *pied à terre*.' This *pied à terre*, he said, must be at Buckingham House. 'There are early associations which endear me to the spot.'

All, or some, of this modest plea may have been eyewash. Even today, when there is a greater concern among historians to examine and expound the better qualities of George IV, who has certainly in the past had more than his fair share of censure, it still seems to be assumed that he proposed a simple repair and enlargement of Buckingham House purely to obtain a grant from Parliament; but that thereafter, he and Nash ignored Parliament's intention and began what was virtually a new building. In the end, the King himself obtained neither *pied à terre* nor palace; for the work was nowhere near complete when he died in 1830.

One historian of the Palace thinks that Nash's work on it deserves to rank as one of the classic muddles of history; for although all the money provided, and a great deal more, had been spent, the building was in such an unfinished state that hardly a room was completed, the decorations were scarcely begun, and it was 'unfit for human habitation'. George's successor, his brother William IV, had the work completed, but he did not care for the result, and preferred not to live in it. When the Houses of Parliament were burned down in 1834, he offered the Palace to take their place; but the Lords and Commons found it no more to their taste than did he. Nevertheless, it is to a great extent Nash's building in essence that forms the building we know today, a building that is certainly world-renowned, as instantly-recognisable on a picture postcard or a book illustration as any piece of architecture in the world, though few would credit it with outstanding architectural importance. For the British, and certainly for the English, it is almost a shrine, an embodiment of their history, a focus for the people when they feel and are moved as one entity, as they have been, for example, in the great wars that have been waged during the Palace's relatively-short history, in the rejoicings of victory or in sombre times of national crisis or mourning. Nash did, it seems, for all his tearing down and building up, retain some hold on history. Some of that original eighteenth-century Buckingham House was incorporated in his work and remains to this day; but I have never been able to find anyone who could point it out with certainty. William IV's architect, Edward Blore, covered almost the whole of Nash's exterior work with a new façade; and in 1913, yet another new façade by Sir Aston Webb replaced Blore's; but the great State rooms which give the Palace its undoubted grandeur are essentially the work of Nash, with the exception of the huge and often-photographed ballroom which was added in the eighteen-fifties. Though it was disliked and bitterly criticised when it was first built, and has often been sneered at by knowing aesthetes over the years since, there is a disposition nowadays to regard Buckingham Palace as by no means architecturally negligible. Indeed, one universally-respected, and never sentimental, modern critic, Sir Nikolaus Pevsner, might be held to suggest that it is very well suited to its State function; for he praises its 'great Englishness'. Nash, he says, succeeded in keeping it a country house—'surely the only royal palace in any major capital which has its lawns and lake and faces a park and not an urban square'.

It was during Queen Victoria's long reign that Buckingham Palace became firmly associated in the public mind with the whole idea of the Monarchy, part of the mythology which expressed a successful industrial and imperial nation's own good opinion of itself. However, it is interesting that most of Victoria's biographers record her as being pleased with the Palace in a lightly domestic sense when she arrived there to live on 13th July 1837. She went for a walk round the garden with her mother and noted that her favourite spaniel, 'dear' Dashy, seemed to feel quite at home there. In fact, by modern standards, the Palace had many grave domestic faults. It was at that time furnished largely with a collection of pieces that might well have been described as 'cast-offs' from Windsor Castle, because William IV had firmly put aside George IV's estimate of £100,000 for furnishing the Palace and decided to exercise all possible economy. Today, however, some of this collection remains in the Palace among the most valued and valuable of the Queen's possessions. The young Queen Victoria found the soft furnishings of her new London home so dirty that a thousand yards of material had to be washed and more than five hundred yards sent to the dyers. Not a clock in the place worked, and she had to borrow one while they were repaired, though some of them survive in the Palace today keeping good time. But there were worse difficulties than these, some indeed that it is hard to believe could ever occur in the home of a Queen. For instance, the Palace had few bathrooms and their taps supplied only cold water. There was a special hot-water supply for the Queen's own bath, but the bath had to be filled and emptied by hand. Worse still, none of the fifty lavatories had proper ventilation, and their plumbing was so cracked and leaky that fumes in one of them caused fresh white paint to tarnish overnight. The basement floor of the Palace provided the roof for what was otherwise an open sewer serving the entire neighbourhood, so that a blockage, or heavy rain with a high tide in the Thames, could bring sewage into the Palace kitchen. Smoking chimneys made some rooms, including the Throne Room, frequently uninhabitable. No one had thought to provide dustbins, so rubbish was dumped in the courtyard. Buckingham Palace stank.

A highly-complex system of privilege, precedence and perquisites in the Royal Household, including demarcation disputes of hardly credible pettiness between high officials of the Court, made it impossible to transform this chaos quickly into order, comfort and decency. In fact, there was little radical change until after the Queen's marriage, when Prince Albert applied intelligence, method and a tenacious sense of mission to the running of the royal homes. But he was still battling for some of the reforms he wanted until the day he died.

For the nearly forty years during which Queen Victoria acquired the sobriquet 'the Widow of Windsor', Buckingham Palace, once the centre of London life, retreated into the shadows. On her rare visits to the Palace, the Queen deplored any change. As is well known, she insisted that the Prince Consort's rooms must remain exactly as they were when he died.

Buckingham Palace might well have remained in eclipse after Victoria's death. So accustomed are we to regard it as a focus for the British people at dramatic times in their history that it is strange to note that it played almost no part in the nationwide, deeply-genuine mourning for the death of the old Queen. She died at Osborne and was buried at Frogmore near Windsor. The new King, Edward VII, lived at Marlborough House at the time he succeeded to the throne and he was proclaimed at St James's Palace. His Queen, Alexandra, loved her own home and often said how much she regretted leaving it for Buckingham Palace after Edward's accession. Edward himself had memories of the Palace too closely associated with the strict régime of his youth to be entirely pleasant. He called it 'the sepulchre', partly, it may be, because of the musty smell that people who knew it during its years of relative disuse have said it acquired, and partly because of his revered but formidable father's ghostly rooms, preserved like a corpse in a glacier, unchanged by time but wholly dead. It was well known that the place depresssed him, and it is on record that he seriously considered making Hampton Court Palace the royal residence in its stead, but was advised that to do this would be too expensive.

The King was essentially genial, gregarious and a lover of life; so since he had to accept Buckingham Palace as his London home, he exercised these qualities in the extremely thorough, even ruthless, reorganisation he carried out there and in the other royal residences. At the Palace, an army of workmen moved into the faded and bereaved labyrinth of corridors and State rooms. Painters, carpenters and plumbers brightened, rationalised and modernised to the standards and taste of the one-year-old twentieth century. According to Sir Lionel Cust, Surveyor of the King's Pictures at that time, Edward liked to be personally involved when he could, sitting 'in a roomful of workmen giving directions'.

Under the new King, magnificence and a high degree of formality remained; but there was a new ingredient, a kind of male benignity, exemplified, possibly, in the whiff of expensive

Napoleon III and the Empress Eugénie visited Queen Victoria at Windsor in 1855

The first British King to hold a pilot's licence, George VI made his test flight over Windsor, home of kings for many centuries

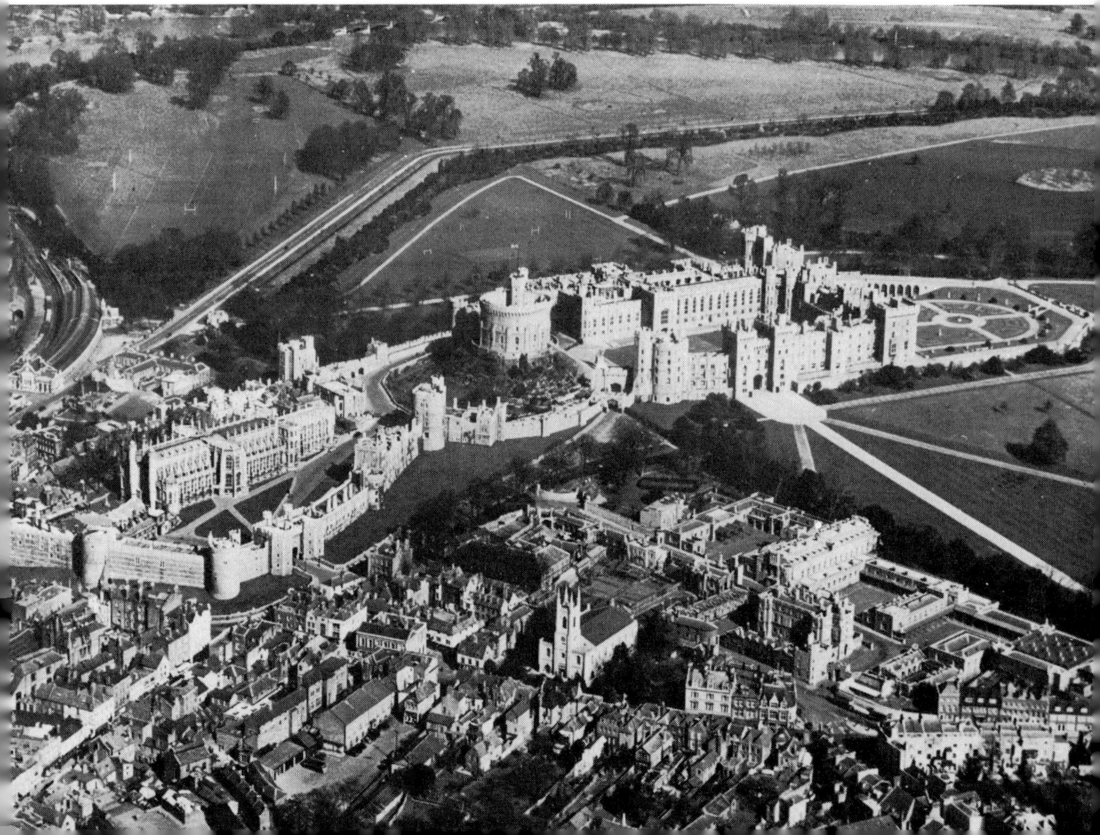

Balmoral was the favourite home of the young Queen Victoria. Carl Haag's romantic eye sees her welcoming Albert home from the chase

The drawing room at Balmoral in 1855. The Queen had a passion for designing tartans

cigar smoke which was sometimes detectable about the Palace now as it had never been in the days of the old Queen. What was more important as a piece of social history was that an entirely new kind of person began to be received regularly at the Palace. As before—as indeed to this day—those personages went there who did so by custom, if not precisely by right. These were the holders of high office, the ministers and diplomats, and others whose names were in the 'representative lists'; but now, too, came those new men of the new century and their ladies—the financiers and industrialists, the Press lords and sportsmen among whom the King had made his own congenial world when he was Prince of Wales. Above all, Buckingham Palace was now truly alive, and in a special way—in spite of the mystery which it retained and retains for the ordinary people—it became a centre of the national consciousness as it is to this day.

In spite of the new broom, of the new brightness and aids to more genuine comfort and better hygiene, the general appearance of the great State rooms did not change startlingly. Indeed, the photographs taken in 1893, when Victoria allowed a magazine to send in a reporter and a cameraman—'for the first time', says the magazine—show an interior entirely recognisable as the one to be seen today, give or take a potted palm or two and the disposition of some of the furniture, though no doubt greater differences might have been apparent had those old pictures been in colour.

Certainly, in the next reign, Queen Mary, a connoisseur of the decorative arts and a noted antiquarian and collector, brought about enormous improvements in the arrangements and furnishing of all the Royal Palaces, although it seems she was unable to do anything about uncluttering the study in which the Sovereign, her husband, George V, liked to work in the midst of hundreds of little personal treasures covering every surface. In the State Apartments of Buckingham Palace she made only such changes as would restore the coherence and unity of their original Regency style. For the private rooms, she traced and installed as much of the furniture originally designed for the Palace as she could. In this new reign, too, Buckingham Palace became a family home in a way which it had not been since the death of Prince Albert in 1861; for the King and Queen, he forty-five and she forty-three, were young enough to have a growing family of which the eldest was sixteen and the youngest five. That atmosphere, of being a home as well as a great State edifice, has remained with the Palace ever since. There was, of course, during George V's reign, the important exterior alteration to the Palace brought about by the completion of Aston Webb's new façade. If *The Times* newspaper may be regarded as reflecting the taste of the day, this work was popular. At the present time, more people would probably agree with Sir Nikolaus Pevsner's verdict, '. . . a tasteful but insipid performance rather in the French idiom.'

However, in his more general praise of the Palace, Sir Nikolaus notes the effect created by its gardens, a triumph for 'the English delight in the country house and a humanized countryside'. The gardens are probably best-known to the outside world as the place where the Royal Garden Parties are held in the summer, tea-parties on the grand scale, intensely English, with the Queen, the Head of the Church of England, playing in a sense the role of hostess played by vicars' wives on so many sunlit vicarage lawns all over England at about that time of the year. It is pleasant to think that something so very English as 'a nice cup of tea' is at the centre of the occasions on which the Sovereign entertains her subjects in the greatest numbers—about eight thousand at each party—and in the widest variety from all sections of the population, civic leaders, trades union leaders, workers for welfare organisations, scientists, doctors, schoolmasters, journalists, athletes, clergymen. It is pleasanter still to note the opinion of Mary Spencer-Warren, expressed in an article about the site of Buckingham Palace, that 'here the first cup of tea drank in this country was made; brought here in the year of the Great Plague by the Earl of Arlington, he having paid sixty shillings per lb for its purchase in Holland'.

King George VI and Queen Elizabeth were both keen and knowledgeable gardeners, and made great improvements in the Palace gardens, clearing rather boring Victorian shrubberies to create long vistas and pleasing views from the Palace windows and the main lawn. Our present Queen, then Princess Elizabeth, with her sister, Princess Margaret, used to be particularly fond of the little island in the gardens' large lake. They used to take an old punt out to it, pitch a tent, and camp there during the day, but begged unsuccessfully to be allowed to sleep there at night. There is a story that Princess Elizabeth fell in the water on one of these excursions, and had to be taken back to the Palace, mud-stained and dripping, by her Governess, Miss Crawford, the famous 'Crawfie'. At one time there were no fish in this lake; that there are some now is an accident of the last war. After a bomb had fallen in the Serpentine in Hyde Park, a grid was left off a pipe which leads from that lake to the one at Buckingham Palace. Chub, roach and perch swam through and astonished the royal gardeners the following day by an apparent startling instance of spontaneous generation.

In fact, much more recently, the Palace gardens were found to be full of other natural surprises. In the autumn of 1974, a team from the B.B.C. radio programme, *The Living World*, found types of wild life there that astonished the experts, for instance a kind of moth normally associated only with Africa, where it lives on cotton plants. There may be some significance in the fact that it made its appearance shortly after a visit from some Commonwealth Prime Ministers who were holding a Conference in London. There were also several other rare species of insects and spiders, including one normally found only in French wine cellars, which had possibly come over in a case of wine. There were also three times as many birds as in other royal parks. The reason for the natural peculiarities of the Palace gardens is probably their great seclusion in spite of their being in the heart of London. There are no cats at the Palace and the high garden walls with wire along their tops keep out any that might try to intrude. The birds seem to know this. A blackbird risked building its nest on the ground there and successfully reared its young.

In the 325 days that he reigned before his abdication, King Edward VIII was in residence at the Palace for only a few weeks. Most of the time he used it simply as a work place, and even for this chose an unimportant room on the ground floor which had the practical advantage of being close to the offices of those Household officials with whom he was likely to be most often in consultation. He said in his book, *A King's Story*, that when he did at last take up residence at the Palace, he did so without pleasure; and he made no physical changes. 'One never tinkers much with palaces,' he said. 'Like museums, they seem to resist change. Besides, a curious presentiment induced me to leave the rooms as they were. Somehow I had a feeling that I might not be there very long.' However, he did introduce some economies at the Palace, following the precedent of both his father and grandfather in their own first days upon the throne.

King George VI and his Queen also left the structure of the Palace much as they had found it, apart from some small practical improvements, such as the installation of a much-needed service lift from the kitchens and the building of a new summer-house in the gardens. Two actions by the King in the early years of his reign looked the one romantically back at the past and the other rather grimly into the future. The first was his granting permission for part of a film about Queen Victoria to be made at the Palace; and there were still some Palace servants old enough to remember seeing the old Queen herself leave the Grand Entrance for her Diamond Jubilee Thanksgiving Service at St Paul's, and able to vouch for the authenticity with which Anna Neagle re-enacted this piece of history. Not many months later the King anticipated history still to come when he gave instructions for the strengthening with timbers and steel girders of the lower rooms at the Palace as an air-raid precaution. The Palace was indeed bombed. It was among the first buildings in London to receive direct hits. In one week of September 1940, it was struck seven times. The King and Queen were in residence during the worst raid of that week which wrecked the Palace chapel. Queen Victoria's Bible, in which all births in the royal family are recorded, was recovered from the rubble. The King and the Queen spent part of that day visiting the homes of fellow Londoners who had also been bombed. The Queen said, 'I'm glad we've been bombed. It makes me feel I can look the East End in the face.' Her demeanour during the bombing inspired this verse from a Chicago American:

> Be it said to your renown
> That you wore your gayest gown,
> Your bravest smile, and stayed in Town
> When London Bridge was burning down,
> My fair lady.

Later in the war the Palace was struck twice more, once by a flying bomb. It was not until 1962 that the last of the damage was made good. By then, Queen Elizabeth II had been installed at the Palace for ten years with her husband, Prince Philip, and their children.

During their tenure, Buckingham Palace has retained its grandeur for the appropriate grand occasion, its atmosphere of history enshrined for those who seek that or are sensitive to it, its suitability as the recognised centre of what is still the most glamorous of the world's remaining monarchies. But it can also seem, according perhaps to the particular reason for one's attendance there, both a busy and notably efficient place—exemplifying Prince Philip's often-quoted remark, 'We live over the shop'—and a very evident family home.

Prince Philip is also said to have referred to the Palace as 'the museum' and 'our tied cottage', though with a certain affection, I understand. Both these attitudes towards it are reflected in the way the royal family use it. I have discovered this for myself during my regular visits there on journalistic business and on those occasions when I have had the honour to be there as a guest.

I suppose one would have to be very unimpressionable and self-consciously cynical—and so, almost by definition, unsuitable for journalism—to be able to visit Buckingham Palace for the first time without experiencing some degree of awe. I was rather pleased when I first went there to find that the taxi-driver who delivered me to the Privy Purse Door was also experiencing a sense of occasion. He got out of the driving seat to stare round him, and said, 'You've made my day. I've never brought anyone here before.'

Inside, I was impressed, as many others have been, by the relaxed and friendly atmosphere, and the curious way in which the breezy and sociable efficiency of what might be called the business side merged imperceptibly with the museum, the old and deliberate regality and magnificence, and the family home. I thought it was fun—and I still do—to pass through corridors lined with pictures that I had seen before only as reproductions in books, to call on Ronald Allison, the Queen's Press Secretary, and my predecessor as B.B.C. Court Correspondent, and to find him sitting at an early Victorian desk that would have delighted Christie's, and backed by a couple of Dutch seventeenth-century *genre* paintings of striking merit. These days his office wall is decorated with one of the best Canaletto townscapes

I have ever seen, and he calms my envy by telling me that it is only there because it is waiting to be cleaned. But that office, like most of the rooms of the Queen's Household officers, has also its battery of telephones, its filing cabinets and shelves and trays, and its intercom box, bristling with keys and knobs, which I am told results from one of Prince Philip's earliest efficiency drives.

Along those working corridors the doors are always open, exemplifying the general, friendly accessibility of the people who work there, although nothing seems casual. To get to some offices I have sometimes had to pass between the door of the lift that goes up to the Queen's private apartments and the steps and exit to the garden normally used by the royal family; and it is pleasant to see there a homely clutter of small pedal-cars and bicycles, for which even the youngest of the royal children, Prince Edward, is now, undoubtedly, rather too old. Near those steps there is always a little pile of neatly-folded white towels, which puzzled me for months, until I was told they are for drying the feet of the royal corgis if they are taken out in the wet. It is not only old masters that decorate the corridors. There are quite a few pictures that must be purely of family, though that also means historical, interest, and all manner of slightly mysterious small objects, someone's mementoes or treasures of the past, for which no one has been able to give me an explanation. For example, what is the origin of a piece of fixed ammunition—from a naval Q.F. gun, I would guess—which stands all by itself on one small table? What circumstance brought to the Palace a slightly sentimental statuette of a recumbent girl, apparently dead, under a little glass case nearby? Who was she?

The Palace servants, too, are an amiable body, most strikingly lacking in flunkeyism, only properly deferential, never servile; and they all belong, as do the rest of the employed Palace staff, to a trade union. If one of them, on retirement, were to open a school of instruction to teach some of the worst head-waiters of some of London's best restaurants how things are done at the very top, he would do a great service to the capital. The records show that it was not always so. For instance, it is clear that being a royal servant must have been a nerve-testing business in Victoria's day. With the exception of a favoured very few, such as John Brown, her legendary Scottish factotum, no servant might in any circumstances address her directly. There is a story that she caused to be severely reprimanded a maidservant who drew her attention to a red-hot twig which had sprung unnoticed from the fire and was smouldering in the royal skirts. The composer, the late Dame Ethel Smyth, has told of Victoria's horror of encountering anyone unexpectedly, and of how a Maid of Honour at Windsor just escaped such an unscheduled meeting, and hid behind a curtain, crouched and trembling, for half an hour, while Victoria supervised the placing of some tributes from an Indian Prince. Dame Ethel also recalled, as 'one of the most appalling blunders I ever committed in my life', how she once nearly stood on the hearth-rug at Windsor when the Queen was herself standing on it, but was fortunately headed off from this sacrilege by 'dear, human Princess Christian, who had come more in contact with low life than the Queen'.

It is quite evident that no one at the Palace nowadays feels constrained to pussy-foot about the place as in Victoria's day, though a certain caution is observed to avoid needless intrusion if the Queen is likely to be in the vicinity; and you certainly do not address the Queen unless she addresses you. But in fact she is not very likely to be encountered unexpectedly in the office corridors of the Palace; however, on a few occasions when I have had business there, the Duke of Edinburgh has come striding briskly by, with a manner not unlike that of an amiable orderly officer, or whatever is the naval equivalent, doing his rounds, and he had a 'Good morning' for those he passed. An arranged meeting with him in his study at the Palace is also by no means a formal affair, although he maintains so full a programme and works to so tight a schedule that it is not easy to secure.

In his fascinating reminiscences, *Of Carriages and Kings*, Frederick John Gorst, a royal footman in Edward VII's day, described a banquet given in honour of King Alphonso XIII of Spain. 'The Crown gold was used throughout . . . masses of orchids and lilies of the valley . . . the Royal guard, with halberds in hand, rigidly posed like living statues . . . King Edward in full dress uniform . . . Queen Alexandra in white satin with the blue ribbon of the Garter and a glittering tiara . . . ladies resplendent in gorgeous gowns . . . the gentlemen in knee breeches and with all their decorations and orders . . .

the table illuminated by golden candelabra bearing hundreds of candles whose light sparkled in a sea of priceless jewels.' Clearly, in those times, there was plenty to spare of everything, including adjectives. But even though Britain is now in very much leaner times, the Palace can still, as part of the Queen's job, so to speak, more than hold its own in the matter of regal display when the Foreign Office has indicated that the entertainment of some foreign Head of State is politically desirable—which is one reason, no doubt, why there is always a long queue of potentates who have made it clear that they would welcome an invitation to pay a State Visit to Britain as the guest of the Queen. I imagine that the main difference between such an occasion now and what it was in Edwardian times is that today everything is much more carefully costed than it has ever been. The Palace is not extravagant, and I have noticed that it reacts more quickly and more evidently to appeals for national frugality than do the offices of the Government's own ministries and departments. I think it must have been in the winter of 1973 and 1974 that I first began to notice that the Palace was just a little chillier than it used to be and that not so many lights shone. It was warmer in Downing Street.

Just the same, the Palace has forgotten nothing of what it has learned over the years about formality, ceremonial, etiquette and organised magnificence. A good occasion for watching it operate its well-drilled and impeccably-organised dazzle routine is the evening reception that the Queen gives every year for the Diplomatic Corps. Most of the great State rooms are used for these occasions, one of which was the first great reception of her reign. They follow a pattern, are very regal indeed, and are quite obviously a source of enormous gratification to the diplomats and their families. With ceremonial and evening dresses, gowns and tiaras, medals and stars, sashes, ribbons and collars of all degrees of colour and glitter, gorgeous and interesting national costumes, they stand, each country forming its own group, waiting for the arrival of the Queen, making, I would guess, quite as brave a show as anything Footman Gorst saw all those years ago. Members of the Honourable Corps of Gentlemen-at-Arms stand by in all the rooms, with scarlet coats with velvet facings and gold lace, ornamental halberds, white gloves and white-plumed, gilded helmets. At last, preceded by the Lord Chamberlain, bearing his white wand of office, the Queen comes with Prince Philip; and then, at intervals, follow other members of the royal family who are able to be there. Almost all of the grown-up members were present, I think, on the occasion that I was fortunate enough to be invited to this reception. All of them spoke to everyone in all the diplomatic groups, and were apparently at pains to seem to give equal time and attention to all. Though I am glad to have seen it, it was a lengthy affair, and I was not sorry when a Palace servant selected the first possible moment to whisper in my ear and lead me and a friend in the direction of a bottle of champagne and some glasses. I do not accuse him of chauvinism but merely credit him with compassion when I disclose that what he whispered was, 'Better get in there quick before all them foreigners cut you off.'

The Diplomatic Receptions demonstrate how well Buckingham Palace is suited to the grand and formal kind of entertainment required of the Queen as Head of State, the symbol of the nation, extending its hospitality and goodwill to the outside world. But the Palace has, of course, seen many much less formal parties, too, given for the family and for personal friends. The Queen's father, George VI, could be lively and schoolboyish on such occasions, shedding his natural reserve when he was with people to whom he felt close or whom he knew well. He is said to have been a skilled ballroom dancer, and he also liked to take the leadership of a long, hilarious snake of family and friends, dancing the conga up and down the great staircases and the labyrinthine corridors of the Palace.

Queen Elizabeth and Prince Philip not so long ago hit upon a new kind of Palace party which pleasantly combines the royal and formal with the relatively informal, a type of evening reception to which an Osbert Lancaster of entertaining might give some such title as 'Mid-Twentieth Century Regal'. Many, though by no means all, of the people invited were connected with the stage, radio and television, and the arts generally. It seemed at first that it was all going to be rather formal. After toiling up the Grand Staircase, surrounded by scores of faces of people one seemed to know intimately, but few of whom one had ever met—a slightly dream-like experience in itself—it seemed total unreality to find at the top, and first glimpsed between the large shoulders of Peter Ustinov and the rather narrower ones of a celebrated disc-jockey, the Queen, the

Queen Mother, Prince Philip and Prince Charles, poised in a glittering tableau to receive the guests. Entering the State Rooms after the bows and curtseys, my wife and I heard a woman say, 'It was like seeing them suddenly at Madame Tussaud's.' That does sum up the feeling of the occasion which to some extent remained.

From then on it was essentially a large, informal drinks party with a buffet, and very enjoyable, too; but it does not seem like real life to talk first to the Prime Minister—Harold Wilson at the time—and immediately afterwards to Ernie Wise; and to wonder, perhaps not with total insanity, how long it would be before the latter had the former in one of his plays, being asked who he was by Eric Morecambe, who also, of course, was at that remarkable party. In those grand rooms one saw unlikely combinations of the famous that gave deep delight. There were 'Precious' Mackenzie, the weight-lifter, and Sir John Betjeman, the Poet Laureate. There was Mr Jimmy Savile, of the 'pops'. There were Sir Robert Mark (Commissioner of Metropolitan Police); Mr Alistair Maclean, who writes thrillers; and Mrs Marjorie Proops, for whom other people write thrillers. There were Mr Tommy Steele, Mr Emlyn Williams, Sir Alec Guinness, Mr Jack Hulbert, Dame Cicely Courtneidge, Mr Albert Finney and Mr Roger Moore. There were Mr Edward Heath, Mr Jeremy Thorpe, and Mr Harold Macmillan. There were many others. And through this name-dropper's paradise moved from group to group the Queen; the Duke of Edinburgh; Queen Elizabeth the Queen Mother; the Prince of Wales; Princess Anne; Princess Alice, Duchess of Gloucester; the Duke and Duchess of Kent; Princess Alexandra and her husband; and Earl Mountbatten of Burma.

For those who grew tired of collecting names to drop, there were arranged here and there to be examined some of the curiosities of the Royal Library and archives and, indeed, some of the treasures. I remember the autographed score of a choral work written by Mozart at the age of ten; the shirt Charles I wore at his execution, and the bullet that killed Nelson; letters from Queen Victoria, including one opposing a tax which would bear hardest on those with smallest means, and another demanding action about bad housing; a letter from William IV, offering Buckingham Palace, which he disliked, as a replacement for the Houses of Parliament after their destruction by fire; and another from Disraeli, thanking Queen Victoria for a bunch of snowdrops.

Only the Queen, of course, could give a party like that, and I think everyone there was delighted by it. It continued into the small hours of the morning, a long time after the Queen herself had left.

So then, in a building of six hundred rooms and one and a half miles of corridor, probably the most stared-at place of its kind in the world, the Queen, with a staff of about two hundred, spends most of her working life and her private life as a wife and mother with her husband and family. When the Queen is in residence there, and only then, the Royal Standard, as most Londoners know, flies over the Palace. Quite often it is not to be seen there at week-ends; because the Queen likes to be in the country, or as near as possible to it, when she can; so she goes to her other working home, Windsor Castle, in Berkshire, about twenty-two miles from London.

Windsor is very much Royal Windsor. Kings have reigned in Old or New Windsor for almost half of Christian history. Edward the Confessor was the first ruler to recognise its suitability as the site of a royal dwelling, though his Palace was not where the present Castle stands, but in Old Windsor, a Saxon settlement then called Windlesora, by the river bank and on the fringe of the forest, ideal as a base for hunting. William the Conqueror liked hunting, too; so he continued to use Old Windsor; but he needed security and protection greater than the old Palace could offer, and built for this purpose on a hilltop about three miles further upstream. What he built has developed over more than nine centuries to become the world's largest lived-in fortress and has been used by every English sovereign from his time to the present.

Of sovereigns who have reigned within living memory, it is Victoria who springs most readily to mind in connection with Windsor. She went there as a child to pay her respects to her uncle, George IV, and recalled afterwards that he was 'large and gouty but with a wonderful dignity and charm of manner' and that he wore a wig. He took her by the hand, she recalled, and said, 'Give me your little paw.' It was he who had made Windsor Castle by his extensive restoration a place comfortable enough for a sovereign to live in, creating from a vast muddle of ancient and delapidated structures the coherent unity we know today, one of the most romantic architectural silhouettes in the world. For Victoria it was to take on romantic associations of another kind; for it was there that she waited for Prince Albert on the day she proposed marriage to him. She went there as a bride. There she watched by Albert's bedside during the most terrible days of her life as he lay dying in December 1861.

Albert liked Windsor and its surroundings, and he did a great deal of work there. He managed its farmland so well that it showed a profit; he planned new gardens and new avenues of trees; and he adapted rooms to make a library. He showed less than his normal urgency in pressing for the completion of work started fifteen years before on the Castle drains, some of which were worse than inadequate and probably fouled the water supply. They very possibly killed him. One of the physicians who attended him, Dr Jenner, wrote to a friend, 'The Prince of course had typhoid fever. . . .' Not far from Windsor Castle was Frogmore, where there was a little lake on which Albert had enjoyed skating while Victoria and her mother, the Duchess of Kent, occupant of Frogmore House, watched him admiringly from the shore. It was at Frogmore that Victoria built a mausoleum for his body to rest in; and thereafter spent a great part of her waking life longing for the day when her own would be placed beside it. That happened thirty-eight years later.

It is from those years that the legend of the Widow of Windsor derives. Victoria was present in St George's Chapel, Windsor, when the future King Edward VII married Princess Alexandra of Denmark; but she still wore the black streamers of widowhood. An observer commented, 'Not a gleam of joy at her son's marriage illumined her desolation.' Another discordant note was sounded by a four-year-old nephew of the bridegroom, who when his uncles Prince Alfred and Prince Leopold tried to stop him from flinging across the choir an ornament that was part of his costume, 'showed his displeasure by biting them hard on the legs'. This child grew up to become even more unpleasant under the title of Kaiser Wilhelm II of Germany. After the wedding, the Queen went down to Frogmore to have a good cry at the mausoleum.

As the years wore on, and Victoria continued to be sunk in her widowhood, some of the people and some of the newspapers began to complain that she was not doing her job and that the royal family was not worth the money it cost the nation. There was probably more genuine and active republicanism at about that time than there has ever been since. Before Albert's death all manner of grand people had been entertained at Windsor, including the Tsar Nicholas I of Russia and King Louis Philippe of France, the first French King to visit England since 1356. In a single year before Albert's death, the year 1841, 113,000 guests were entertained to dinner at Windsor; and blind envy not being at that time the fashionable sin of the working man, the people were delighted and proud that they were being so splendidly represented by their ruler. After Albert's death there was hardly any royal entertaining at all, and difficult as this is to understand in our more egalitarian times, the people felt that the Queen was letting them down. The sombre atmosphere of the Widow's Windsor did gradually lighten a little over the years, but as late as 1896, at Windsor the newly-married Duchess of Marlborough—the lovely American heiress, Consuelo Vanderbilt—was made to feel by the Queen that 'any warmth she might have possessed must have been buried with the Prince Consort'.

Windsor Castle and its precincts are credited with a legion of ghosts—Herne the Hunter, who hanged himself on a tree in the Park in Tudor times; George III, whom a sentry claimed to have seen pale and demented peering from a window; Anne Boleyn, also at a window, overlooking the cloisters, which are themselves said to be haunted by the husband who had her beheaded, Henry VIII; the first Queen Elizabeth, whose ghost has allegedly been seen in the library; and an unidentified 'little grey man'. But if there are ghosts in the Castle, one of them surely ought to be the little old lady in 'a white tulle cap, black satin dress and shiny black boots with elastic sides'—Queen Victoria at Windsor as recalled by a little boy who called her 'Gangan', her great-grandson who succeeded her three reigns later as Edward VIII, and who was the favourite uncle of the present Queen.

By the end of the century republicanism had faded, and the old Queen, surrounded in the four rooms she used at Windsor by hundreds of photographs and mementoes of the dead, playing at patience and fumbling through bundles of old letters, had become a central part of the new nationalism and imperialism of which the Boer War was the most violent expression. During that war, on the day of the Relief of Mafeking, when Victoria had just about nine months to wait before at last rejoining Albert, some boys from nearby Eton College came to sing patriotic songs under her window. When she leaned out to thank them, they were interested to see one of her Indian servants hand her a Scotch and soda.

The masculinity of Scotch and soda, with an attendant rich aroma of expensive scalp-lotion and good cigars, might well be said to express the essential atmosphere created in the Castle by its next occupant. Edward VII, sixty years old, grey-bearded, stout and ebullient, set breezily to work there, as at Buckingham Palace, to clear away the clutter and bring in the new age. He installed new bathrooms and ventilation and extended the telephone system which had been introduced at Windsor sketchily about five years earlier. He changed some of the coach houses into garages for his Mercedes and Daimler motor-cars. He rearranged and redecorated almost every room, and again as at Buckingham Palace, liked to supervise the work himself on the spot as often as he could. Etiquette became less formal than under Victoria, and guests found, as they had not at Windsor for nearly forty years, that dinner there could be positively enjoyable. Naturally, after so long a time under a régime very set in its ways, not everyone liked the changes. Lord Esher, son of one of the old Queen's most distinguished justices and soon to become Deputy-Governor and eventually Governor of the Castle, feared that the 'sanctity of the throne' had disappeared. He said, 'The King is kind and debonair and not undignified—but too human!' When everything was ready to the King's satisfaction, proper entertaining began again. A ball on the grand scale was given in the Waterloo Chamber in 1903, the first to be given in the Castle for half a century. The King modernised the business affairs of the Castle, insisting on better accounting and more efficient methods, and in consequence produced considerable economies. Though the King's Court at Windsor cannot precisely be described as democratic—indeed he liked the British aristocracy far more than had his mother, who considered that too many of them lived for nothing but pleasure—he did make it far more open. He had made friends among the new successful men, and welcomed them to Court because he admired them or found them amusing, and apparently cared little about their antecedents. He may even be said to have struck a blow for women's rights; for he restored the practice, centuries in abeyance, of admitting ladies to the Order of the Garter, which of course is especially associated with St George's Chapel.

The restoration of St George's Chapel, always acknowledged as one of the great masterpieces of fifteenth-century Perpendicular architecture, was one of the most important works carried out at Windsor in George V's reign. Every stone in the ceiling was removed and inspected and some were replaced, and the whole structure was cleaned. Expert opinion seems to be that it now looks much as it must have done five centuries ago. Here are buried many English sovereigns, and the Garter Knights convene for their yearly service and have their stalls surmounted by their coats of arms; for it is primarily the Chapel of the Order, and the Sovereign when in residence normally worships in the domestic chapel adjoining the State Apartments.

Once again, with the new reign, there came a change of style at Windsor. George V did not care for Windsor at first, because he associated it with ceremonial and lavish entertainment, things for which he had little liking. He had venerated his father, but was aware that he was of a different mould. When he acknowledged this in a remark that has often been quoted, he at the same time summed up, many commentators think, the essence of his own character. He said, 'England is good enough for me. I like my own country best, climate or no, and I'm staying in it. I'm not like my father. There's nothing of the cosmopolitan in me. I'm afraid I'm insular.' So it was in character that at Windsor he should give much of his personal attention and interest to the development and working of the estate, which acquired a genuine reputation for the stimulus it gave to scientific agriculture and ideas on the breeding of better cattle.

He and his descendants were fortunate in the fact that his Queen Consort used her taste, knowledge and discretion as skilfully at Windsor as she did at Buckingham Palace, even though she had to overcome gently the King's conservative dislike of change in the appearance of things to which he had become accustomed. Where the King was a source of change was in his preference for a quieter style of life at the Castle than had prevailed under his father. He was firmly domestic. Lord Esher was naturally pleased. 'We have reverted to the ways of Queen Victoria,' he wrote in his diary. The undoubted charm of the ancient Castle gradually began to work its spell on the King; and it is understandable that when during World War I he decided to renounce for his family all German titles, he chose to adopt for it the name of Windsor. It is even more understandable if one considers some of the other names suggested by the Royal College of Heralds—'Guelph', 'Wipper', 'Wettin', 'Fitzroy' and even just plain 'England'. Interestingly in this connection, George V's granddaughter, the present Queen, used to call him 'Uncle England' when she was a small girl.

In his short reign before his abdication, Edward VIII does not appear ever to have lived in the Castle, though it is known that he had a great affection for it. But as his own father had reverted instinctively to a style of life at the Castle similar to that of his grandmother, Victoria, so Edward looked back with affection on what he had seen there in his grandfather's day, a world of fashionable, exciting, often clever and beautiful people, smart, well-dressed, cosmopolitan. Something akin to this kind of world he built up around himself as the immensely-popular Prince of Wales at his own country house, Fort Belvedere, not far from Windsor. As King, he took some of these friends, including Mrs Wallis Simpson, whom he renounced the throne to marry, in a party to view the Castle, and he gave at least one dinner party there. It was from the Castle that he made his broadcast over the B.B.C. announcing his decision to renounce the throne.

The first British King to hold a pilot's licence and wear airman's wings was King George VI. He earned these when he took his test flight one day in the summer of 1919, and when as Duke of York, he had no expectation of ever being King. In an Avro 504J one hundred horse-power aircraft he was required to fly unaided a cross-country course of eighty miles, and he chose to make that flight over Windsor Castle, a place that he loved. Windsor was also associated with the deep happiness of his early married life, because he went there to live with his family in the Royal Lodge, a grace-and-favour residence in the southern recesses of Windsor Great Park. There his elder daughter, now the Queen, and her sister, Princess

Margaret, spent some of the most lovingly-recalled days of their childhood. When the family moved into the Castle after the dramatic accession to the throne which so deeply dismayed the King, they were able to settle comfortably into at least that part of their new life, for they knew the Castle as well as they knew their own nearby home. Once again the style of life was one of settled domesticity, though much of the formality of George V's day was abandoned. For much of the War the King stayed each night at Windsor. For Princess Elizabeth and Princess Margaret, living at Windsor must be their predominant wartime memory, for they lived there for almost the whole of the war years from 1940.

The home farm at Windsor is said to be one of the chief off-duty interests of the Queen, though the administration of it is one of the responsibilities that Prince Philip has taken on to lighten the Queen's heavy load. Windsor for them and their children is a much lived-in home. Their domestic life there, one is told, has developed patterns, some of which are carried over from the days when the Queen lived there as a young Princess. Windsor is important, too, particularly for the Queen and Princess Anne, because it has always been associated with the breeding, training and riding of horses. However, Windsor, like Buckingham Palace, is for the Queen a place of work as well as a home. The Castle, Buckingham Palace and the Palace of Holyrood House in Edinburgh, her official Scottish home, where she spends at least one week each year, usually in early July, are crown property maintained by the Government. When she is in any of them she is not on holiday. Strictly speaking, the Queen is never on holiday, because her constitutional duties and the state papers follow her everywhere.

8. The Queen's Own Homes

The two residences of the Queen that are her private property are Balmoral Castle in Aberdeenshire, in Scotland, and Sandringham House in Norfolk. Each year, she spends two fairly long spells away from London and the almost-London of Windsor so as to have a change, a rest, much-desired almost complete privacy, and as much outdoor life as she can contrive.

The royal family usually move to Sandringham for the New Year celebrations and the month of January, after spending Christmas at Windsor. The house was originally acquired by King Edward VII when he was Prince of Wales, so that he could, as his parents wished, have a retreat from the distractions of London, where he had his principal and official residence at Marlborough House. The search for a suitable place was still going on when his father, Prince Albert, died. But about two months after that, Edward inspected the Sandringham property, which belonged to Charles Spencer Cowper, a stepson of the Prime Minister, Lord Palmerston. A report to Queen Victoria said the house was certainly ugly on the outside, but it was pleasant within, and the surrounding estate was in good order. The Queen decided to buy it, and did so a few days later.

The house itself was not very old, but it was on an ancient site. Sandringham was listed in Domesday Book as Sant Dersingham. Before taking it over, the Prince of Wales became engaged to his future Queen Consort, Alexandra, and after that he went on a tour of Southern Europe. He then made one brief stay at Sandringham before his marriage at Windsor, and he took Alexandra there shortly after that. In the years following, as the Prince's family grew, piecemeal additions and alterations were made, but proved to be inadequate; so at last, it was decided to demolish the old building and start a new one. Professor Pevsner seems to have no opinion of it as a piece of architecture, though in his volume on Norfolk he describes it at some length. However this may be, successive royal occupants seem to have liked it. Queen Victoria, who only visited it twice, even described it in her diary as 'handsome'. A great deal of work was done on the grounds. An ornamental lake felt to be too close to the house was resited and two new lakes were constructed. The landscape gardener, W. B. Thomas, who was given the commission, broke his leg in carrying it out and had to stay at Sandringham until it healed. He was so moved by the kindness that the Princess of Wales showed him while he was there that he sent her white roses on her birthday for the rest of his life.

The Prince of Wales, with his usual love of what was modern, included among new farm buildings a gasometer to supply gas to the whole estate. He wrote proudly to Queen Victoria to tell her of this, but added, '. . . of course, not in the living rooms!' Queen Victoria, it seems, detested gas, and even disliked coal, so that she would have only wood fires in her homes.

In the early eighteen-nineties, a succession of misfortunes, one a real tragedy, afflicted Sandringham. The upper floor was severely damaged by fire in 1891 and, as a result, the Prince celebrated his fiftieth birthday under a temporary roof of wood, tarpaulins and corrugated iron. But he seems to have regarded the whole mishap as at least an adventure, and even rather a joke. What happened a few days later was very far from a joke. The Prince's son, Prince George (later George V) became ill and had to be moved from the damp building to Marlborough House in London. His illness was diagnosed as typhoid, and so, with the tragic fate of Prince Albert in everyone's mind, there was a grave anxiety. But early treatment brought about a cure. The tragedy came a few weeks later when his elder brother, Albert Victor, Duke of Clarence, in direct line of succession to the throne after the Prince of Wales, caught influenza at Sandringham and died at the age of twenty-eight. Not long before, he had become engaged to be married to Princess May of Teck, who subsequently married the younger brother and became Queen of England as his Consort.

When they married, they were given a house on the Sandringham estate called Bachelor's Cottage, but renamed York Cottage. George VI and all the other children of George V and Queen Mary, except the future Edward VIII, were born there. On the death of Edward VII, Queen Alexandra became the occupant for life of the main house at Sandringham, the 'Big House', as it is usually called. In the intervening years, the history of the estate has been for successive generations of the royal family blissfully lacking in drama and a place where they can feel happy and free. Various improvements have been made through several reigns; it has been carefully administered and made to pay its way. Today it has arable, stock and fruit farms run on modern lines. Part of the Queen's thoroughbred stud is kept at Sandringham and nearby Wolferton, and both places have produced many famous racehorses, including several Derby winners. In front of the stables on the Anmer Road at Sandringham stands a bronze statue of Persimmon, winner of the 1896 Derby for the Prince of Wales. Contemporary newspaper reports show that this must have been one of the most popular successes in British racing history. The statue was presented to the Prince of Wales by the Jockey Club.

During his brief reign, Edward VIII felt some anxiety about the economics of the Sandringham estate. He says in his book, 'My inquiring gaze fell upon the Sandringham accounts and the figures startled me.' To his recently-dead father, George V, Sandringham had been the place he regarded as home, and he had written of it, 'Dear old Sandringham, the place I love better than anywhere else in the world.' In Edward's view, his father's love for the property 'had defied the encroachments of time'. As the young King put it, 'There, in remote Norfolk by the Wash, his private war with the twentieth century had ended in almost complete repulse of the latter. Sandringham had been allowed to suffer but few changes since my grandparents' days.' Edward noted that only by prodigal dipping into the Privy Purse had Sandringham been maintained as a model property, and he regarded himself as having inherited 'a voracious white elephant'. So he asked his brother, the Duke of York, to survey the estate and report on how running expenses might be reduced.

This 'excellent report', no doubt, formed the basis of reforms the Duke himself carried out after he so soon, and so reluctantly, took his brother's place on the throne. As George VI, he inaugurated not only administrative improvements but also changes in the grounds, so as to widen vistas, show particular trees to better advantage, create a new flower garden and widen lawns. The Queen's most historic contribution to the history of Sandringham has been to enable the general public to have a greater share in its beauties. She made the first moves to this end in 1968, when it was decided to set up the Sandringham Country Park over several hundred acres, where the people are welcome to walk in the woods and have access to areas set aside for recreation and picnicking. As *The Times* newspaper noted some years ago, the public can now enjoy the delights of the estate all year round, while ironically, its royal owners' duties permit them only six weeks a year at Sandringham. There is also now at Sandringham a museum for the more than 250,000 people who visit the property every year. In it are shown big game trophies, most of them obtained by various members of the royal family between 1880 and 1930; rugs and skins given to the Queen during her many Commonwealth tours; a display of Himalayan game birds, which used to stand at the foot of the main staircase in Sandringham House; motor-cars formerly used by members of the royal family, including the first it ever bought, Edward VII's Daimler Tonneau; items to do with horse-racing history; local archaeological finds; and china, uniforms and other objects relating to Sandringham's history.

The gardens had in fact been opened to the public as early as 1908, in the time of their first royal owners, King Edward VII and Queen Alexandra. They decided that a variety of charities should benefit from the entrance fee paid by visitors, which was set at sixpence (equivalent to 2½ new pence). Naturally enough, the fee has increased over the years. King George VI watched over the disbursement of this money, seeing that it went not only to organised charities but also to individuals in need who were brought to his notice.

At the time of writing, changes are in progress or being planned at Sandringham, and there is some uncertainty about the precise manner in which the royal family will continue to use this favourite home of several generations. The 'Big House' allegedly had 365 rooms when the Queen inherited it; and it is well known that she sees it as inappropriately large for a private house for anyone in times such as our own. Because of rising costs and the general economic situation, she was advised to give up a plan for making it smaller and more modern. After there had been some demolition in furtherance of this plan, it was decided to make what remained weather-proof as it stood.

Buckingham Palace announced that the house would eventually be opened to the public. It was unclear whether or not the royal family would still be resident there during their own visits to Sandringham, or whether they would permanently adopt some other, smaller house on the estate. The Queen took a close personal interest in the repair and improvement of Wood Farm, a thirteen-roomed house, formerly the home of the local doctor, which had been empty and unused for some time; and she and other members of her family have stayed there during recent visits.

Balmoral, the other royal residence at which the Queen and her family have at least the sensation of being 'away from it all' is, of course, especially associated with Queen Victoria, who celebrated the happy days she had spent there with her beloved Albert by writing a book about them, *Leaves from a Journal of Our Life in the Highlands*. Her pleasure in her production of this very interesting book introduced a small ray of light into her long, dark widowhood. She was proud of it, and pleased, no doubt, when Mr Disraeli, prolific novelist as well as Prime Minister, casually spoke to her of 'we authors, Ma'am'. He always knew the right thing to say. But it is, indeed, very far from being a book to be sneered at. Ivor Brown, an eminent critic as well as the author of a book on Balmoral, says, 'The *Journal* is one of the happiest books ever written, despite the fact that in its second volume it covers a period of intense grief and mourning. It is a record of "unforgettable days", an appreciation not only of the scenic sublimities of Upper Deeside and the Cairngorms, but of family fun.'

The Prince Consort bought the Balmoral estate from the Earl of Fife, completing the purchase in 1852. The Castle as one sees it today was built in 1855, in the Scottish baronial style, as it has been called, and it cost at the time £100,000. It replaced a rather messy building already on the site. Its 100-feet-high tower looks on to some of the most enchanting scenery in all Scotland.

Queen Victoria's life-long love affair with Scotland began when she was a girl of twenty-three, and saw it for the first time as a piece of coastline—'so dark, rocky, bold and wild'—viewed from the deck of the yacht *Royal George*. That was in 1842. She stayed only about two weeks, seeing Edinburgh and a few other places, but expressed her sadness at having to leave.

She was back again two years later at Blair Atholl to stay for a few weeks, at the end of which she was writing about 'the dear Highlands' and complaining that the English coast appeared terribly flat. Next, in 1847, she made a fairly extensive tour of the Scottish west coast which ended in foul weather, with the Mull of Galloway seen through driving rain from the rolling decks of the royal yacht. 'I was very ill,' wrote Victoria, but nevertheless, added lovingly, '. . . and this was our last glimpse of dear Scotland.'

Queen Victoria firmly sets apart these three tours as 'visits to Scotland', in contrast to 'Life in the Highlands', the heading she bestowed on all her doings in Scotland after the diary entry of Friday, 8th September 1848, which begins with the words, 'We arrived at Balmoral at a quarter to three.' From then on, for her Balmoral was Scotland and Scotland was Balmoral. She loved Scotland, it might be said, by extension from the Deeside mountains which she explored with her adored Albert.

Probably very few people nowadays have read the book prepared from Victoria's journal; certainly not as many as will have some mental image of her against the setting of Balmoral. One may speculate that she is imagined firstly as an ultra-feminine young thing, skipping about the braes, dotingly attendant on Albert. He, dressed in an incongruous kilt, lies on his stomach in the heather taking inaccurate pot-shots at assorted game in a distinctly un-British manner. This image fades into that of a dumpy little black-clad widow on a pony, allowing herself to be bossed about by her uncouth gillie, John Brown, and spending her spare time covering everything within reach in tartan of her own design. Occasionally Palmerston, Gladstone and Disraeli call, the first two complaining bitterly about the distance they have had to travel. In a quiet corner, Landseer sketches industriously.

If these fantasies of the modern mind owe a lot to the evocative, gently-mocking Palace plays of Laurence Housman, and something to the inspired nonsense of Brahms and Simon's *Don't Mr Disraeli*, they nevertheless have an element of surrealist truth, which is supported by pictures painted with highly-serious intent in Victoria's own day. My own favourite is one called 'Evening at Balmoral'. In this, a forecourt of the Castle, dramatically lit by flaring torches held by kilted gillies, is littered with the corpses of slaughtered stags. A kilted Albert, left leg thrust forward in a heroic attitude, holds up by the antlers the head of one of the stags to show it to Victoria. She stands admiring from a regal strip of carpet on the porch steps, and judging by the expression on her face, is saying something like, '*Who's* a clever boy, then?' This work, by Carl Haag, presumably pleased her, because it is—or was—somewhere in the Royal Collection. What is more to the point is the probability that it would have been equally acceptable to most of her subjects, including her Scottish subjects.

Both the modern satirical vision of Victoria at Balmoral and the nineteenth-century creation of Mr Haag, loyal and well-intentioned though he was, are travesties because they miss the essential truth that Victoria's love for Scotland was entirely genuine and neither a modish joke nor a pantomime romance. Certainly the happy days she shared with Albert in the Scottish Highlands must have coloured her attitude at the start; but as long as she remained active, her efforts to achieve a real knowledge of Scotland and its people were far more than a sentimental amusement. Her exploration of Deeside when she was a young woman took her on energetic and taxing expeditions to some of the highest and most formidable peaks in Scotland, starting with mighty and majestic Lochnagar which looks on Balmoral. On her first climb there her mountaineering ardour might have been damped for ever by the mist which developed into thick clouds of fog near the summit and was followed by a wind of almost hurricane force. For hours Victoria and her party were lost on the mountains. 'It was cold, wet and cheerless', she wrote in her diary; but in succeeding years she returned to the mountains again and again. When she was over forty she climbed Ben Muich Dhui which, at that time, and until 1870, was believed to be the highest mountain in the United Kingdom. The last of the Queen's mountain expeditions with Prince Albert was in 1861 when they visited the high table-land between Aberdeenshire and Forfar. Perhaps an interesting small historical discovery awaits someone at the place, 3,000 feet above sea level, where they took their lunch. Prince Albert wrote a note recording the lunch, and put it in a soda-water bottle which he stuck in the ground. The faithful and indefatigable Carl Haag also commemorated this occasion in a drawing that used to be well-known.

Victoria's enthusiasm for Scotland had early on survived the avuncular scepticism of her revered first Prime Minister, Lord Melbourne, who remarked that the drawback to Scotland was that the Scots thought so highly of it. She continued all her life to apply this Scottish opinion not only to Scotland but to the Scots, to whom on a personal, human level she seemed able to draw closer than she did to the English among whom she spent so much more of her time. Though the blood of both 'Butcher' Cumberland and Bonny Prince Charlie ran in her veins, it was with the latter that she chose to be associated, never allowing him to be spoken of as the Young Pretender, and proclaiming herself an ardent Jacobite. At Balmoral there was a relationship between the Sovereign and the ordinary people living in the country around which certainly had no parallel elsewhere in her realms. Uniquely it achieved affection and respect on both sides which obviated any intimidating remoteness on the Queen's part or undue obsequiousness from the Scots. The note is struck exactly, and to my mind touchingly, by the words of welcome when the Queen called at the house of the mother of one of the gillies. Old Mrs Grant said, 'Is that you, my Sovereign? I am happy to see you looking so nice.' In more general terms, it is perhaps especially worth noting at a time when efforts for greater Scottish autonomy have reached a peak, that Victoria always made a sharp distinction between her two kingdoms, never referring to Scotland as if it were in some way a province of England, a solecism not uncommon her in day. At the same time, in the opinion of Sir Reginald Coupland, 'she forged a personal link between the British Monarchy and Scotland such as none of her predecessors since the Union had even thought of.'

As Prince of Wales, and after his marriage, Edward VII also chose to emphasise his Scottish responsibilities by establishing a residence on Deeside, an area which many lovers of Scotland, including Mr Ivor Brown, regard as ideally suited as a centre for royal interest, because it is in many ways a microcosm of all that is best in Scotland. Edward used to go every year to Abergeldie Castle. There, and at Balmoral when he came to the throne, he liked to entertain large shooting parties. His mother had seen to it that Scotland should form part of his identity. He was entered in the High School of Edinburgh, and received private instruction for a time in Edinburgh University.

In his meticulously well-ordered manner, George V followed

the now established family custom of spending some time each year at Balmoral, where he could lead the outdoor life he liked, deer-stalking, shooting game-birds, fishing, riding the hardy little Highland ponies. As always, even when at Balmoral for rest and recreation, he was an early riser, and was often seen out of doors at six o'clock in the morning.

Edward VIII, though in his own book he is several times insistent about how much he enjoyed what he called 'the bracing air and the healthful days "on the hill" ', had some mixed feelings about Balmoral. He seems to have been slightly depressed by evidence of his great-grandmother's 'craving to immortalize her own private memories and ward off the encroachments of time'. He wrote, 'The hills and crags above the River Dee lent themselves to a profuse display of these tangible signs proclaiming her dedication to the dead,' and he described memorial cairns on nearly every hilltop, statues and inscribed objects of granite in the grounds, 'dedicated to the memory of a relation or a faithful retainer or even a pet dog'. He also remembered that it was at Balmoral that his father gave him and his brother, the future George VI, a mathematical test 'of brain-racking complexity'. The problem, which George V maintained '*anybody* over ten years old should be able to solve', was to work out the average weight of the stags killed by the King in the previous stalking season, and it kept the two boys a whole day at their desks in the schoolroom. However, Edward records that after he came to the throne he was able to please Queen Mary, his mother, with the news that he intended to spend the last two weeks of September at Balmoral. 'She hoped,' he said, 'now that I had become head of the family, that I would return more to the ways of my father.' He said he sometimes found the transplanted routine of the Court at Balmoral a trifle too formal for his tastes, so he decided to confine his first house-party there as King largely to friends to whom he felt he was indebted for hospitality over the years, rather than to 'a succession of Cabinet Ministers, archbishops, admirals, generals, and so forth'. He speculated that a white marble statue of Prince Albert in the Castle might have disapproved 'whenever the tray of cocktails was carried into the drawing room before dinner', but that he might have applauded his being able to play the bagpipes, the first member of the royal family to acquire this accomplishment.

Mr Hector Bolitho accuses Edward VIII of parsimony at Balmoral on the grounds that he used one of the rooms normally occupied by an upper servant, took only half the usual number of servants to the Castle with him, and ordered the Highland servants not to line the avenue for his arrival, as they had done in his father's day. This charge—made in a book published in 1937—seems more than a little unfair in the lean late-Seventies. Edward in some things went too fast, no doubt, but economies and some streamlining of pomp and circumstance, as well as a reasonable insistence in living their private lives in freedom in their private homes, such as Balmoral, are matters in which the royal family to this day may be said to have followed the lead he gave.

For George VI, Balmoral was often the place that he and his Scottish-born Queen chose for rest and recuperation after spells of particularly trying public duties or after times of crisis. Several family events of importance to them also took place while they were in residence there. The King liked entertaining at Balmoral in a warm, domestic way, a taste that his daughter, the present Queen, and Prince Philip are said to share. But for a man able to be so quietly strong in his duties, he could, as a private person, be touchingly diffident. Dorothy Laird reports the recollection of someone close to the King that when he was arranging his first guest list for Balmoral, he asked doubtfully, 'Do you think they will really want to come?'

After their Coronation and the strenuous round of official activities that followed it, King George VI and Queen Elizabeth went to Balmoral for two months of well-earned rest. Several of their subsequent sojourns there were disturbed by various turns for the worse in the state of international affairs as the growing totalitarian madness in Germany brought the world closer to the brink of war. When the War was approaching its last phase in the autumn of 1944, the royal family went to Balmoral with a special security guard, because it was thought possible that there might be a desperate, last-minute attempt by the Nazis to seize the King in some such manner as they had rescued Mussolini from his imprisonment in the Abruzzi mountains the year before. This highly-exceptional and wholly secret 'Sovereign's Escort' included, in addition to a Household Cavalry detachment and some Scottish Home Guards, the Fifth Battalion the Manchester Regiment (Territorial Army), which provided the occasion for the Queen and the two Princesses to become members of a little-known and exclusive club. This is the 'Tha' Wha'' Club. 'Tha' Wha'', it was explained to them—as it had to be; for television was still then in its infancy—is Lancastrian for 'Thou What?', meaning roughly, 'What did you say?', but chiefly used to express astonishment or incredulity. The expression had given its name to the Regimental concert party and then to the Club. The Queen presented the Manchester Regiment with a silver cup inscribed 'Tha' Wha'—Balmoral, 1944'.

Earlier in the War, in August 1942, news of a family tragedy came to the royal family at Balmoral. It was there that they learned that the King's youngest brother, the forty-year-old Duke of Kent, who was on active service with the R.A.F., had been killed in an air crash on his way from Scotland to Iceland in bad flying weather. He had been staying with the King and Queen only a few days before. By coincidence, his body was found on a Scottish hillside by a shepherd whose son was a servant at Buckingham Palace. At the end of the War in Europe, the King and Queen took a few weeks' respite at Balmoral, as they did again a few months later when peace came with the final defeat of Japan. During the Balmoral holiday of 1946 a young man seen regularly with the royal family over several weeks began to be noticed by the public for the first time, and became the object of speculation in connection with Princess Elizabeth, which for once turned out to be well-founded, because he was Prince Philip of Greece and Denmark. The Princess's engagement to him was announced the following summer.

At Balmoral the King rested after the operation carried out in 1949 to relieve obstruction in the arteries of his legs. He was at the Castle for the last time when doctors were summoned to see him there in the autumn of 1951. A few months later he died.

At the present time, Deeside is as popular as ever with the royal family, as an area in which they can be together and be free. From early in Elizabeth II's reign there has grown up a family custom of gathering there in the summer, with the Queen and Prince Philip and their children at Balmoral and Queen Elizabeth the Queen Mother and Princess Margaret at nearby Birkhall, and two house-parties intermingling frequently for picnics, fishing and other sports, and for walks and drives through the hills in a privacy unusual for all of the royal family for most of the rest of the year.

At Balmoral then and at Sandringham the royal family find their greatest freedom to be a family and to feel like a family, though hardly an ordinary family, even if they may sometimes wish, as probably they do, that they could be just that. But what citizen of a Monarchy, who liked living in that system, would really want the royal family to be ordinary, 'just like everybody else'? A sound, sensible and reasonable case for the usefulness and sheer practicality of constitutional Monarchy as a system of Government uniquely suitable for Britain can be, and has often been, made out. However, a mystical quality, a kind of magic, if you like, which is attached to the idea more than to the person of the Monarch, though it can apply to both, is essential to this system, and is perhaps itself highly practical; for it could be contended that it answers to something inherent in human nature. 'Majesty' is the word that most precisely expressed this quality. It is foolish to want something mystical, magical and majestic to be, at the same time, 'just like everybody else'.

9. The Monarchy and the Press

A great many people alive today have lived in the reigns of six British monarchs and throughout those of four of them. Only the young, born in the last twenty-five years, will be able to take for granted the irreverence with which the British Press frequently feels free to treat the Monarchy and the Queen, and the royal family as persons. Queen Victoria in the later half of her reign was relatively sacrosanct, for most of her subjects the mystical embodiment of their own appraisal of themselves as a nation, a great power, the centre of an empire and an imperial idea. Though you might castigate the policies of her ministers and the ministers themselves, you did not make fun of the Queen. This same restraint, which seems, on the whole, to have been instinctive, rather than consciously self-denying, carried over with astonishingly-little apparent effort into the reign of Edward VII, and continued during those of George V and George VI, whose unchallenged probity won natural respect and each of whom was a focus for national loyalty and endeavour in a world war. During the less than eleven months that Edward VIII occupied the throne before abdicating to marry a divorced American lady, Mrs Wallis Simpson, the Press found plenty to write about in the Monarchy, but generally, Fleet Street saw the King's dilemma as a dilemma for the Kingdom and the Empire to be treated with high seriousness, and if there were journalistic jokes on the subject, they did not get into print.

As we know now, Edward VIII enlisted the help of the two most powerful newspaper barons of the day, Lord Beaverbrook and Esmond Harmsworth, later Lord Rothermere; and they persuaded others in the newspaper world to preserve a gentleman's agreement to avoid 'sensational publicity' about some of the events that led up to the abdication crisis. Malcolm

Muggeridge, in his book on the Thirties, recalls that even the *Daily Worker* (a Communist publication which survives under another name) scrupulously observed the self-denying ordinance, though of course the idea of deliberately suppressing inconvenient news can hardly have presented a problem in itself to an editor whose mentors were *Pravda* and *Isvestia*. To the rest of Fleet Street—and not least the circulation managers—it did, particularly when the American papers were playing the story for all it was worth and more. The storm broke in the end; but after the abdication of Edward, the British Press returned with surprising speed and apparent contentment to what Edward called its 'long-standing reticence where the privacy of the royal family was concerned'. It maintained it with ease throughout the dignified and praiseworthy reign of Edward's younger brother. Historically, of course, the reticence was not really of 'long standing'. It continued, though, through the early years of the present reign; but later, keeping roughly in pace with those changes in society to which society itself has given the rather indefinite label, 'permissive', there was a gradual change in the degree of latitude in treatment of the royal family that the Press felt its readers would accept.

The Monarchy, and particularly the Queen herself, are most certainly held in high regard by the majority. Even most critics of Monarchy in Britain agree about this. The Silver Jubilee celebrations will probably show that there is also widespread and genuine affection both for the Crown as a symbol and an institution, and for the Queen as a woman and the mother of a family, as well as Head of State, esteemed because she represents the nation's self-esteem. Nevertheless, a great many who can still become misty-eyed on a royal occasion will also be able to laugh at a joke about royalty. Even some of the more tasteless jokes—and there have been a fair number of these in recent times—have no longer the shock value that they would have had, even a decade ago. All this is, in fact, a return to a freedom that the British Press permitted itself in the earliest days after it had won the right to describe itself as free. It is true that in 1813 Leigh Hunt and his brother were fined and sent to prison for libelling the Prince Regent in their newspaper, the *Examiner*; and that in a sense they were martyrs to the cause of Press liberty. Nevertheless what they wrote undoubtedly was libellous; it would probably have been held to be so even had it been directed against a less exalted personage; and it is very likely that a court today would come to a similar conclusion—though it is unlikely that its sentence would be so severe. Also, fellow writers and some of the greatest men of the day in other spheres did not hesitate to express their sympathy for the Hunts in the most public manner. At about the same time, Gillray and others caricatured George III and George IV with a savagery not yet attempted by any present-day cartoonist. Even *Punch*, later to become so loyal a supporter of the Monarchy as to seem almost part of it, was from the start of the paper in 1841, and well into the 1850s, an outspoken opponent of the Royal House and a severe, and often unfair, critic of the young Victoria.

Queen Elizabeth II had been on the throne for twelve years before she started to be the subject of cartoons. An early one—it may have been the first—appeared in the *New Statesman* in 1964 during the Shakespeare Festival. In this, Wally Fawkes, 'Trog', depicts the Queen yawning politely on a commemorative postage stamp of which Shakespeare and the balcony scene from *Romeo and Juliet* form the background. He was interestingly echoing precisely the kind of attack that *Punch* in its infancy used to make on Victoria and Albert, suggesting that their court was philistine and uninterested in the arts and learning.

I have noticed that this particular barb is used against the royal family less often nowadays than it used to be, although quite a few books about the Monarchy, or on various periods of the present reign, have tended to enshrine the notion that the authentic Palace sounds are the neighing of horses and the yapping of corgis, that the Queen's only leisure reading is *The Sporting Life*, and that all the pictures in the Royal Collection were bought by someone else or acquired by accident. It is an idea that, as part of the bowler-hat-and-umbrella set image of the British, occasionally filters into those parts of the French Press that seem to cater for a public convinced that culture is a commodity and that France invented it. In general, though, the British Monarchy and particularly the Queen herself, is an immensely popular subject in the French Press as well as in the Press of other Western European countries; and their editors may be assumed to know what their readers like. One of them, George Higgins (a Frenchman by blood, birth and

Foreigners were astonished at the freedom with which the British Press sometimes treated the royal family in earlier centuries. A Gillray cartoon of the Prince Regent

Press freedom in 1964 credits the Queen with an unlikely, if understandable comment as she opens Parliament

Near the end of her life, and still in love with Balmoral, Queen Victoria sat for a family photograph in the grounds. The Duke of York (later George V) is on the extreme right and his Duchess (later Queen Mary) holds their eldest son (later Edward VIII)

Sandringham grounds in the snow. The royal family usually celebrate New Year on the estate

breeding, despite the English-sounding name) has written of this with authority as a former editor of *Paris-Match* and of the mass-circulation *France-Dimanche*. He said, 'On the Continent the Queen enjoys wild and dazzling success. In France, Germany and Italy the mere fact that her photograph appears on the front of a newspaper or magazine virtually ensures its success. *France-Dimanche*, *Jours de France*, *Paris-Match*, *Stop*, *Oggi*, *Stern*, are the living proof of this. On the Continent, if a popular magazine reaches a low in circulation and its head of sales is interrogated about the best way to stop a further falling off, it is odds on that the confident reply will come: "Elizabeth".' Higgins disclosed that at one period he featured the Queen on the front page of seven successive issues of *France-Dimanche*, and gained readers with every issue.

It is a pity that in the valuable compilation, *The Monarchy and Its Future*, in which M Higgins was writing, its editor, Jeremy Murray-Brown, apparently took it for granted that anyone who cared about such matters would regard our present royal family as philistine, and simply said soothingly that this was preferable to having a court with highbrow pretensions. 'Better far a charmed circle of jockeys, punters and yachtsmen, than one of *literati* and eggheads!' Philistinism is hard to define, an abstraction that defeats dictionaries. Judging where it applies is even harder, except for those who wear naturally what Browning calls, 'that hateful smile of boundless self-conceit'. Under the heading, 'Intellectuals: It's All in the Mind', Bernard Levin, in one of his *Times* pieces, posed this problem for the man of feeling playfully but well. He wrote, 'Is Mr Benn an intellectual? Is Prince Charles? Probably yes, probably no, though don't forget that the latter plays the 'cello and the former has for years been steadily doctoring his *Who's Who* entry to conceal the fact that he had a good education. Are 'cellists, then, intellectuals, and those who affect to despise the intellect not? Or not?'

Those who feel they can draw a conclusion in spite of Levin's inability—or, more probably, reluctance—to establish a 'Levin's Law' in this important and delicate field may care to consider some possibly-relevant facts about the royal family and some of its forbears. Prince Charles does indeed play the 'cello, as well as some other instruments; he likes going to concerts, and is friendly with Rostropovitch and Yehudi Menuhin; he has, as a history graduate, published some slight historical writings which have been praised by competent judges; and he is interested in painting, having some skill as an amateur water-colourist.

Musical talent runs far back in the family, but for convenience, one might start a list of its musicians with George IV, because he, too, played a stringed instrument, the violoncello, rather well. Max Beerbohm (An intellectual? Yes? No?) also thought that George was 'a splendid patron', who 'inspired society with a love of something more than mere pleasures, a love of the "humaner delights." '

Queen Victoria was a good enough pianist to realise what was happening when Jenny Lind sang for her, and the accompanist, who was from a rival theatre, tried subtly to spoil the performance. The Queen took over the accompaniment herself with total success. It is true that one of her granddaughters once surprised the old Queen practising at the piano, and said, 'Why grandmamma, how can *you* practise now, and *what for*?' Perhaps that was a philistine question, coming from a royal child. Victoria's husband, Albert, showed talent as both a performer and a composer of music. He and Victoria could draw well, and amused themselves with etching. As a patron, he was among the first in England to be attracted to the Italian Primitives, and he acquired the Duccio Triptych, a Fra Angelico and a Gentile de Fabriano which are now important in the Royal Collection. *Punch* sneered at him; but those were the days when it also sneered at the Parthenon.

Edward VII first sponsored the series of excellent catalogues and portfolio books on the royal art collections which still continues and this was his own idea. His sister, the Princess Royal, who was later Empress Frederick of Germany, became a painter of real quality, as a young girl tackling with considerable success large, crowded pictures of historical subjects in the manner of the day, and when she was older studying problems of structure, form and light in landscapes, of a kind regarded as advanced at the time. Another of the sisters, Louise, was a sculptor who exhibited at the Royal Academy.

It has to be admitted that George V wanted to abolish the 'King's Musick', and was prevented from doing so only by Sir Edward Elgar's horrified protest. The loyal assurance of the Windsor Castle Librarian, Sir Owen Morshead, that George was 'much attached' to his pictures is not a very weighty encomium; but possibly Queen Mary's activity as a connoisseur and patron over a wide field of the arts balances her husband's deficiencies.

George VI, preoccupied by World War II and its aftermath for a large part of his relatively short reign, had little time to do much for the arts; but it was he who shortly after the War was the prime mover in the Royal Academy's Exhibition of the King's Pictures, possibly the greatest public display of royal paintings ever seen. His consort, now the Queen Mother, likes paintings, and judging by those I have seen on her walls at Clarence House, has an eclectic taste. I remember a dazzling Matthew Smith still-life, a Lowry which was not one of his usual townscapes, some Augustus John, an Ethel Walker seascape. The Queen Mother also owns pictures commissioned from John Piper. Whether it was she or George VI who said to him: 'What awfully bad weather you seem to have, Mr Piper,' or whether this was ever said at all, seems to be a matter of dispute. I have been told that she also likes the work of Edward Seago as well as that of the insufficiently-appreciated Sussex landscape painter, Claude Muncaster, a few of whose pictures hang at Clarence House, though I gather the Queen Mother has others elsewhere.

As to her daughter, Queen Elizabeth II, her activity as a patron of the arts has already provided the material for a book. She is no painter herself, but her enthusiasm for painting takes her when she can spare the time on private visits to London galleries and exhibitions and to the premises of art auctioneers on the eve of interesting sales. She is said to be knowledgeable and she buys discreetly, benefiting from the advice of the four eminent men in the world of the visual arts who hold appointments in the Royal Household which are not sinecures. At the Queen's wish, and under their direction, the Royal Collections have had more scientific expert attention than ever before. She lends pictures and other objects of art generously to exhibitions all over the country. She plays the piano very well indeed, as do the Queen Mother and Princess Margaret. They sometimes play duets when the occasion offers.

Prince Philip has notoriously said that artists think of him as 'an uncultured polo-playing clot'. But he mixes with artists, is friendly with a few—Topolski is on 'Dear Philip' terms as a correspondent—and he is attracted by the honesty and directness he finds among them. When sitting for a portrait, as he and the Queen have to do from time to time, he has been known to amuse himself drawing the painter. He is a painter himself, how good, people can judge for themselves, because some of his landscapes have been exhibited and reproduced in the newspapers.

Prince Philip keeps at Sandringham a collection of cartoons which Basil Boothroyd says are 'largely insulting'. Probably even the most ardent monarchist nowadays would be little bothered by the early cartoons about the royal family, if only because far greater liberties have been taken since by other publications than the *New Statesman*. In particular, *Private Eye* several years ago started to publish its frequent cover photographs of members of the royal family with ballooned utterances superimposed, sometimes making a valid political point—as for instance, in one of which the Queen, with an unlikely choice of phrase, disclaims authorship of the Speech from the Throne—but more often having that touch of lavatory humour which may have prompted the playwright, John Osborne, when he described *Private Eye* as 'a public school giggle'.

However, I think not even *Private Eye* among publications of the present day has gone quite as far in its treatment of royal personages as did some of the cartoonists in the days of the Georges, although it is an authentic revival of their bawdy, barnyard manner in most other respects. For example, William Heath, a political cartoonist of the first decades of the nineteenth century, could surely, were he alive today, walk straight into a job with *Private Eye* and, as Wodehouse says, 'no questions asked', although he might prefer to rival them with a magazine of his own, which he could well call *Private Parts*. This would reflect the tone of his cartoons, which were popular in the gentlemen's clubs of his day, and published close to them—as well as to the Court of St James's and Carlton House—from Panton Street, off the Haymarket, an old, away-from-Fleet Street shrine of London journalism.

Typical of Heath's *oeuvre*, and now a collector's item, is the drawing he printed in August 1820, three days after the opening in the House of Lords of what amounted to the 'trial' of Caroline of Brunswick, George IV's estranged Queen, for alleged adultery and scandalous behaviour involving her Italian chamberlain, Bergami. The case was dropped after three months had been spent on it, mostly in hearing hilarious evidence. Heath's cartoon shows two pear trees against the distant background of Windsor Castle. In one reclines the King and in the other Bergami. Queen Caroline squeezes two pears positioned in unmistakable conjunction with Bergami, and comments: 'They are more juicy than the Windsor.' Doing the same thing in relation to the King and some pears, Lady Conyngham, the companion of his riper years, puns horribly: 'How *Cunning* I am to gather the Windsor . . .' Onlookers contribute other remarks to make quite certain that the point of these subtle pleasantries is entirely clear to everyone over the age of puberty.

It is interesting to discover that at this time freedom of the Press carried to such lengths was astonishing to an American observer. The United States Minister reported, 'The most remarkable aspect of this fierce encounter was the rage of the Press and liberty of speech. Every day produced its thousand fiery libels against the King and his adherents and as many caricatures that were hawked in the streets. This tempest of abuse was borne for several months without the slightest attempt to check or punish it.'

Less than seventeen years later Queen Victoria came to the throne.

No doubt some of *Private Eye*'s little squibs about the royal family have caused offence to many; but curiously, they can have a beneficial effect in demonstrating to an often-doubting world the extent to which the Press in Britain is really free. I used to subscribe to the paper when I was the B.B.C.'s Moscow Correspondent largely so that I could leave it about to be read by the K.G.B.-sponsored translators, who are the only kind that foreign journalists are allowed to employ. One of them, evidently enraged by the fact that you can publish things about the Queen in Britain which you could not possibly publish about President Podgorny in the Soviet Union, once came to me with the current copy and threw it crossly on my desk. She said, 'We *know* this thing isn't really published in Britain. It is printed by your Government for people like us abroad to make it seem that you have freedom of the Press.' I am quite sure that she did not really believe this; but could she, perhaps, have been the first person ever to accuse *Private Eye* of belonging to the Establishment?

So far as I know, if the Palace has ever been seriously annoyed by anything that has appeared in that paper, there is no evidence of its having done anything about it, except that it possibly has helped Prince Philip to swell his cartoon collection. In my experience, the Palace is much less ready than Government ministries and Members of Parliament to complain about what appears in the Press, and seldom does much more than point out errors of fact which may have appeared in publications which it presumably regards as responsible.

This is very far from saying that the Monarchy is loftily unconcerned about the Press and the image which it presents through it. As far back as the Press has existed the Monarchy has always been interested in what it chose to print. For instance, by good fortune, we know with some precision what were Victoria's views on her relations with the Press at almost the very end of her reign of sixty-three years, and by the same means we have an insight into what one influential magazine thought was the proper way to deal with her at that time when she was regarded as the living and apparently immortal symbol of British greatness, power and empire. The magazine was *The Strand Magazine* which—to paraphrase the words of one of its later editors, Reginald Pound—was the image in print of the English middle-classes for more than half a century, 'confirming their preference for mental as well as physical comfort', and faithfully mirroring their tastes, prejudices, and intellectual limitations. These were much the same as those of the Queen herself; and from soon after its foundation in 1891, the magazine found her very approachable. She read and revised an article they submitted to her about the dolls she had played with as a child; but she deleted nothing. Her corrections were simply printed with the article in the form of footnotes. Further articles were submitted to the Queen at intervals and treated similarly. In a sense, she had become an unpaid contributor to *The Strand Magazine*, and this was very good for its circulation and advertising. In due time, the magazine's editor, George Newnes, became a baronet—for 'political services' and work 'in the cause of healthy popular literature'. The last of the articles which may be regarded as having Victoria's endorsement was written before her death, which was in January 1901, submitted to Court, returned with some deletions, and published in April 1901. A reproduction of her signature appears at the end of it, but the precise significance of that is not made clear.

About Victoria's relations with the Press, the article says that she had portions of *The Times* and other newspapers read to her daily after breakfast, seldom made any comment on reports about public or political affairs, but would express sympathy or grief about bereavement or calamity. Illustrated papers 'afforded her much amusement'. But she was 'annoyed if any inaccuracies appeared in the papers concerning herself or her family'. The article says, 'The Queen never undervalued the influence of the Press, and like her husband, Prince Albert, who was of opinion that "a really good article did untold good," she attached due importance to the power of journalism. Of "Society" papers with a scandalous gossiping tendency she had a perfect horror.'

Plenty of cartoons had been drawn of Victoria, but as her reign progressed, they became increasingly decorous; so that in 1900, *The Strand Magazine*, in spite of its sensitivity to her opinion, was able without qualms to bring out a twelve-page article, called 'The Queen in "Punch"; 1841-1899', which reproduced forty-two cartoons of her, none of which could possibly have caused her offence.

By now there was a whole world of respectable, positively fashionable cartoonists. Most of the critical bite and all the vulgarity had gone out of the business, and there were men to whom members of the royal family would sit to be cartooned. As Prince of Wales, Edward VII, at a time of life when he knew that he was fat, sat to Leslie Ward, the famous 'Spy', as he signed himself, and warned him, 'Now let me down gently.' Ward, ever tactful, said: 'Oh, but you've a very fine chest, sir.' Looking back through the files, it seems that it was all right to poke fairly gentle fun at foreign royalties, and by 1905, you could already be pretty rude about Kaiser Bill.

Journalism and the status of the journalist had come a long way since the start of Victoria's reign. It is well enough known that it was during this period that the 'popular' Press came into existence with the wider spread of literacy and more efficient methods of printing and distribution. It was probably not quite so generally understood that all this was accompanied by a greater appreciation of the power of the Press by those who managed the country's affairs, and that this led to their accepting socially those who wielded this new power. In the 1830s it is possible to detect in the work of a good many writers of ability resentment of the fact that they were not yet so accepted. For instance, Thackeray, Dickens and Albert Smith—all of them journalists before they were novelists—frequently convey the impression that they have suffered from a sense of inferiority. Robert Graves, in the Foreword to his *The Real David Copperfield*, makes a good deal of the effect on Dickens of 'the gentleman-obsession which, first formed at the age of ten, seems to have become the ruling element in his life. . . .' The atmosphere that was so much resented is conveyed very well in something written by the Editor of the *Spectator*, Stephen Rintoul, in 1831. 'The tone in which newspapers are usually mentioned in the House of Commons is absurd. Men who cannot breakfast without one, in the evening pretend to be hardly cognizant of the existence of such things. Men who in private life look to them almost for their sole stock of opinions, are found in public sneering at their contents. . . . Newspapers are far above the contempt of Members of Parliament in ability, and in power are scarcely beneath the Honourable House itself.' Trollope's political novels demonstrate the manner in which all this gradually changed. The attitude towards the Press that Victoria allowed herself to be credited with at the end of her reign, and which she also demonstrated practically, was one she would have been unlikely to hold when she was first on the throne. The Queen had changed because the times had changed. What would nowadays be called 'the Establishment' had put into operation its own very English variant of an American formula, and in relation to the Press it was saying in effect, 'If we can't lick 'em, let 'em *join us*!' As a result, much of the Press —including *The Times*; the Queen's old enemy, *Punch*; and her new friend, *The Strand Magazine*—had become, to quote Reginald Pound again, 'as much a symbol of immutable British order as Bank Holidays and the Changing of the Guard'. This is not at all a bad thing if the order has its own integrity, as it has had in Britain on the whole. Such change typifies a civilised process which is always better than revolution; for revolutions usually make things worse before they get better and frequently create conditions that are lastingly retrograde.

The British Monarchy, then, changes with the times in its attitude to the Press as in many other things, even if, for long periods, it proceeds just a step or so behind. It is possible that the progress might have been faster had Edward VIII not abdicated; for bringing the Monarchy closer to the people was a cause that appealed to his temperament while he was still Prince of Wales; and of course, the Press—the 'media' as we say nowadays, so as to include sound radio and television—would have been important to him had he sought seriously to promote this as King. Lady Longford calls him 'the first royal communicator', and heads her chapter about him with those words. Whether or not he had a real understanding of what was to be communicated is open to question; for as she makes clear, he seemed unable to distinguish between the deference paid to royal office and a purely personal popularity. When he was told as Prince of Wales that he had become 'too accessible', he said: 'I do not agree. Times are changing.' Trying to guess what would have happened to the Monarchy had he remained on the throne is a fascinating game to play, but it can provide no sure answers. But did he, as Lady Astor told him he would, when he was Prince of Wales, make the way easier for his successors?

A mechanism for the dealings of the Palace with the Press had been evolving even in Victoria's day. Principally it concerned itself with the important but uncomplicated matter of giving out news about royal activities; and this was done in the main through the relationship established between Court officials and the Court Correspondents, accredited to the Palace, of the then two domestic news agencies, the Press Association and the Exchange Telegraph. Today, that is still the basis of the system, except that only one agency, the Press Association, remains, and the Queen employs as her Press Secretary, and a member of the Household, a journalist widely experienced in newspaper work as well as in radio and television. There are two Assistant Press Secretaries, one of them usually from a Commonwealth country, and three other members of the Press staff.

It is difficult to see how, in the days of the mass media, an institution as much in the news as is the Monarchy could deal with the demands of the Press without some such organisation. Of course, there are elderly journalists who recall, in relation not to the Palace alone, 'the days when there was no such thing as a Press Officer, and you could make a direct approach to the person you wanted'. It is true that such direct approaches did sometimes pay off. One of the most striking instances of this is recounted by Sir Philip Gibbs, writing (in *The Journalists' London*) about George Smith—'Royal' Smith, as he was called—who was the Court Correspondent of the Press Association for thirty-three years from 1894. Sir Philip Gibbs says that when the Boer War ended, Smith went to Windsor to collect the proclamation he felt sure Edward VII would make to his people; and he asked the King's Secretary, Lord Knollys, about it, only to be told rather stiffly that it had not occurred to the King to compose such a message, and anyway, he was out in Windsor Great Park and likely to return late. Smith said he would wait. While he did so—for some hours—he amused himself by drafting the kind of Royal Proclamation he thought would be suitable, and eventually persuaded a reluctant Lord Knollys to submit it to the King. After an interval it came back with a few small changes; but it had been signed, 'Edward, R.I.'

Perhaps the existence of an organised Press Office at the Palace nowadays will make it impossible for either of the two Court Correspondents at present accredited there—Douglas Dumbrell, for the Press Association, and myself, for the B.B.C. —ever to be able to claim the distinction of having personally drafted a Royal Proclamation; but I think that in similar circumstances we would also have been spared the wait of some hours that 'Royal' Smith experienced. The Palace Press Office is as efficient and useful as anything of the kind I have ever encountered and better than most. Members of the Queen's Household have not been made less helpful and approachable because the Press Office exists; on the contrary, it acts as an excellent and courteous intermediary. Its task is, of course, much larger and more complex than the mere giving out of news in London. To give an example, before Princess Anne's wedding in 1973, the Press Office had to undertake a great deal of rapid but thorough organising to meet the complex needs of the vast hosts from the Press, sound radio and television, foreign as well as British, who would be descending on London on 14th November. Without imaginative planning and split-second timing the media could produce chaos on that day, instead of the smooth but eye-catching British pageantry that was expected by many millions of television viewers, a world-wide radio audience listening to reports and commentaries in forty languages, and uncountable readers of newspapers.

I went to one of the Palace's planning meetings. Fifty or so people sat round a table in a pleasantly-Gothic room in the precincts of Westminster Abbey; it was in fact the immensely-historic Jerusalem Chamber, said to be named after some tapestries depicting the history of Jerusalem which once hung there. Shakespeare mentions this room. Henry IV was carried there after he collapsed while praying at the Shrine of Edward the Confessor before his intended departure for the last of the Crusades. When he asked where he had been brought, he was told, 'To the Chamber called Jerusalem.' He said: 'Laud then be to the father of Heaven. Now I know that that shall come true which hath been prophesied of me that I shall die in Jerusalem,' or as Shakespeare put it later:

> But bear me to that Chamber,
> There I'll lie; in that Jerusalem shall Harry die.

I rather enjoyed the continuity by which the twentieth century brought to such a place a group of people who embodied —and in some cases looked as if they did—some of the most bizarre developments of that century, the men from the media; for what could be at the same time more incongruous and more right than that they should meet there to plan their part in the wedding celebrations of a young princess of so ancient a line?

Also present were officials of the Household, demonstrating an entirely twentieth-century grasp of organisational problems; people from the Department of the Environment; representatives of the local authorities in whose area the wedding processions would take place; high-ranking police officers; someone to speak for everybody likely to be concerned. The Queen's Press Secretary was in the chair.

It was not their first meeting, and they were simply trying to tie up loose ends. But some of the questions they posed, and answered, give an idea of the amount of detail that has to be taken into account when planning a royal, national occasion. How could those who wanted to do so get a look at the royal glass coach at a time when it was in fact up in Edinburgh, dismantled and being gone over by craftsmen to get it ready for the wedding? In precisely what places did regulations require that drapery used on stands must be fire-proof? How much extra did that cost? Who was going to be required to pay for it? Where might motor-cycle dispatch riders position themselves in the Abbey precincts to take film from the cameramen inside, while causing the minimum disturbance and threat to security? What complex system of passes could be arranged to satisfy the police that Press people going into the Abbey were the right people, during a period when, because of the Irish troubles, security was of major importance all over London? Where and how would the wedding presents be put on show so that all the world could know what they looked like? Who, in what circumstances, could get a glimpse of the wedding breakfast scene? Everyone present, and not least the people from the Palace Press Office, demonstrated a lively conviction that all these matters were of interest and importance to millions.

It was all a rather remarkable demonstration of the Palace's being very much abreast of the times, while the coming events that were the core of this activity were the celebrations of a sacrament as old as Christianity, the panoply of an ancient royal house and an ancient kingdom, something that was not of these times but yet not out of-date, amenable to these times but in essence timeless.

Much the same kind of organisational grasp and efficiency has to be demonstrated by the Palace to a greater or lesser degree several times during the year, often in a number of different countries and over several days or weeks, for example, when the Queen, or another member of the royal family, or several members together, undertake a foreign official tour, or when there is a State visit to this country by some foreign Head of State. The Press Office is indispensable on such occasions.

Perhaps, then, it is the times, and the irrefutable demands of the times, that have brought about those changes in the style of the Palace that some writers have seen—with much exaggeration, in my view—as a kind of royal descent into the market place and a piece of deliberate policy. Bernard Levin, with thought and wit as always, seems to share the opinion of these writers. In his book about the Sixties, *The Pendulum Years*, he says: '. . . the royal family abruptly decided to give themselves a new public image, more in tune with the decade. . .' He notes that 'suddenly, from, roughly, the moment that the formal investiture of the heir-apparent as Prince of Wales was decided upon, a torrent of intimate and authorized publicity about the royal family began to pour out'. Well, this did happen; but I am not at all convinced that it was because of some abrupt decision by the royal family to create a new image. Surely the Palace was simply responding to an increased demand by publishers for books that they thought the public might want to read because of the Investiture—in just the same way that publishers have commissioned books to appear in the Jubilee year, such as this one.

I do not think it remarkable that at about this time there appeared a full-length television documentary on the lives of the royal family 'which, a full year in the making, portrayed them with an intimacy never before attained except in the unreliable below-stairs gossip that had been peddled for so long'. I do not think it 'perhaps more remarkable still' that the Duke of Edinburgh and Prince Charles gave direct television interviews preceding and following the documentary film. All this had to be done at some time; for no doubt the Palace thought, as Mr Levin clearly does, and I do, that 'unreliable below-stairs gossip' is a bad thing. What better time to do it than when greater attention was going to be focused on the Monarchy because of Prince Charles's Investiture?

I doubt, too, if there is any truth in the idea that following these broadcasts, the royal family drew back in fright, earnestly advised that the divinity that doth hedge a king disappears when the public gets too close to him. I do not agree for one moment that 'the symbol of the decade's end', as far as royalty was concerned, 'was the Queen's decision, at the time of the last Christmas of the Sixties, to dispense with the Monarch's annual broadcast to the nation, a tradition which had been unbroken, in peace or in war, since it was first instituted by George V in 1932.' As a matter of cold fact, Prince Philip explained that the broadcast was being given a miss only for that year, which had already seen the royal family film and the Caernarvon Investiture. That seems reasonable to me. There have been regular Christmas broadcasts since, some of them quite elaborate. The Duke of Edinburgh has appeared on television, just as he had in the past, long before this period that Mr Levin sees as so crucial. Prince Charles has appeared several times, with great success. Just recently—as I write this—B.B.C. television crews have been swarming all over Buckingham Palace making a film about the Royal Collection. Here we are, well into the Seventies, the 'pendulum years' tucked behind us, and still 'no serious republican movement' has arisen, and there are some of us who do not see in sight even yet 'a real possibility that the Monarchy might one day wither away'.

With all these abrupt decisions, and indecisions, and earnest warnings, Mr Levin makes the Palace much more exciting than I have found it, almost sinister. It seems to me an interesting place, sometimes an amusing place, occasionally an impressive place; but exciting?—well, let us say that I have covered more dangerous stories. There is no one behind the arras.

In the meantime the Queen and the Duke are doing their best to be friendly to the Press, and even if they have scars from the way it has treated them and their family in the past, they are not letting them show. One of the jolliest royal occasions I have reported for years was the visit they paid to Fleet Street in February 1976. The late Lord Beaverbrook would have been interested in their paying their first call at Beaverbrook Newspapers, from which he directed much fulmination against the Palace in the past. They were also at the *Daily Mail* and *Evening News* offices, at the *Daily Telegraph* and the *Sunday Telegraph*—where they attended a planning conference, and even made some polite suggestions—and at the *Mirror* group of newspapers. It was pleasant to see some of the reputedly hard-boiled ladies of Fleet Street as much in a delighted frenzy over the visit as were the girls pushing the tea-trolleys.

It is perfectly true, of course, that as Elizabeth Longford says, 'our Royal Family have been dissected' at the hands of writers 'with a freedom that was conceded only to cartoonists during the last century'. I agree with her that, on the whole, this is an advantage, but that also, 'the more royalty can speak for themselves the better'. They have, indeed, started speaking for themselves. They are a little late in doing so; but as I have already suggested, the Monarchy, although changing with the times, tends to be a step or so behind them. The politicians—trust them!—got in on the act much earlier, but have not, I think, made as good a showing.

From its early days, television has felt itself obliged, because it is a visual medium, to bring the viewer, in its news and current affairs programmes, the actual event, the actual person. The journalist, the intermediary, who in newspaper journalism reports, selects, relates, describes and analyses, is subordinate to this need. 'Let the man speak for himself' seems, superficially, the most honest policy. Politicians learned very quickly that this was greatly in their favour. When the amount of viewing time that can be devoted to a given topic is small, as in a news bulletin, and a government minister concerned knows that the nature of the medium requires him to be given a large part of it, he soon learns how to use that to his best advantage; to stress those aspects that are most favourable to his case; with any luck, to run out of time before much, if anything, can be said about other aspects.

The interview, obviously, is the basis of this kind of television. It is very time consuming. It is also capable in the long run of discrediting politicians. In the fullness of time, people can, for example, come to recognise 'old so-and-so, who never looks as if he means what he says', 'old such-and-such, who always dodges the question', 'old this-and-that, who is always so bloody patronising'. I believe this is already happening, and that it may have a lot to do with the reports that, increasingly, politicians and their politics are held in disrepute among the ordinary people of Britain. I am not suggesting that if this is really happening, it is necessarily a good thing. I am inclined to agree that it may also be very unfair to individuals; for an honest man should not in justice be blamed if he has the misfortune to look and talk like a rogue, but he probably will be. So coming down into the market place on television and radio may in the long run prove to have damaged the credibility of politicians. But if all this is true for politicians, might it not be true also for the royal family? In my view, it need not be so, and so far, is not so.

That verse of the National Anthem which no one ever remembers or sings says:

> Confound their politicks,
> Frustrate their knavish tricks. . .

So much for the politicians. Of the Sovereign, the next verse says:

> May she defend our laws. . .

The anthem sees the elected representatives of the people as a tricky, politicking lot. The Sovereign, above politics, is seen as the defender of the people's laws. But the defender against whom? Well, it is not impossible to visualise a situation in which the answer could be: 'Against a particularly tricky, politicking and knavish lot of ministers who were seeking to violate or misuse the laws, the Constitution.' The politicians can be regarded, then, as coming into the market place on radio and television to hawk their wares, and *caveat emptor*! The Sovereign, and those close to her, are not selling anything at all, but using a modern means to carry out the ancient duty of showing themselves to the people, demonstrating that the Sovereign is there—above politics and to defend the laws, not power in herself, but the symbol of the power of the people. The Monarchy has not, in my opinion, lost anything by being brought closer to the people in this way. It is keeping up with the times, reminding the people in a modern way that it is still there to serve them. Nevertheless, the question of publicity is —as Sir Harold Nicolson has pointed out—one of the most difficult problems that assails parliamentary kingship in the present age. 'Too much publicity,' he says, 'will stain the mystery, even the dignity, of the Crown. Too little publicity will be regarded as undemocratic and will render the gulf that yawns between the sovereign and the ordinary subject an unfortunate barrier rather than a necessity of segregation.' Sir Harold concludes: 'I am grateful to destiny that I have not been chosen as public relations officer to Buckingham Palace, which is in truth a nightmare task.'

10. Royal Progress

'Britain may not be a super-power compared with America or Russia, but we offer the rest of the world an example of achievement through the character of the British people. So long as this is true, we shall have that self-confidence which earns us the respect of the rest of the world.' That was said in 1969 by Mr Edward Heath, who was then the Conservative Prime Minister. He was boasting. At about the same time, Mr Kenneth Tynan said, 'England is a much more perverse and decadent country than the United States.' He was boasting, too.

The common ground in these two statements by two very different characters is an apparent assumption that, whatever else may be said about them, the British are always interesting enough to merit study by other countries and comparison with the greatest of them. If this was true in the past, there is very little truth in it today.

British perversity and decadence add up simply to the routine 'permissive' apparatus that is to be found nowadays in the larger cities of most developed countries of the Western world, and a continental Christopher Isherwood would be no more likely to find the authentic essence of Sally Bowles and Mr Norris in London than he would in Lisieux or Lourdes. But unhappily he would be able to find plenty of testimony to the existence of many of the corroding economic uncertainties and certainties which made possible that half-world of Berlin in the early Thirties which Isherwood found so fascinating—the effects of inflation, too high a level of unemployment, lack of success in trade, waning confidence, fear of the future. We are not today, as Mr Heath suggested that we were in 1969, offering the rest of the world 'an example of achievement through the character of the British people'; and if anything still makes us interesting to those beyond our own shores, it is not the economic struggle that has been the core of our existence as a nation since the end of World War Two. Most foreigners think the British have been stupid and lazy about their troubles, and for a long time—perhaps since as long ago as 1969—they have found us in this context faintly comic but on the whole boring.

In spite of all this, there are still some things about Britain that continue to attract the interest and attention, even sometimes the admiration, of other peoples. For example, although our political prestige in international affairs has undoubtedly declined greatly, British ministers and diplomats still have an influence which is out of proportion to the reality of British power. This is because we still benefit to some extent from credit won in the relatively recent times when we were truly one of the world's great powers. The workings of the British parliamentary system can yet excite some admiration, although observant foreigners will have noted the fears of some in Britain that the trades unions threaten to usurp its function, and Lord Hailsham's more sophisticated theory that what we have now is really an elective dictatorship. The continued British inventiveness and creativity in the sciences and the arts, especially in the theatre, are highly regarded abroad. A certain air of relaxation about the present British way of living can be envied by some visitors, though more would probably detect in it today a symptom of national fatigue and loss of drive. Interestingly, the one essentially British institution which is almost unreservedly admired by people in other countries, and especially by those well informed, is the Monarchy. It is seen partly, of course, in a romantic light, surrounded by all the glitter and fun of ceremonial and tradition. But it is also seen—if one may judge from articles in a great many magazines and newspapers abroad—as being, perhaps, itself the most stable institution in British life, able to communicate some of its own stability to the nation, and yet, at the same time, presenting no barrier or discouragement to social reform and economic change, capable itself of adapting to change and changing times without any loss of its essential quality and function.

This is how the Monarchy appears also to many responsible and thinking people in Britain itself, and they most certainly outweigh in numbers those equally articulate among whom it is the fashion to regard it as outmoded, useless, and for them, not even decorative. The small number of outspoken opponents of the Monarchy agree that, to their regret, it still commands the affection, loyalty and interest of the great body of ordinary British people. Few would dispute the contention that there is little demand for a republic, and many would admit that events in a number of countries suggest that a republic offers fewer guarantees of freedom, justice, protection and well-being for the individual than does the kind of monarchy we have in Britain.

That all this is so says a great deal, of course, for the character and ability, as well as the integrity, of those individuals who constitute the Monarchy, and particularly the Monarch herself. The British people have now had a long time in which to formulate their feelings about their Queen; for she has been a reigning monarch for more than half her life. Two of her children are now older than she was when she came to the throne. Having achieved the age of fifty very gracefully, the Queen is still an attractive woman, and the famous smile she inherited from her mother warms and dazzles no less than when she was the pretty girl who took up the burden of Monarchy in 1952.

After the euphoria of the early years of the reign, a spirit of criticism of the Monarchy made itself felt at various times; and though it did not at any time reflect widespread feeling in the country, it made a real impact, and this was, perhaps, exaggerated in the Press because the Monarchy is always a good story, but a better story when it is criticised than when it is praised—at least, this seems to be the line of commercial reasoning followed by much of Fleet Street.

The peak period for picking holes in the Monarchy came when the Queen had been on the throne about five years, in the summer of 1957. Looking back on that year, it is hard to see just what the Monarchy might have done, if it did anything, to provoke attack. The Queen and the Duke of Edinburgh did quite a bit of travelling, with visits to France and Denmark, which caused no trouble, and one to Lisbon which caused some. As I have already described, a visit to Canada produced some antagonism there. No one seems to have been bothered by the announcement in February of the Queen's decision to grant the style of Prince to the Duke of Edinburgh, so that he would henceforth be known as Prince Philip, Duke of Edinburgh; and there could surely have been no general dismay about the ending of the Queen's Bounty of £3 for triplets, even though it had been running since 1849. For the first time, the Queen made her Christmas broadcast over television as well as radio, but the minor storm had broken before that.

Mr John Grigg, the political journalist, who was then Lord Altrincham, seems to have been the main cause of the bother through an article he wrote in the *National and English Review*. What he criticised was not Monarchy itself—which he supports—but the way he thought it worked in practice at that time. In fact, a great many other supporters of Monarchy would have thought then that a good number of the points he made were valid. As the saying goes, it wasn't so much what he said as the way that he said it. He disliked the manner in which the Queen spoke in public; and some people, though not all, would have agreed with him. But some kindly and more helpful phrase than 'a pain in the neck' might have been recommended by a kindlier critic and would have kept the blood pressures steadier in Cheltenham. Equally, although it was easy to quarrel with the wording of the Queen's speeches, it was certainly using the sledge-hammer to say as he did, 'The personality conveyed by the utterances which are put into her mouth is that of a priggish schoolgirl, captain of the hockey team, a prefect, and a recent candidate for Confirmation.' He also made a number of suggestions for improvements in the style of the Monarchy. Many of them were undeniably sound, and though no doubt he was unaware of this, some of them—such as the abolition of the debutantes' presentations—were already being carried out.

The Press swooped on the unfortunate Lord Altrincham like piranha fish. 'Lord Altrincham's Crime' was the headline of one literary sub-editor. Reporters dogged his footsteps. One furious monarchist threatened to horse-whip him. The really unfortunate result of the whole affair was that a number of other magazines took up a theme that seemed to them to attract readers, but some of them were unjust in their allegations as well as abusive in their choice of phrases.

It is all history now; but something else that Lord Altrincham wrote remains worth quoting, because it is still relevant. He said, 'The basic virtue of Monarchy is that it appeals to the imagination. It emphasises the unity of the living with the living, of the living with the dead, and of the living with those yet unborn; for tradition reaches forwards as well as backwards. Thus, when we cheer the calm, dignified, serious and self-improving young woman who is now the Head of the Commonwealth . . . all citizens of the Commonwealth can share the excitement of creating a common tradition for the future; and in that process of creation Elizabeth of Windsor is the central figure. She deserves the thoughtful support of all who are not swept off their feet by republican slogans; who see in Monarchy a form of government at once more ancient and more modern, more colourful and more practical, more romantic and—without prejudice to hard-won liberties—more dynamic than a republic can ever hope to be.'

In his criticisms, Lord Altrincham was urging in essence that the Monarchy to fulfil its task fully must change with the changing times. It is, in fact, the greatest virtue of the British Monarchy that it has been able to do this and survive. During and after World War I, most of the other European monarchies disappeared largely because they did not change. It is interesting that in the days when all monarchies were despotic, the idea of constitutional monarchy, though without that name, was visualised by one of the greatest of the scholastic theologians, the 'angelic doctor', Thomas Aquinas. F. C. Copleston, the English Jesuit philosopher, says of Aquinas in his book about him, 'What is certain, however, is that though he did not regard any particular form of government as divinely ordained for all men, and though he did not attach primary importance to the form of constitution and government, he gave the palm to a "mixed" constitution in which the principle of unity, represented by monarchy, is combined with the principle of administration by the best and with some measure of popular control, as, for example, by the people electing certain magistrates. Aquinas thought that monarchy is most conducive to unity and that it is the most "natural" form of government, possessing analogies with God's rule over creation and with government in communities of insects like bees. But at the same time the constitution should be such that the likelihood of tyrants arising or of rulers acting tyrannically is diminished as far as possible. So we can say, if we like to use modern terms, that Aquinas favoured constitutional monarchy.'

No doubt we know more now than Aquinas did in the thirteenth century about the habits of bees and other insects, and may not be particularly anxious to copy them; but generally his formula for good government does have a striking resemblance to what the British monarchical system has become as the result of trial and error, war and revolution, one flirtation with a kind of republican dictatorship, and gradual change over the centuries.

As I have said in previous chapters, there is no great movement towards republicanism in Britain; and where there has been criticism of the Monarchy it has been concerned with the manner in which it operates rather than with its value as an institution. Even more, it has been concerned with personalities. In the course of diverse reading about the British Monarchy, some of it exceedingly tiresome, I have come to the sad conclusion that what might be called 'middle-of-the-road' monarchists are either very few or distressingly inarticulate. Almost all that is written about Monarchy these days, apart from occasional editorials when it is in the news because of some constitutional matter, appears to come from extremists who, obsessively fascinated by it, either hate it or adore it in a manner that sometimes seems, to say the least, intemperate.

Outstanding among the haters is, of course, Mr Willie Hamilton, whose book, *My Queen and I*, gained considerable notoriety, although, whatever may have been its intention, it supplied little ammunition for those who might wish to attack constitutional Monarchy as a system, and seemed to many reviewers to be mainly yet another expression of the author's already well-known distaste for various members of the present royal family.

So long as it has enemies like Mr Hamilton, the Monarchy is not desperately in need of support from friends. Indeed, I fear it is ill-served by some of its more ecstatic partisans, particularly some of the ladies of Fleet Street, writing on royal occasions as if they were about to swoon with excitement, even though they sometimes give us little gems to treasure, as did the lady in the *Daily Express*, who said when Princess Anne's engagement was announced, 'She's shied away, backed off, and reared up when we mentioned Mark Phillips's name. She's bared those big beautiful white teeth at any suggestion of a love affair . . . Then tonight Anne comes blushing down the straight to announce that it's ON.'

After that kind of thing, and Mr Hamilton, it is a refreshment to look back upon the dispassionate analysis of Bagehot, or to read, among modern writers on the Monarchy, the English common-sense of J. B. Priestley and the anxious, but clear-eyed, scholarship of Harold Nicolson.

Noting that during the quarter of a century that King George V reigned five Emperors, eight Kings and eighteen minor dynasties disappeared, while the British Monarchy emerged more firmly established, Nicolson says that this stability was not due solely to King George's straightforwardness and wisdom, but also to 'the elasticity of our constitution, to the capacity possessed by this ill-defined assortment of laws, customs and conventions to adjust itself, without strain or rupture, to fundamentally altered conditions'.

Fitting this English capacity to cope with change into his general contention, about which he is far from complacent, that the secret of Englishness is to be reasonable rather than rational, taking into account what is instinctive and intuitive as well as the dictates of despotic intellect, J. B. Priestley (in *The English*) considers the Monarchy thus: 'It is restored after the Civil War and the Protectorate, but without any pretensions to divine rights, with monarchs more or less being tried on as if they were hats.' Then he describes what he calls 'irrationality triumphant' in the bringing from Hanover of George I, who knows no English, and so cannot attend Cabinet meetings, and is a King 'reigning in bewilderment, wondering what his subjects are saying'. Priestley concludes, 'It seems utterly ridiculous. Yet we know that the stature of this nation is now immensely enlarged in the minds of men of sense and goodwill everywhere, and that for several decades London is the Mecca of the new Enlightenment. Rationality, a logical scheme of things, a clear-cut intellectual system, may have vanished from the English scene, but with this victory of the reasonable the possibility of civilised government, with some guarantee of individual liberty, came closer to the whole Western world. It owes an enormous debt to Englishness.'

The British Monarchy is seen then as the achievement through acceptance of change, of something which may not seem always logical and rational, but is reasonable because it manifestly works. Emotion does not have to enter into it, nor even that 'magic' of the Monarchy, Bagehot's 'nice and pretty events' which sweeten politics for the mass of the people. In this connection it is interesting to read the diary note of Nicolson, written on 17th January 1950, while he was working on his official biography of George V. He said, 'I fear I have no mystic feeling about the Monarchy. I regard it merely as a useful institution.'

Why does the Monarchy work? For Bagehot its value seems to have been chiefly in the fact that it prevented the people in political power—the Government of the day—from having in their own ranks the Head of State, and from seeking to introduce their own nominee into that position. There is clear advantage in having as the person who holds the ring, 'the referee', in Mr Nicholas Ridley's words, someone who is above party politics, and who can clearly be seen to represent not just those who have been elected into power, but the whole nation. Consideration of this provides a large part of the answer to the question which is often asked: If we abandoned the Monarchy, what better could we devise to put in its place? It seems to me, as to many others, to invalidate the notion that some kind of elected or nominated figure-head President would be either more rational or more reasonable for a country such as Britain. In addition, no such person could personify, as does a monarch, the nation both in its past and in its present. For many, even in a post-Christian Britain, there is a lingering, if not entirely conscious, awareness that Monarchy is a holy mystery, that the Sovereign's crowning is a consecration, that a Christian monarch is Christ's deputy, and that Elizabeth II is what her Proclamation stated her to be, Queen by the grace of God.

Nicolson says that in 'limited' or 'constitutional' Monarchy, the British people, with their political aptitudes and their congenital dislike of all logical extremes, developed by compromises a system which, without any rupture of continuity, was sufficiently elastic to admit of recurrent change. The changes that we have seen in the first twenty-five years of Elizabeth II's reign have been carried out without disturbance of that continuity, or of the cohesion, permanence and stability which are among the Monarchy's most vital contributions to the British system of government. They continue a process, a royal progress in another sense, which was already apparent when Victoria celebrated her great Diamond Jubilee, and some of this has been reflected in the foregoing chapters.

When Edward VII succeeded Victoria in 1901, Bagehot's statement of the rights and duties of the Sovereign was thirty-four years old and required reading for the Duke of York, studying to become a king. The power of the people was no longer something that the Monarch merely acquiesced in, but something he embodied and defended. King George V, in character and training a man of the Victorian age, eased the first Labour Government into office. Clement Attlee, who became leader of the Labour Party in George V's Jubilee year, described the King as 'a rallying point of stability' and a focus for 'sympathy with new ideas'. He said, 'He knew and understood his people and the age in which they lived, and progressed with them.'

George VI, when he came to the throne after his brother's brief reign and abdication, observed his constitutional position scrupulously during the years that he was on the throne in times clouded by war and the changes brought about by war. It has been said that in him the nation found the image of the way of life for which it was fighting. In his reign, the Monarchy survived the immense change which made him the last British Sovereign to be Emperor of India and the first to have the title of Head of the Commonwealth, the symbol of association in a body all of whose members did not owe him allegiance.

Queen Elizabeth has accepted change and also instigated change, altering nothing of the essence of the Monarchy, but formulating a new style that accepts the demands of a new age. Her husband, the Duke of Edinburgh, has said that voluntary change is the life-blood of the crown. Prince Charles has been educated in a manner calculated to bring him closer to the life of the people than any previous Heir Apparent. Britain has at the head of its national life something that many not so long ago might have thought a contradiction in terms, a modern Monarchy. All the indications are that the great mass of the British people accept it and support it far more fully, perhaps, than they understand it. Their cheers for their Queen in her Jubilee year will be just as enthusiastic and heartfelt as were those for Victoria and George V, and there will be conviction in the cries of, 'God Save the Queen!'

Select List of Sources Consulted

The following list contains sources mentioned or quoted in the text or others to which the author feels greatly indebted; it does not attempt to include all the large number of books and periodicals that he consulted in writing the book.

ALEXANDRA, H.M. Queen Alexandra of Jugoslavia. *Prince Philip* (1960)

ARTHUR, Sir George. *Queen Alexandra* (1934)

AVON, EARL OF (Sir Anthony Eden) *Full Circle* (1960); *Facing the Dictators* (1962)

BAGEHOT, Walter. *The English Constitution* (2nd edition with additional chapter, 1872)

BARNETT, Correlli. *The Collapse of British Power* (1972)

BATTISCOMBE, Georgina. *Queen Alexandra* (1969)

BENSON, E. F. *King Edward VII: An Appreciation* (1933); *Queen Victoria* (1935)

BENTLEY, Nicolas. *The Victorian Scene 1837–1901* (1968)

BERE, Brigadier Ivan de la. *The Queen's Orders of Chivalry* (1961)

BLYTHE, Ronald. *The Age of Illusion: England in the Twenties and Thirties 1919–1940* (1963)

BOLITHO, Hector. *Albert the Good* (1932); *King Edward VII, His Life and Reign* (1937); *The Romance of Windsor Castle* (1946)

BOOTHROYD, Basil. *Philip—An Informal Biography* (1971)

BOWLE, John. *The English Experience: A Survey of English History from Early to Modern Times* (1971)

BROWN, Ivor. Balmoral The History of a Home (1955)

CAMPBELL, Judith. *Anne: Portrait of a Princess* (1970); *Elizabeth and Philip* (1972)

CATHCART, Helen. *Her Majesty* (1962); *The Married Life of the Queen* (1970)

CLARK, Brigadier Stanley. *Palace Diary* (1958)
COLE, G. D. H. and POSTGATE, R. *The Common People 1746–1946* (1938)
COLLIER, John, and LANG, Iain. *Just the Other Day; An Informal History of Great Britain Since the War* (1932)
COWLES, Virginia. *Edward VII and His Circle* (1956)
CRAWFORD, Marion. *The Little Princesses* (1950); *Queen Elizabeth II* (1952)
DENT, H. C. (Editor). *Milestones to the Silver Jubilee: A Diary of the Nation* (1935)
DUFF, David. *Mother of the Queen: The Life Story of Her Majesty Queen Elizabeth the Queen Mother* (1965)
DUNCAN, Andrew. *The Reality of Monarchy* (1970)
FISHER, Graham and Heather. *Elizabeth Queen and Mother* (1964)
FLETCHER, Ifan Kyrle. *The British Court, Its Traditions and Ceremonial* (1953)
FULFORD, Roger. *George IV* (1939)
GIBBS, Sir Philip (Editor). *The Book of the King's Jubilee* (1935)
GORE, John. *King George V: A Personal Memoir* (1941)
GORST, Frederick John (with ANDREWS, Beth). *Of Carriages and Kings* (1941)
GRAEME, Bruce. *The Story of Buckingham Palace* (revised edition, 1970)
GRAVES, Robert, and HODGE, Alan. *The Long Week-End: A Social History of Great Britain 1918–1939* (1941)
HAMILTON, Willie. *My Queen and I* (1975)
HEDLEY, Olwen. *Windsor Castle* (1967); *Royal Palaces: An Account of the Homes of British Sovereigns from Saxon to Modern Times* (1972)
HIBBERT, Christopher. *The Court at Windsor: A Domestic History* (1964)
His Majesty's Speeches: The Record of the Silver Jubilee of His Most Gracious Majesty King George V (1935)
HOPKINS, Harry. *The New Look: A Social History of the Forties and Fifties in Britain* (1963)
HYDE, Douglas. *I Believed: The Autobiography of a Former British Communist* (1950)
INGRAMS, Richard (Editor). *The Life and Times of 'Private Eye'* (1971)
JENKINS, Alan. *The Twenties* (1974)

JENNINGS, Sir Ivor. *The Queen's Government* (1960)
JUDD, Denis. *George V* (1973); *The House of Windsor* (1973); *Eclipse of Kings: European Monarchies in the Twentieth Century* (1976)
LAIRD, Dorothy. *How the Queen Reigns: An Authentic Study of the Queen's Personality and Life Work* (1959); *Queen Elizabeth the Queen Mother and Her Support to the Throne During Four Reigns* (revised edition, 1975)
LEE, Sydney. *Queen Victoria: A Biography* (1902)
LESLIE, Anita. *Mrs FitzHerbert* (1960)
LESLIE, Doris. *The Great Corinthian* (1952)
LEVIN, Bernard. *The Pendulum Years, Britain and the Sixties* (1970)
LONGFORD, Elizabeth. *Victoria R. I.* (1964); *The Royal House of Windsor* (1974)
LYND, Helen Merrell. *England in the Eighteen-Eighties: Toward a Social Basis for Freedom* (1945)
MACKENZIE, Compton. *The Windsor Tapestry, Being a Study of the Life, Heritage and Abdication of H.R.H. The Duke of Windsor* (1938)
MACMILLAN, Harold. *Riding the Storm 1956–1959* (1971); *Pointing the Way 1959–1961* (1972); *At the End of the Day 1961–1963* (1973)
MARIE-LOUISE, Princess. *My Life in Six Reigns* (1956)
MARSHALL, Dorothy. *The Life and Times of Victoria* (1972)
MAUROIS, André (translated by Hamish Miles). *King Edward and His Times* (1933)
MAXWELL, Sir Herbert. *Sixty Years a Queen* (1897)
MELVILLE, Lewis. *The First Gentleman of Europe* (1906)
MIDDLEMASS, Keith. *The Life and Times of Edward VII* (1972); *The Life and Times of George VI* (1974)
MORRAH, Dermot. *The Work of the Queen* (1958); *To Be a King* (1968)
MUGGERIDGE, Malcolm. *The Thirties: 1930–1940 in Great Britain* (1940)
MURRAY-BROWN, Jeremy (Editor). *The Monarchy and Its Future* (1969)
NEWTON, W. Douglas. *Westward with the Prince of Wales* (1920)
NICHOLS, Beverley. *The Sweet and Twenties* (1958)
NICOLSON, Harold. *King George Fifth, His Life and Reign* (1952); *Monarchy* (1962)

NOWELL-SMITH, Simon (Editor). *Edwardian England 1901–1914* (1964)
PEACOCKE, Marguerite Dorothea. *The Story of Buckingham Palace: The Royal Home through Seven Reigns* (1951)
PELLING, Henry. *Winston Churchill* (1974)
PINE, L. G. *Princes of Wales* (1970)
PONSONBY, Arthur. *Henry Ponsonby, Queen Victoria's Private Secretary. His Life from His Letters* (1942)
PONSONBY, Sir Frederick. *Recollections of Three Reigns* (Edited by Colin Welch, 1951)
POPE-HENNESSY, James. *Queen Mary 1867–1953* (1959)
POUND, Reginald. *The Strand Magazine 1891–1950* (1966)
PRICE, R. G. G. *A History of Punch* (1957)
PRIESTLEY, J. B. *The Prince of Pleasure and His Regency 1811–1820* (1969); *The Edwardians* (1970); *Victoria's Heyday* (1972); *The English* (1973)
Punch files from 1841–1976
PUNNETT, R. M. *British Government and Politics* (1968)
RICHARDSON, Joanna. *The Disastrous Marriage. A Study of George IV and Caroline of Brunswick* (1960); *George IV, A Portrait* (1966)
ROWSE, A. L. *Windsor Castle in the History of the Nation* (1974)
SHERIDAN, Lisa. *The Queen and Princess Anne* (1959)
SHEWELL-COOPER, W. E. *The Royal Gardeners: King George VI and His Queen* (1952)
SITWELL, Edith. *Victoria of England* (1936)
STEEGMAN, John. *Consort of Taste 1830–1870* (1950)
Strand Magazine files from 1891–1950
STUART, D. M. *Regency Roundabout* (1943); *Portrait of the Prince Regent* (1953)
THOMSON, David. *England in the Nineteenth Century 1815–1914* (1950); *England in the Twentieth Century 1914–1963* (1965)
TREVELYAN, G. M. *English Social History* (1942)
TURNER, E. S. *The Court of St James's* (1959)
WAKEFORD, Geoffrey. *His Royal Highness Charles Prince of Wales* (1962)
WATSON, Vera. *A Queen at Home: An Intimate Account of the Social and Domestic Life of Queen Victoria's Court* (1952)
WEBB, R. K. *Modern England from the Eighteenth Century to the Present* (1969)

WHEELER-BENNETT, John W. *King George VI, His Life and Reign* (1958)
WHITELOCK, Dorothy. *The Beginnings of English Society* (1952)
WILKINS, W. H. *Mrs. FitzHerbert and George IV* (1905)
WILSON, Harold. *The Labour Government 1964–1970. A Personal Record* (1971)
WINDSOR, H.R.H. THE DUKE OF. *A King's Story—Memoirs of H.R.H. The Duke of Windsor, K.G.* (1951)
WINDSOR, The Duchess of. *The Heart Has Its Reasons: The Memoirs of the Duchess of Windsor* (1956)
WULFF, Louis. *Queen of Tomorrow: An Authentic Study of H.R.H. Princess Elizabeth* (1946)
YOUNG, G. M. (Editor). *Early Victorian England 1830–1865* (1934)
YOUNG, Kenneth. *Sir Alec Douglas-Home* (1970)

Index